Charles Brockden Brown
and the *Literary Magazine*

THE LITERARY MAGAZINE,

AND AMERICAN REGISTER.

No. I.]   SATURDAY, OCTOBER 1, 1803.   [Vol. I.

THE EDITORS' ADDRESS TO THE PUBLIC.

IT is usual for one who presents the public with a periodical work like the present, to introduce himself to the notice of his readers by some sort of preface or address. I take up the pen in conformity to this custom, but am quite at a loss for topics suitable to so interesting an occasion. I cannot expatiate on the variety of my knowledge, the brilliancy of my wit, the versatility of my talents. To none of these do I lay any claim, and though this variety, brilliancy of solidity, are necessary ingredients in a work of this kind, I trust merely to the zeal and liberality of my friends to supply me with them. I have them not myself, but doubt not of the good offices of those who possess them, and shall think myself entitled to no small praise, if I am able to collect into one focal spot the rays of a great number of luminaries. They also may be very unequal to each other in lustre, and some of them may be little better than twinkling and feeble stars, of the hundredth magnitude; but what is wanting in individual splendor, will be made up by the union of all their beams into one. My province shall be *to hold the mirror up* so as to assemble all their influence within its verge, and reflect them on the public in such manner as to warm and enlighten.

As I possess nothing but zeal, I can promise to exert nothing else; but my consolation is, that, aided by that powerful spirit, many have accomplished things much more arduous than that which I propose to myself.

Many are the works of this kind which have risen and fallen in America, and many of them have enjoyed but a brief existence. This circumstance has always at first sight, given me some uneasiness; but when I come more soberly to meditate upon it, my courage revives, and I discover no reason for my doubts. Many works have actually been reared and sustained by the curiosity and favour of the public. They have ultimately declined or fallen, it is true; but why? From no abatement of the public curiosity,

Charles Brockden Brown and the *Literary Magazine*

Cultural Journalism in the Early American Republic

Michael Cody

McFarland & Company, Inc., Publishers
Jefferson, North Carolina, and London

Frontispiece: The first page of the first issue of Charles Brockden Brown's *The Literary Magazine, and American Register* (October 1, 1803). Special Collections and Archives, Kent State University Libraries.

LIBRARY OF CONGRESS CATALOGUING-IN-PUBLICATION DATA

Cody, Michael, 1958–
  Charles Brockden Brown and the literary magazine : cultural journalism in the early American republic / Michael Cody.
    p.   cm.
  Includes bibliographical references and index.

  ISBN-13: 978-0-7864-1784-1
  (softcover : 50# alkaline paper) ∞

  1. Brown, Charles Brockden, 1771–1810. 2. Literary magazine, and American register. 3. Journalism — Pennsylvania — Philadelphia — History — 19th century. 4. Periodicals — Publishing — Pennsylvania — Philadelphia — History — 19th century. 5. Philadelphia (Pa.) — Intellectual life — 19th century. 6. Novelists, American — 19th century — Biography. 7. Journalists — United States — Biography. I. Title.
PS1136.C63   2004
813'.2 — dc22   2004002800

British Library cataloguing data are available

©2004 Michael Cody. All rights reserved

No part of this book may be reproduced or transmitted in any form or by any means, electronic or mechanical, including photocopying or recording, or by any information storage and retrieval system, without permission in writing from the publisher.

On the cover: (foreground) Charles Brockden Brown, engraved by I. B. Forrest from a miniature by William Dunlap in 1806; *(background)* pages 4 and 5 of the first issue (October 1, 1803) of *The Literary Magazine, and American Register* (Special Collections and Archives, Kent State University Libraries)

Manufactured in the United States of America

McFarland & Company, Inc., Publishers
  Box 611, Jefferson, North Carolina 28640
  www.mcfarlandpub.com

For my family

Acknowledgments

This book had its beginning as a dissertation in the Department of English at the University of South Carolina, Columbia. I am grateful to Ezra Greenspan, now at Southern Methodist University, who as my director challenged and encouraged me throughout my research and writing and, in the end, became a mentor and friend. My fine committee of readers deserves particular mention as well: Joel Myerson, whose example as a scholar and teacher was never short of inspiring; Benjamin Franklin V, whose guidance, especially in the classroom, provided a solid foundation for my understanding of early American literature; and Constance B. Schulz, whose perspective as a historian influenced my understanding of Brown's *Literary Magazine* as a work reflecting a particular place and time. I also owe a debt of thanks to Martin Brückner (now at the University of Delaware), who, in his brief time at the University of South Carolina, was instrumental in helping me define my approach and refine my ideas in regards to this project. Other faculty members with whom I studied at USC played important roles in my still-continuing development as a scholar; they are Matthew J. Bruccoli, Paula Feldman, Cynthia Davis, and Steven Lynn. I would also like to thank the Graduate School at the University of South Carolina for granting me a Summer Dissertation Fellowship in 1999; this financial support allowed me to focus on research and writing during the important early stages of the project.

My research took many forms as I traveled to some institutions and corresponded with others. My particular appreciation is due to Sydney J. Krause, Sidney W. Reid, and Robert Trogdon of Kent State University. I am also indebted to numerous research librarians and staff at Kent State, the American Antiquarian Society, the Harry Ransom Humanities Research Center at the University of Texas at Austin, the University of Virginia, and the Library Company of Philadelphia.

My colleagues in the Charles Brockden Brown Society continue to be a source of inspiration and support. I owe particular gratitude to Alfred Weber of the University of Tübingen (for his unwavering transatlantic support), and to Fritz Fleischmann, Mark Kamrath, John Holmes, and Janie Hinds. I look forward to our continuing work together.

The following is a miscellany of names — in no particular order — of people who have in one way of another, at one time or another, befriended and supported me during my work on this project: John McMichaels, Gary Leising, Missy Lewis, Lee Davinroy, Jim Nicholl, Hal Farwell, Jim Byer, Brian Railsback, Bill Higgins, Carol Boggess, Peter Murphy, Warren Edminster, Sean Goudie, and Andy Doolan. For current friendship and professional support, I thank Judy Slagle and the rest of my colleagues in the Department of English at East Tennessee State University.

I would not be here without the gift of family, both immediate and extended. In particular, my parents, Dorothy Reeves Cody and Plumer J. Cody (1931–1996), and my brother, Jerry, have suffered my life's twists and turns with steadfast faith and hope. My sons, Lane and Raleigh, have been a blessing, bearing with great patience my hours as a "bookworm" and filling my hours as a father with joy. Finally, my wife, Leesa, has so faithfully borne with my pursuits — this book included — that the symbols and sounds of words can only partially express my gratitude and love.

Contents

Acknowledgments		vii
Introduction		1
ONE	"The Task of an Editor"	11
TWO	The Republic and the Liberal Individual	37
THREE	The Mockingbird, the Mirror, and the Makings of an American Character and Culture	81
FOUR	Fragments of Fiction	127
Afterword		155
Notes		161
Bibliography		189
Index		197

Introduction

From 1803 to 1807 Charles Brockden Brown (1771–1810) served as editor of and chief contributor to a popular Philadelphia monthly miscellany called *The Literary Magazine, and American Register*, the second of his still largely unexplored journalistic ventures.[1] Although Joseph Dennie, the flamboyant editor of *The Port Folio*, was America's most popular magazine editor during the first decade of the nineteenth century, he has not come down to us as the most important man of letters from the period. That honor belongs to Brown, whose minor but secure position in American literary history is, of course, as America's first important novelist. But what has been largely forgotten about Brown is that during the last ten years of his literary career — and of his life — he was also a talented and important magazine editor and journalist.[2]

Traditionally separated from his complex, brooding quartet of major novels — *Wieland* (1798), *Ormond* (1799), *Arthur Mervyn* (1799, 1800), and *Edgar Huntly* (1799) — Charles Brockden Brown's work in the years between 1801 and his death in early 1810 has been, when not completely ignored, generally misunderstood and at times altogether denigrated. Why does this bifurcation exist in Brown's career? William Dunlap — the author's friend and first biographer — may be in part responsible. In *The Life of Charles Brockden Brown* (1815), Dunlap identified a change that occurred in Brown between the latter years of the eighteenth century and the early ones of the nineteenth: "From the regions of poetry and romance; from visionary schemes of Utopian systems of government and manners, Mr. Brown ... became a sober recorder of things as they are..." (2: 68). Unlike many of the critics who would follow, Dunlap applauded the change, seeing in it, as Berthoff says, "a clear and necessary rejection in maturity of that rash Jacobinism (stemming from wrong-headed, however good-hearted, youthfulness) which had infiltrated Brown's fiction" ("Literary" 17). This perceived shift became the basis for most general interpretations of Brown's career since Dunlap's *Life* appeared, although the nature of the change itself has been interpreted differently over the years.

In an essay originally published in *Spark's American Biography* (1834), William H. Prescott followed Dunlap's understanding of Brown's later career:

> In the year 1801 Brown returned to his native city, Philadelphia, ... and in 1803 undertook the conduct of a periodical, entitled *The Literary Magazine and American Register*. A great change had taken place in his opinions on more than one important topic connected with human life and happiness, and ... in his general tone of thinking, since abandoning his professional career.... Instead of a mere dreamer in the world of fancy, he had now become a practical man... [42].

Prescott, like Dunlap, seems to view Brown's metamorphosis from "a mere dreamer in the world of fancy" to "a practical man" as a positive change. As much as this echoes Dunlap's assessment, however, there is an important new note sounded here, a note that would be picked up and rebroadcast by most Brown critics through the remainder of the nineteenth century and much of the twentieth. This is that in ceasing to publish novels Brown was "abandoning his professional career." Viewing letters in the early republic from a period of burgeoning romanticism, Prescott promotes the idea that imaginative writing and the making of books is a profession while magazine writing is the site of the professional writer's apprenticeship, the realm of the amateur man of letters.

Brown's perceived abandonment of fiction as a profession for journalism and political pamphleteering has often led disappointed twentieth-century critics to treat the second half of his career harshly. William Charvat, for example, has claimed that after 1801 Brown "spent the rest of his life storekeeping and doing hack work for Philadelphia publishers" (28). Similarly, Frank Luther Mott has written of Brown during his last decade that "[f]ailure in his most ambitious literary attempts, the unfaith of his promising friends, the responsibilities of marriage, the lectures of his conventional brother, and — finally — physical illnesses, tamed his high spirit and made him a hack" (222).

The mid–twentieth–century biographies of Brown by Harry Warfel and David Lee Clark are divided over the worth of the *Literary Magazine, and American Register* in particular. "The title," Warfel writes, "...appealed to the nationalistic predilections of the American people, but the magazine itself lacked nativistic bias" (221); in addition, it "lacked point, direction, intellectual elevation" (222). According to Warfel, the magazine simply provided Brown with a way to keep writing while earning a reasonable salary, and the job for which Brown was paid "was not so much one of composing new tales or new moralizing essays as of translating, adapting, or excerpting from books and periodicals" (224).[3]

Clark, who provides a more detailed analysis of the *Literary Magazine*, is kinder, making note of Brown's "sound judgement and catholicity of taste" in his capacity as editor. "In evaluating Brown as a writer," he says, "we must accordingly remember that for the first quarter century of our national life, he was not only America's leading novelist and critic but also ... her outstanding journalist" (244). Clark was particularly impressed by Brown's reviews:

> As a reviewer, Brown was well equipped; his classical education, his knowledge of French and Italian literatures, and, what was more rare, of German literature, his own work as a writer of fiction, and the Quaker honesty and high seriousness that were so much a part of him — all these, combined with a conscious endeavor to create and foster a native literature in which all Americans could take pride, marked Brown as the greatest critic in America before Edgar Allan Poe [245].

This may sound a bit extravagant, but while Brown's criticism is not particularly intense by today's standards, it is often more intricate and intuitive than other American literary criticism from his time.

Warner Berthoff recognizes the *Literary Magazine* for what it was: "a public forum for the concentration of literate intelligence and the diffusion of knowledge" ("Literary" 304). Berthoff understood, as Warfel did not, that Brown's "theme of public usefulness" represents a "fundamentally political purpose," despite Brown's claims to the magazine's political neutrality; taking this into account "helps to explain what would otherwise seem a chaotic editorial policy" (305). As for the lack of "nativistic bias," Berthoff writes that Brown

> conceived the community of letters and knowledge as international and made room for European literary news and reprints.... And in an important sense this did not betray the cause of American national literary culture. For if such a culture were truly to provide stability, it would have

> to keep abreast of the European model, to become as rich and as enterprising. On the other hand Brown persistently encouraged manifestations of literary nativism [306–07].

In order to help American writers and readers break away from the provincialism practically dictated to them by the country's physical isolation and then participate in the international community of letters, Brown discussed British culture and authors with the underlying motive that such information should be understood as a means to American improvement.

More recent biographical criticism dealing with the period during which Brown worked on the *Literary Magazine* has tended toward Warfel's point of view. "On or about April 1800 Charles Brockden Brown changed," Steven Watts writes in his 1994 book on Brown, *The Romance of Real Life*. "The burst of novel writing over the previous few years had fulfilled his literary agenda" (131). According to this thesis, Brown, who began his career as a "youthful utopian radical," spent the last decade of his life as a "stodgy middle-age conservative" (25). Likewise, Donald Ringe has said that "[t]he other writing Brown did in the last years of his life was largely nonliterary," and while it "should certainly not be dismissed as insignificant, it does represent a falling off from the truly important fiction he had already written" (*Charles* 108, 109). Ringe's identification of the later writing as "other" and "nonliterary" necessarily marginalizes it, privileging Brown's fiction without taking into account that Brown would have adhered to a much broader definition of what was literary than critics generally recognized through most of the twentieth century.

As is evident from this brief survey, the relatively small amount of criticism treating Brown's *Literary Magazine* has varied broadly. Part of the problem in interpreting Brown's career as a whole — and his later work in particular — has to do with the question of what texts are literary. Focusing predominantly on belles lettres, much criticism since Brown's time — from that of Samuel Taylor Coleridge and Edgar Allan Poe in the nineteenth century to that of T. S. Eliot, Cleanth Brooks, and Robert Penn Warren in the twentieth — has been governed to some degree by various manifestations of formalism. It is no wonder, then, that those Brown scholars whose critical sensibilities are influenced by a formalist orientation would draw a line through the middle of his career, thus separating the novels — with their specialized, poetical language and forms — from the journalism — with its more ordinary, "practical" language and forms.

This separation of a career is not only unnecessary but also detrimental to our interpretation of Brown and his work. In *Rethinking Intellectual History: Texts, Contexts, Language* (1983), Dominick LaCapra argues that even apparently simple, factual texts such as "a tax roll, a will, and the register of an inquisition"—and in Brown's case, I believe, the various journalistic items in his miscellany—can involve both "documentary and worklike components that should be examined in a critical historiography." LaCapra explains:

> The documentary situates the text in terms of factual or literal dimensions involving reference to empirical reality and conveying information about it. The "worklike" supplements empirical reality by adding to and subtracting from it. It thereby involves dimensions of the text not reducible to the documentary, prominently including the roles of commitment, interpretation, and imagination. The worklike is critical and transformative, for it deconstructs and reconstructs the given, in a sense repeating it but also bringing into the world something that did not exist before in that significant variation, alteration, or transformation. With deceptive simplicity, one might say that while the documentary marks a difference, the worklike makes a difference — one that engages the reader in recreative dialogue with the text and the problems it raises [30].[4]

LaCapra continues by pointing out that "it is only by investigating what a thinker did not explicitly or intentionally think but what constitutes his still question-worthy 'unthought' that a conversation with the past enters into dimensions of his thinking which bear most forcefully on the present and future" (31). To apply LaCapra's ideas to the reading of Brown's *Literary Magazine* is to discover in almost every issue work of real and relevant value to a study of Brown and the American political and cultural structure of his time.

The opening of relatively new fields of study such as the history of the book will be especially useful in revising our view of Brown's life in letters by helping bridge the gap between the major novels and the juvenilia, journalism, pamphlets, and ephemera. Susan Belasco Smith and Kenneth Price, for example, point out that

> the history of the book is a study of the context of printed texts in a variety of forms (books, magazines, newspapers, journals, reviews, and pamphlets) and how those texts are produced, received, and interpreted. Strongly antiformalist in origin and intent, the theory and practice of book history draws on a variety of disciplines, ranging from history to anthropology, sociology to linguistics, and literature to politics [7].

Brown read, wrote, and published in all of these disciplines (some, of course, decades before they became formal disciplines). During his twenty years as an author, he participated in disseminating texts of cultural and literary worth; in addition to this, his published literary essays and book reviews assisted in the establishment of literary education and reading habits in America and influenced the public reception of offerings from the early American press. To assess his work according to the methodology of the history of the book seems natural, but few such attempts have been made by Brown scholars.

To move from studying print culture in Brown's day in general to studying Brown's career in particular is, in part, to shift focus from the history of the book to the more specific area of the profession of authorship. To analyze Brown's later writing in terms of this approach is to find that — although Prescott and Charvat, for different reasons, declare Brown's professional career at an end when he finished writing his novels — Brown remained a career author, a writer of some reputation and celebrity beyond the novels. His work with the *Literary Magazine* was a professional collaboration between himself as writer and editor, John Conrad as publisher, and the early American literary market. Understood in this context, Brown neither sold out nor became a hack but continued to reach a readership. It is true, as Ringe and Watts suggest, that the forms and approach of which Brown made primary use changed around the turn of the century. Rather than return to the novel after resettling in his native Philadelphia, he chose the miscellany as the medium through which he would both make the majority of his living and participate in the diffusion of information and knowledge considered vital to the stability of young republican America. But even with this dramatic shift, Brown's commitment to letters and to the improvement of his fellow citizens never wavered. As Carol Cyganowski has written, Brown "edited the magazine toward the values evident in his own fiction: distinctively American subjects, interest in science, and belief that work of quality could appeal simultaneously to the American intellectual and common reader" (3). Viewed in this light, Brown's career, far from being segmented, was organic, and the sheer volume of his post–1800 work — written even while being involved with his brothers' business, marrying, beginning a family, and declining in health — indicates that he maintained his creative and intellectual energy until finally forced to his deathbed.

Recent revisions in cultural theory will also be useful in returning to Brown's career a sense of balance. The rise of cultural studies has led to a broadening of our understanding of what literature is and what it does; as a result, the range of what are today considered by many to be meaningful subjects of literary study more closely aligns with the breadth of reading material that was in Brown's time considered literature. "In that day," Larzer Ziff points out in *Writing in the New Nation* (1991), "most who thought about the matter defined literature as all of written knowledge, which is to say that belles lettres constituted a very small part of what they regarded as literary" (ix). Cultural studies, like book history, reopens to critical investigation the entire expanse of what an author such as Charles Brockden Brown read and wrote, providing a platform on which high and low culture, the genteel and the practical, meet and contest.

One particular cultural approach that seems especially significant to an understanding of Brown and the literature of the early American republic is postcolonial studies. In their historical relationships to Great Britain, the United States, Canada, Australia, and New Zealand can be identified as "settler colonies" (Ashcroft et al. 133); in their similar colonial pasts, these countries came into, and existed within, the British Empire in obviously different ways than did, say, India and the nations of Africa. But the literature and culture of the United States has only recently begun being considered in light of postcolonial theories. The chief reason for this may be that, having gained independence earlier and less peacefully than other settler colonies, the United States has far more often — and for far longer — been associated with its own imperial ideologies. Still, Ashcroft and his colleagues argue that "[t]he literature of the USA should also be placed in [the postcolonial] category":

> Perhaps because of its current position of power, and the neo-colonizing role it has played, its post-colonial nature has not been generally recognized. But its relationship with the metropolitan centre as it evolved over the last two centuries has been paradigmatic for post-colonial literature everywhere. What each of these literatures has in common beyond their special and distinctive regional characteristics is that they emerged in their present form out of the experience of colonization and asserted themselves by foregrounding the tension with the imperial power, and by emphasizing their differences from the assumptions of the imperial centre. It is this which makes them distinctively post-colonial [2].

Brown and his American literary contemporaries were — in as real a sense as those authors writing in the other settler colonies have been in the twentieth century — postcolonial authors. They wrote on that "important site of conflict within post-colonial literary cultures" where "the backward-looking impotence of exile and the forward-looking impetus to indigeneity collide" (136).

In *Writing and Postcolonialism in the Early Republic*, Edward Watts identifies "the process of decolonization" as "the exploration of local conditions and self-awareness" (10). In order for the literary culture of the American people to come into its postcolonial own, the new nation's authors and readers needed not only to investigate the localized physical, cultural, economic, and political conditions but also to begin conducting this investigation from an American point of view. The people of the United States must learn to locate themselves in the world according to their Americanness on both individual and national levels. The evolution from Federalist republic through Jeffersonian republic to democracy was the result of this rather slow process of localization. "For something to be *post*-colonial," Watts writes in reference to Lawrence Buell's identification of writing in the American Renaissance as postcolonial, "some process of decolonization must have occurred or at least begun between the years of the early republic and the middle of the nineteenth century" (5).[5]

In the early stage of this vital period of transition, Charles Brockden Brown established the *Literary Magazine*. When he returned to Philadelphia from New York in 1801, his career as an American man of letters — only some three years of which were spent writing the novels for which he is best known — was little more than half over. The attitudes and interests displayed in his continuing work as editor and author of the magazine shed light on him as an individual, on authorship and magazine editorship in the early nineteenth century, and on American culture in those crucial years when the second-generation citizens of the United States struggled to realize the ideas and ideals of the Revolution. An investigation of the magazine is, I believe, requisite for the fullest understanding of Brown as an American author. I do not mean to imply by this assertion that Brown's novels should be considered less significant than either Brown studies or general literary history have claimed them to be, for the novels represent his greatest literary legacy and remain the primary source of our interest in his work. What I hope to prove by this study is that Brown's *Literary Magazine* is far more significant than has previously been understood to our knowledge not only of Brown as a man of letters but also of American literary, political, and cultural history in that important first decade of the nineteenth century. And with the rise of recent literary and cultural theories, a vocabulary now exists for asking and seeking to answer the important questions regarding Brown and his most successful journalistic venture.

Is it reasonable, for example, to believe as Warfel seems to that Brown — so purposeful and complex in his novels and political pamphlets — was so undirected and simple-minded in his magazine work? Can he be merely an editor? If not, what is his role in the relationship between magazine editorship, American culture, and republican politics? Does Brown develop a persona in his magazine that overtly marshals its contents into a single monologic text in the same way that the Federalist republicanism of Joseph Dennie's "Oliver Oldschool" rules *The Port Folio*? Or is Brown's persona subordinate, allowing the miscellany to be more dialogic in the hands of its readers? Is the *Literary Magazine*, as Smith and Price ask, "a single text or is it the sum total of the many texts that appear in competing columns and pages" (9)?

Furthermore, in the postcolonial environment of Brown's time, what was the relationship between authorship and authority, and how was this relationship affected by depersonalization and negation as they existed in anonymous or pseudonymous miscellaneous literature? Does the *Literary Magazine* localize its subject matter — in relation to the old imperial center — for decolonization of its translocalized American readers? That is, in keeping "abreast of the European model" of literary culture, as Berthoff says, while at the same time promoting "manifestations of literary nativism," is Brown able to avoid recolonizing the infant American intellectual and cultural life of his readers? Could it be that out of the miscellany Brown develops a voice — either overt or covert — that is nationalistic and democratic rather than classically republican?

It seems obvious in light of such questions that no single critical approach will be adequate to the task of analyzing Brown's work as an editor and a journalist. The approach itself must be of a miscellaneous nature. But my thesis can be presented without the coloring of a particular theoretical palette: the material in the *Literary Magazine* shows Brown in his most direct participatory role in what was already a fading republic of letters and represents his most mature literary service in the name of a nascent American cultural nationalism. Analysis of the magazine reveals that, despite criticism portraying him as having disengaged himself — after finishing *Edgar Huntly* and *Arthur Mervyn*—from those vital transformations taking place in the early American republic, Brown used the *Literary Magazine* to remain active in America's shifting ideological and cultural life between 1803 and 1807. He was more serviceable to his country in his capacity as editor than he had ever been before, more directly influential and financially successful than at any other time in his career as an American author.

ONE

"The Task of an Editor"

In the 27 April 1805 issue of *The Port Folio*, Joseph Dennie's noted Philadelphia weekly, the following appeared as part of an anonymous review entitled "Conrad's Magazine":

> The Editor is a young man, who, for a series of years, has exhibited a perseverance in literary labour very rarely witnessed in America, and a style purer than that of the generality of his compatriots. Although his figure appears extenuated by his ardour of application, and his face pallid, not by the midnight revel, but by studious vigils, yet his alert and robust mind seems not to sympathize with its valetudinary companion. He employs many a vigilant and inquisitive hour, in reading what deserves to be remembered, and in writing what deserves to be read, and with his literary enthusiasm added to his facility of style, he appears well qualified for the task of an Editor [125-26].

The "young man" praised here was thirty-four-year-old Charles Brockden Brown, and the monthly miscellany he had been editing for almost two years when the review appeared was *The Literary Magazine, and American Register*.

Having left New York and returned to his native Philadelphia early in 1801, Brown published *Clara Howard* in June and *Jane Talbot* in the following December, thus concluding his "series of performances" in the novel genre (C. B. Brown, *Wieland* 3). In addition to seeing these books through the press, he joined the mercantile firm of his brothers James and Armitt, James Brown and Company. "But," as Harry Warfel writes, "that he could remain away from printer's ink was impossible. Once soiled with that black substance, a man cannot remove the stain or the ambition to influence the thoughts of his fellow men" (221). True to this supposition, by late summer 1803 Brown was readying his return to the "republic of letters" via the vehicle of the *Literary Magazine*. And less than two years later, Dennie's weekly could say that

> The Literary Magazine and American Register, a journal conducted by Mr. Charles B. Brown of this city, and published by John Conrad and Co. has reached its eighteenth number, and now appears in a vigorous and adult state. The Magazine for the past month was composed of materials entirely *original*, and the beauty and good sense of many of its papers were not less attractive than their novelty [125].[1]

Thirty-three more issues would appear beyond the "eighteenth number" the *Port Folio* reviewer mentions. As editor and chief contributor, Brown saw the publication through a total of fifty-one monthly issues—a particularly impressive run in a period when few American magazines survived beyond a year. Month by month between October 1803 and December 1807—"in reading what deserves to be remembered, and in writing what deserves to be read"—he compiled a miscellany of original and selected pieces that averaged eighty pages per issue, which made it, along with Brown's earlier *Monthly Magazine*, "the most imposing magazine that America had yet seen" (Clark 218).[2]

Why did Charles Brockden Brown subject himself to this perpetual, difficult work? Like many of his fellow citizens and men of letters Brown thought it by no means certain that the experiment in republicanism begun by victory in the Revolutionary War would be successful. The survival of the new nation depended first upon stability rather than a distinct American identity, and to create this stability in the political realm, a certain amount of social and cultural cohesiveness was necessary. Brown and others believed that a wide diffusion of useful knowledge—of politics, education, science, and the like—would help create the stability, order, and national identity necessary for the union's survival. He seems, in part, to have turned from the book market because of the greater opportunity offered by magazines for this diffusion of knowledge in the young republic, a mission that was, perhaps, his only career-long concern as a professional author. As Warner Berthoff correctly noted in his 1954 Harvard dissertation,

> The generation of Charles Brockden Brown ... had the custody of a critical era, and if ... its members may claim only a minor place in the history

of literature, they must bulk rather larger in the history of American culture.... Brown's primary significance, historically, is as a register of that era, for which we have perhaps no more comprehensive American spokesman and about which we certainly do not know as much as we should ["Literary" 1].

Although critics have far more often and more thoroughly explored Brown's fiction to the near exclusion of the extensive remainder of his canon, it is through his fiction and journalism together that we have one of the most intellectually stimulating portrayals of the difficulties inherent in the early nineteenth-century effort to establish a United States of America that was truly and lastingly united.

I. Brown's Philadelphia

The City of Brotherly Love was the ideal home for the *Literary Magazine*. With a population of some seventy thousand, Philadelphia was one of the largest cities in the English-speaking world during the 1790s and early 1800s. Dynamic, urbane, and cosmopolitan, it was throughout much of Brown's life the political, economic, and cultural center of America. As David Lee Clark points out,

> Despite Quaker insistence upon a frugal, simple, democratic life, the city became the gayest and wealthiest city in America, teeming with the pomp and chivalry of Colonial days and leading the intellectual life of the nation; here were the foremost schools, newspapers, magazines, and libraries, and here scientific research and philosophical speculation reached new heights; here was the center of trade and commerce with Europe as well as the meeting place of Western fur traders; here met the most advanced ideas in government, science, and religion [12].

For decades before — and a few years after — the 1800 removal of the new nation's capital to Washington, D.C., Brown's native city "was clearly the place for the young American to sharpen his wits, inform his mind, and quicken his literary enthusiasm" (Parrington 186). By 1825, Philadelphia would become "the first major American industrial city," but in Brown's lifetime it was "the Athens of America" (E. Richardson 208).

Brown was born in 1771, and while he was growing up in his liberal Quaker family of merchants, his native city played its well known role in the American Revolution and the founding of the United States: it hosted the Continental Congresses and heard first the Declaration of Independence; it also hosted the Constitutional Convention in 1787; and it served as the new nation's capital from 1790 to 1800. Philadelphia's tenure as the seat of American government was rife with heated political debate as the struggle between Federalists and Jeffersonians gave rise to the first two-party system; at the same time it was a focal point for radical democratic societies. Philadelphia and its environs were arguably the most democratic area in the nation: "The only true democratic community then existing in the eastern States," Henry Adams writes, "Pennsylvania ... contained no hierarchy like that of New England; no great families like those of New York; no oligarchy like the planters of Virginia and South Carolina" (82). The exuberant and progressive intellectual nature of Benjamin Franklin had come to characterize Philadelphia as a whole, and the city rang with the voices of conservatives and radicals, Quakers and deists, politicians and merchants.

Philadelphia was also the home of the American Philosophical Society. The influence of this organization could be felt throughout the city's relatively democratic social structure because the members were not cloistered scholars and scientists but men of business who were part of the community's quotidian life; as Edgar Richardson says, "they were lawyers, merchants, physicians, farmers, clergymen, and publishers who combined their intellectual interests with busy and active careers" (242). They daily met each other and the general population on the streets and in the shops, coffeehouses, offices, and churches. In this way their interests and ideas were diffused and the projects they undertook — such as the establishment of the Pennsylvania Academy of Fine Arts in 1805 — were supported. As a young man, Brown thrived in this intellectually stimulating atmosphere, and its liberality influenced him throughout his career as an author and editor.

From before the Revolution until the nineteenth-century resurgence of Boston and ascendancy of New York, Philadelphia was the hub of the American press, attracting many of the best printers and publishers, writers, scientists, and artists, from Franklin to Mathew Carey, Philip Freneau to Dennie, Charles Willson Peale to Benjamin Rush. Newspapers such as the Jeffersonian *Aurora* and the Federalist *United States Gazette* kept the streets of the city alive with party politics. The shelves of booksellers were stocked with broadsides, ballads, pamphlets, and books of American and European origin. Philadelphia's ambitious press produced several admirable projects around the turn of the century, among which were Thomas

Dobson's *Encyclopaedia*, John Marshall's *Life of Washington*, and the ornate 1807 edition of Joel Barlow's *The Columbiad*, which was the former Connecticut Wit's attempt to write an American epic poem and the Conrad family's attempt "to show that an American publisher could produce a sumptuously beautiful book" (E. Richardson 247–48).³

Furthermore, it was in Philadelphia that Franklin helped pioneer the way for magazines in the New World when he edited and published the *General Magazine* through six monthly issues dating from January 1741.⁴ True to its founding, American magazine culture in the first years of the nineteenth century remained centered in Philadelphia, where Dennie's *Port Folio* and Brown's *Literary Magazine* were published. The intellectually restive environment of the city afforded its magazine editors the opportunity to participate in a culture of letters that was neither as parochial as Boston's nor as hierarchical as New York's, and the result was magazines whose content and tone — as well as format and quality — grew more from the characters and interests of their editors than from commercial and audience considerations (Free 27).

Brown's position as editor of a Philadelphia periodical afforded him the opportunity to observe and comment upon life in America during the heart of the nineteenth century's first decade, a stirring but difficult period. His work with the miscellany reveals his "humane and liberal social ideology," for which, according to Berthoff, Brown was intellectually indebted to the City of Brotherly Love ("Literary" 39). His *Literary Magazine*— indeed, his entire career — reflects Philadelphia's liberality. I would argue that the mixture of voices and ideas that come to inhabit his miscellany between 1803 and 1807 publicly echo the diversity of this city in which he spent the majority of his life.

II. Miscellaneous Literature

"The word *magazine* meant miscellany to most eighteenth century readers," Frank Luther Mott writes in his well regarded history of the medium in America, "and, with certain notable exceptions, the magazines maintained that tradition" (40–41). Contents of the general magazines ranged widely in order to make each issue useful and entertaining to as broad a spectrum of readers as possible. Towards this end, American miscellanies of the colonial and early republican periods typically offered a few "original communications" from their editors and contributors, as well as material reprinted from various British, European, and American sources. The editors' efforts towards a general diffusion of knowledge seem to have been perceived as largely successful; by 1788 George Washington could write to Mathew Carey in praise of the usefulness of magazines to the political, economic, and moral health of the United States: "I consider such easy vehicles of knowledge, more happily calculated than any other, to preserve the liberty, stimulate the industry and meliorate the morals of an enlightened and free people" (qtd. in J. Wood 27).

In the nineteenth century's first decade, American authors continued to utilize magazines for their social, cultural, and political participation in republican life. With over 120 new magazines appearing — if many only briefly — in the United States between 1800 and 1809, the medium was widely available, not only in the urban centers that dotted America's eastern seaboard but also on the western frontier. In addition to Philadelphia, of course, New York and Boston were home to several magazines. Portland, Maine; Hanover, New Hampshire; New Haven and Bridgeport, Connecticut; Baltimore, Maryland; Richmond, Virginia; Charleston, South Carolina; Lexington, Kentucky; and many other locales contributed weeklies, monthlies, or quarterlies of their own. While the periodicals produced by all these places combined do not come near the number established in the following decades of the nineteenth century, their proliferation during this period is striking in comparison to the fewer than 100 that had appeared in America between 1741 and 1799.

Subscription lists were short, but as James Playsted Wood has said, "the influence of the early magazines was probably far greater than the number printed and circulated would indicate.... Every page of every magazine was read carefully by a number of people. Thus the influence exerted by the early magazines was both intensive and extensive" (25). Moreover, these vehicles of useful information were taken seriously by their editors and readers. Encyclopedic in nature, magazines then were not the throwaway items they generally are today. According to the brief "Advertisement" that introduced his *General Magazine*, Franklin clearly intended that each monthly issue be kept: "the Paper and Page will be continued of the same Size, that so the Twelve Months may be bound in one Volume at the Year's End, with a compleat Index or Table, which we shall add to the Month of *December*" (n.p.). Although Franklin's magazine never reached a December issue, the general practice of binding the numbers that made up a magazine's annual or semiannual volumes survived. Lyon Richardson, discussing the view early American magazine editors held regarding their productions, notes that "[t]hey did not look upon the issues as ephemeral; often the intent was to publish periodically a collection of writings later to be appropriately bound and given an exalted place as fit 'furniture' for every man's library" (1). This sense of the magazine's permanence, as well as its relative pervasiveness, drew America's authors to the medium, many as contributors but only a talented few as editors. For this latter group of professed public servants the work of producing a magazine was difficult and often a losing proposition financially, but the opportunity — and, what is more, the duty — to participate in the cultural and political life of the new nation made magazine production worth the effort.

The goal of miscellaneous literature — whether written and collected by the political or the politically disinterested editor — was the improvement of the individual and the concomitant improvement of the nation. Enlightenment ideas of human perfectibility — the American Dream as embodied by the life of Benjamin Franklin, for example — suggested a progressive view of human potential, and editors believed that the reading of their miscellanies played an important part in allowing those Americans who had "genteel and middle-class aspirations to become more polished and cosmopolitan and to approach mastery of a general body of knowledge that embraced religion, history, geography, and natural sciences in addition to public affairs" (R. Brown, *Knowledge* 290). There was a precedent for this belief. According to his *Autobiography*, Franklin had improved his eloquence — and his station in life — in part through reading and imitating the essays of Joseph Addison and Richard Steele in *The Spectator*. American purveyors of miscellaneous literature believed it possible for their readers to do the same.

"The informed citizen," according to Richard Brown, "was in vogue in republican America" (*Strength* 109), and the belief in the efficacy, the necessity, of educating all people in the United States cut across ideological boundaries. The nation's citizens found themselves in a new public role for which they had little preparation. No matter the form of republicanism an individual believed in — whether of classical, liberal, or whatever other stripe — republicans were participants in the national government. Their civic responsibilities included choosing leadership and voting on policies, and in order to fulfill these responsibilities the citizens must have access to the diffusion of information and be educated enough to make choices at the ballot box that would ensure the survival of the republican way of life. In general, early American writers, editors, and readers believed that the useful information distributed through the miscellanies would help provide the necessary educational foundation for American citizens. Furthermore, the provision of similar understandings of history, science, art, and the like, and of similar knowledge for conversation and communication, would lead a republican people to shed regional jealousies, unhealthy political partisanship, and religious prejudices. This, in turn, would aid the government; as Berthoff has noted, the result of a wide diffusion of knowledge, theoretically, would be "the diffusion of certain fixed communal habits of feeling, through which the institution of government might be emotionally secured in the mind, the loyalty, of every citizen" ("Literary" 301).

But this literary effort towards unification raises an important issue regarding the production and reception of early national miscellanies. On the one hand, the dominant elite — among them such literary Federalists as Joseph Dennie and Fisher Ames—feared the revolutionary potential that still existed in the people during the first decades after the Revolution. They saw signs of it everywhere: in uprisings such as Shays's and the Whiskey Rebellions of 1786 and 1794; in the rise of democratic societies and liberal sentiments; in the lack of deferential treatment received from the "common" citizen met on the street. To bolster their social equals and spread their influence among the general citizenry, the literary elite made consistent use of the periodical press. Editors and authors associated with miscellaneous literature released to the marketplace a product intended to unify its audience according to the social, cultural, and political agendas of a learned, authoritative leadership that exercised its power through print. As Edward Watts has pointed out,

> The example of the Addisonian miscellany serves to reveal how republicanism transformed and rephrased British culture to serve its own needs. While the English miscellany was a form suited to experimentation, challenging aristocratic hierarchies but defying classical unity, in the post–Revolutionary United States the same genre served to exhibit the multiple abilities of an eloquent elite [53].

This elite dominated the nation's magazines, promoting the idea of civic virtue in hopes of curbing the increasing individualism and social leveling they saw around them. Once the instructions of these published authorities were absorbed, readers were expected to apply the behavioral patterns represented in the republic of letters to their public and private lives. In this sense, then, the miscellany was, according to Watts's understanding of it, a vehicle for the recolonizing of the American people, attempting to make them a collective of citizens rather than autonomous individuals.

Joseph Dennie's *Port Folio* is a strong example of this Federalist-republican literary tradition, in which the writing of America's men of letters need only play a useful, disinterested role in the public discourse. In doing so, moreover, such writing need not concern itself with portraying any indigenous American qualities. Michael Warner explores Fisher Ames's "American Literature" (1809) as a late example of this particular tradition in American literary history. In Warner's insightful reading of the essay, the "civic orientation" of Federalist Ames "leads to a republican model of literature rather than a liberal one" and an understanding of American writing "in republican rather than nationalist terms." That is, the purpose and "value" of republican literature in America resides in its "public and therefore universalist" nature, and thus American literature's "Americanness" exists only insofar as it "support[s] virtue in the American public sphere" (149).

According to this view, it mattered not that Dennie was an anti-democratic, elitist Anglophile, as well as a colorful dandy.[5] What mattered was that his miscellany promoted civic virtue in a republican sphere of letters not connected, ideally, with nationality. His prospectus for *The Port Folio* was "submitted to men of affluence, men of liberality, and men of letters," who could at that time more easily have been British gentlemen than American merchants, tradesmen, and landholders. The preface's footnotes—more extensive than its text—put on display not only Dennie's learning but also his cultural bias; these notes are full of references to and quotes from classical and British authors such as Virgil, Milton, Dryden, Pope, and Dr. Johnson. "He will not," Dennie writes in the editorial voice of pseudonym "Oliver Oldschool, Esq.," "strive to please the populace," who are "the lower classes of our motley vulgar, too often composed of the scoundrels of all nations, and perpetually restless and rebellious" (n.p.). Dennie's courting of men of affluence and letters and his blasting of "our motley vulgar" participate in that model of miscellaneous literature in which elite authors write in support of republican—as opposed to liberal, democratic, or nationalist—ideals in order to promote civic virtue among those most capable of being good citizens, i.e., the middle classes and above.

On the other hand, the American miscellany may be read as a print representation of informal meetings in the nation's public inns, taverns, and coffeehouses. To approach the miscellany in light of this interpretation provides more understanding of the genre's democratic potential than does the interpretation of it as a redcoated product "of an eloquent elite."[6] According to Edward Larkin in his study of Thomas Paine's editorship of the *Pennsylvania Magazine*,

> If the coffeehouse's combination of a cacophony of voices and a multiplicity of topics served as the ideal model for innovative publishers in the eighteenth century, then the magazine, whose distinguishing characteristics were precisely the broad spectrum of topics addressed, its numerous contributors, and its accessibility to the general public, provided a natural print analogue to the discourse of the coffeehouse [254].

Just as there were natural instigators and moderators in coffeehouse conversations, so there were authors willing and eloquent enough to carry the public conversations, to "speak" their minds in print, and editors able to guide interactions between magazines and their translocalized readers. Miscellaneous literature is, from this point of view, a discussion, a public forum, and not a lecture or a sermon.

Brown's *Literary Magazine* falls in the category of the democratic miscellany. Like inn, tavern, coffeehouse, and street corner conversations, the magazine ranges through topics from politics and literature to yellow fever and dogs. Voices throughout the eight semiannual volumes discuss the values of classical learning, female learning, newspapers, and so on. As editor, Brown most often seems to exercise no authority over the miscellany's contents beyond simple selection, allowing the articles that appear in a given issue to compete on equal terms for a reader's interest and sympathy. Bowing to tradition and opening the inaugural number of the *Literary Magazine* with "The Editors' Address to the Public" (October 1803),[7] Brown set the tone of this unassuming editorial style:

> It is usual for one who presents the public with a periodical work like the present, to introduce himself to the notice of his readers by some sort of preface or address. I take up the pen in conformity to this custom, but am quite at a loss for topics suitable to so interesting an occasion. I cannot expatiate on the variety of my knowledge, the brilliancy of my wit, the versatility of my talents. To none of these do I lay any claim....
> As I possess nothing but zeal, I can promise to exert nothing else; but my consolation is, that, aided by that powerful spirit, many have accomplished things much more arduous than that which I propose to myself [1: 3].

In stark contrast to Dennie's "Oliver Oldschool," Brown's "Editor" is unwilling either to claim authority over his magazine and its readers or to establish any overt, unifying voice. He may moderate the conversations in his literary coffeehouse, but he does not dominate them as Oldschool does.

Editors such as Brown and Dennie — not the readers on their subscription lists — made the early national miscellanies the important institutions that they were to the American audience. Brown's "Address" provides some insight into this aspect of magazine culture during his time:

> Many are the works of this kind which have risen and fallen in America, and many of them have enjoyed but a brief existence. This circumstance has always at first sight, given me some uneasiness, but when I come more soberly to meditate upon it, my courage revives, and I discover no reason for my doubts. Many works have actually been reared and sustained by the curiosity and favour of the public. They have ultimately declined or fallen, it is true; but why? From no abatement of the public curiosity, but from causes [for] which publishers or editors only are accountable. Those who managed the publication, have commonly either changed their principles, remitted their zeal, or voluntarily relinquished their trade, or, last of all, and like other men, have died. Such works have flourished for a time, and they ceased to flourish, by the fault or misfortune of the proprietors. The public is always eager to encourage one who devotes himself to their rational amusement, and when he ceases to deserve their favour, they feel more regret than anger in withdrawing it [1: 3–4].

Although Brown's enthusiasm for miscellaneous literature would eventually fade in favor of the extensive, largely informational reporting of the *American Register*, for more than four years he succeeded with the *Literary Magazine*, a periodical which the *Port Folio* reviewer — most likely Dennie himself — called "a work well calculated, in our opinion, to advance the interests of miscellaneous literature" (126).

III. Brown and His Plan for the *Literary Magazine*

Throughout his twenty years as a published author — from the effusive juvenilia to the often halting and fragmented mature work written in declining health — authorship increasingly became for Brown a public activity. Since the age of sixteen, when he was a leading member of Philadelphia's Belles Lettres Club, he had devoted his life to literature with an eye towards improvement and usefulness. The youthful Brown's intent to serve his country by his writing is evident in his first major publication at eighteen. Adopting in Addisonian fashion an assumed title, Brown in "The Rhapsodist" (1789) recognized the relationship between publication and public service:

> My ambition has already devoted me to the service of my country, and the acquisition of true glory.... If my continual struggles shall at length raise me to a level with mediocrity, and my readers expect not the eccentric genius of a higher sphere, I shall be perfectly satisfied. In the mean time I humbly bespeak their candour and indulgence to well meant endeavours in their service. Every person who commits his writings to the press has by that means voluntarily parted with his ancient liberty and becomes the general vassal; If he brings into his new station spirit and vivacity sufficient to suit himself, at all times, and in every change of disposition, to the humours and caprice of his lord, he may perhaps, though a slave, enjoy a state of splendid vassalage, and reflect with less uneasiness upon the loss of freedom [*Rhapsodist* 2–3].[8]

Dunlap wrote of "The Rhapsodist" that "the title was assumed, [but] the *character* was not. Charles in these essays exhibits himself" (1: 17). Although preoccupied throughout "The Rhapsodist" with his own imagination and its potential for bringing him fame, Brown reveals a sincerity concerning service to his country that is genuine, as it always was in his writing.

Nine years later, in the Advertisement at the beginning of *Wieland* (1798), Brown claims that his work "aims at the illustration of some important branches of the moral constitution of man," and that ultimately "the reader must be permitted to decide" whether or not the novel is successful in this aim (3). These two concerns—"the moral constitution of man" and the informed, intelligent reader, the "lord" of his Rhapsodist—remained with Brown throughout his literary career. At the same time he sought, like many other intellectual Americans in the first sixty years of this country's existence, to promote a distinctly American literature, a literature "opened to us by our own country," as he phrased it in his brief 1799 preface to *Edgar Huntly* (3).[9]

In 1803's "The Editors' Address to the Public," Brown explained in his third-person editorial voice the "motives" and plan for the *Literary Magazine*:

> Useful information and rational amusement being his objects, he will not scruple to collect materials from all quarters. He will ransack the

> newest foreign publications, and extract from them whatever can serve his purpose....
>
> As to *domestic* publications, besides extracting from them any thing serviceable to the public, he will give a critical account of them, and in this respect, make his work an American Review, in which the history of our native literature shall be carefully detailed.
>
> He will pay particular attention to the history of passing events. He will carefully compile the news, foreign and domestic, of the current month, and give, in a concise and systematic order, that intelligence which the common newspapers communicate in a vague and indiscriminate way. His work shall likewise be a repository of all those signal incidents in private life, which mark the character of the age, and excite the liveliest curiosity [1: 5].

News, reviews, and gleanings from other publications were not to be the magazine's only offerings. With typical diffidence, Brown writes that he will "trust ... to the zeal and liberality of my friends to supply" original compositions, and it will be his task as editor "to collect into one focal spot the rays of a great number of luminaries.... My province shall be *to hold the mirror up* so as to assemble all their influence within its verge, and reflect them on the public in such a manner as to warm and enlighten" (1: 3).[10] His trust in his friends, however, was often disappointed, and throughout most of the magazine's life he would write much of the original material himself. He wrote political and literary essays, essays on science and geography, travelogues, biography, Addisonian human interest pieces, poetry, short fiction, history, historical fiction, and so on.

Brown's apparently desultory editorial policy has often frustrated those few critics who have attempted to explore the *Literary Magazine.* Warfel, for example, writes in his 1949 biography that "readers evidently were not expected to read more than five or ten minutes at a time, as if the magazine were a textbook in an elementary class in reading" (222). This is true in a sense; the majority of items—whether original or selected—are brief, and the topics range widely.[11] But this was the nature of the early American miscellany. As Brown had pointed out in his preface to the *American Review*, an earlier periodical with which he was involved in 1801-1802,

> Nothing, it is thought, ... will render the pursuits of knowledge more compatible with those of business, than those periodical publications which impart information in small portions; by which, men engaged in active occupations, may gradually acquire a degree of intellectual cultivation and improvement, without any infringement of the time allotted to their customary and necessary concerns [iii].[12]

In the *Literary Magazine*'s "Editors' Address," Brown recognized "that a work, which solicits the attention of many readers, must build its claim on the variety as well as copiousness of its contents" (1: 5). The widest possible readership would not only support the magazine financially but also allow Brown to extend his intellectual influence as a man of letters: "The project is not a mercenary one," he wrote:

> Nobody relies for subsistence on its success, nor does the editor put any thing but his reputation at stake. At the same time, he cannot but be desirous of an ample subscription, not merely because pecuniary profit is acceptable, but because this is the best proof which he can receive that his endeavours to amuse and instruct have not been unsuccessful.

Americans were busy people, and few of those who were most vital to the stability of the new nation — from government officials to merchants, artisans, and farmers — had the leisure to read either deeply or broadly. But read they must; useful knowledge made useful and stable citizens, a prerequisite for stability in either a republic or a democracy.

Warfel was correct in recognizing that the *Literary Magazine* appears to be something of "a textbook in an elementary class in reading." But it was not published for the education of nearly illiterate masses, as no such masses existed in the largely literate United States of the early 1800s. If the *Literary Magazine* can be seen as a textbook for anything, it is as a reader for a correspondence course in becoming American.[13] As the first settler colony to break away from the British imperial center, the United States of America found itself in the position of being the first postcolonial nation in the modern western world. American society was relatively new and undefined, the land relatively unknown; for all the borrowing from the ancients, the Europeans, and the British, the system of government was new as well. The American was, as Crèvecoeur says, "a new man, who acts upon new principles; he must therefore entertain new ideas and form new opinions" (70). This is certainly what the American needed to do, but the new identity on which to base these actions and thoughts was not yet fully achieved, nor would it be for decades.

A major obstacle to the formation of a distinct national identity was that some of the language brought across the Atlantic to the American wilderness became socially meaningless after the colonies transformed themselves into the United States; barring radical schemes such as Noah Webster's for creating a new American language, an identity crisis was inescapable. That Brown was aware of the inadequacy of England's English to describe the experiences of Americans—to give shape to their thoughts and to their image of themselves and their relationship to the world—had been made apparent in a passage from *Clara Howard* (1801), in which Edward Hartley, a poor young man, speaks to the condition of Americans like himself:

> The ideas annexed to the term *peasant*, are wholly inapplicable to the tillers of ground in America; but our notions are the offspring, more of the books we read, than of any other of our external circumstances. Our books are almost wholly the production of Europe, and the prejudices which infect us, are derived chiefly from this source.... My words were selected and defined according to foreign usages, and my notions of dignity were modelled on a scale, which the *revolution* has completely taken away. I could never forget that my condition was that of a *peasant*, and in spite of reflection, I was the slave of those sentiments of self-contempt and humiliation, which pertain to that condition elsewhere, though chimerical and visionary on the western side of the Atlantic [53].

This problem with language, this need for what Emerson would later call "an original relation to the universe," is in large part responsible for the identity crisis with which the fictional Edward Hartley struggles. Brown would never solve the problem either in fiction or journalism, but as an editor he took steps in this direction with the various reading materials that filled the *Literary Magazine.*

More than any other American writer before Emerson, Brown understood that American readers were needed if an indigenous American literature and culture were to have any hope of becoming a reality. As Berthoff has written, Brown

> took up the life of letters ... out of a sense of public duty.... It was a public duty not only according to the literary assumption that a proper *milieu* must precede the masterpiece, but also according to the political assumption that a nation with unique institutions must also develop a unique national culture. Noting in the first number of his first magazine [the *Monthly Magazine, and American Review*] that the "literary character of America" was "extremely superficial," Brown nevertheless took comfort in a compensatory development, the broader diffusion of the elements of knowledge, obviously appropriate and advantageous to a democratic republic ["Literary" 299].

Thus a primary focus of Brown's career was the cultivation of "a just taste" to be shared by American readers (*Literary Magazine* 5: 163). He attempted to give his audience the critical tools that would steer them away from reading literature from the point of view of a people in exile and towards reading as a search for American indigeneity.

In addition to a native literary culture, Brown perceived that Christianity was a force in stabilizing the American nation, and he included promotion of the national faith among the motives of his *Literary Magazine*:

> In an age like this, when the foundations of religion and morality have been so boldly attacked, it seems necessary in announcing a work of this nature, to be particularly explicit as to the path which the editor means to pursue. He, therefore, avows himself to be, without equivocation or reserve, the ardent friend and willing champion of the Christian religion. Christian piety he reveres as the highest excellence of human beings, and the amplest reward he can seek, for his labour, is the consciousness of having, in some degree however inconsiderable, contributed to recommend the practice of religious duties [1: 5].

This is not a surprising statement from a man with Brown's strong Quaker background, a man little more than a year away from marrying a woman whose brother and father were Presbyterian ministers.[14] But this passage reflects more than Brown's individual religious past and future.

Although the Christian fervor on which life in the New World was founded had been fading in the face of deism and European Enlightenment ideas of human perfectibility, the Second Great Awakening and the concomitant "surge to cultural dominance of evangelical Christianity" (Matthews 26) were well underway when Brown began the *Literary Magazine* in 1803. As he implied in the "Editors' Address," the usefulness of the individual and the improvement of both the individual and the nation was necessarily intertwined with "Christian piety" and "the practice of religious duties." Still, religion was rarely an overt topic in the miscellany. Rather than "champion" any particular Christian doctrine — his native Quakerism, for example — in an age of increasing sectarianism, Brown defined the religious aspect of the magazine according to his editorial prohibitions: "Every thing that savours of indelicacy or licentiousness will be rigorously proscribed. [The editor's] poetical pieces may be dull, but they shall, at least, be free from voluptuousness or sensuality, and his prose, whether seconded or not by genius and knowledge, shall scrupulously aim at the promotion of public and private virtue" (1: 5). This policy placed Brown not only in the long line of American religio-political thinkers that extended backwards to John Winthrop and William Bradford but also in the forefront of a new generation that identified civic virtue with religious piety, an identification that strengthened as the first half of the nineteenth century progressed. "This was the period," Jean Matthews writes, "in which the United States began its career as the most religious of Western nations.... The message from the churches for the next half-century was that the virtue necessary to the republic could be sustained only by religious faith" (126–27). By 1820, only ten years after Brown's premature death, "Christianity ... had become patriotism itself," as Gordon Wood puts it, and America's "republican citizen had become a Christian democrat" (12, 14).

Brown's was a political time, of course, and he did not exclude politics from the pages of his miscellany. But he saw the divisive arguments between the Federalists and Jeffersonians as more destructive than instructive. He reveals his editorial policy in regards to politics in one brief paragraph:

> As a political annalist, [the editor] will speculate freely on foreign transactions; but in his detail of domestic events, he will confine himself, as strictly as possible, to the limits of a mere historian. There is nothing for which he has a deeper abhorrence than the intemperance of party, and his fundamental rule shall be to exclude from his pages, all personal altercation and abuse [1: 5].

It is not to be understood from this, however, that the magazine was to be apolitical. Although his pamphlets from this period are filled with "altercation and abuse," his earlier novels prove that Brown could be a subtle political writer. "Useful information and rational amusement" were his stated objectives in the *Literary Magazine*, but in the republican ideology of his time these objectives—even when not tainted with "the intemperance of party"—had an important literary and political end: the formation of the well-informed citizen, who would be the basic unit in the cultural unity and political stability of the United States.

But for all its clear statements of the values that would inform the miscellany, the "Editors' Address" does not pass without one startling curiosity. At the center of this introduction, Brown makes a declaration regarding his career and the new venture that defies any simple interpretation:

> I am far from wishing ... that my readers should judge of my exertions by my former ones. I have written much, but take much blame to myself for something which I have written, and take no praise for any thing. I

should enjoy a larger share of my own respect, at the present moment, if nothing had ever flowed from my pen, the production of which could be traced to me [1: 4].

In those studies which to some degree take into account Brown's career after his novel period, this enigmatic passage is quoted more often than anything else he wrote. Consequently it seems the most often misinterpreted as well. Warfel sees Brown here "denying merit to himself as an author," Donald Ringe reads this as an indication that "Brown apparently did not regret abandoning fiction," Robert Ferguson believes that "[t]hese fluctuations between creative satisfaction and self-abasement suggest a writer who trusted his own talent but not its use," and Steven Watts reads this "public confession" as revealing Brown's "self-hatred" after his "abandonment of the novel for journalistic enterprises."[15] Perhaps a degree of truth inhabits each of these analyses, but another interpretation of the passage not related to Brown's "failure" as a novelist is possible.

Brown himself offers on the following page a rarely quoted explanation of the first sentence of the passage: "A variety of causes induce me to form such a wish, but I am principally influenced by the consideration that time can scarcely fail of enlarging and refining the powers of a man, while the world is sure to judge of his capacities and principles at fifty, from what he has written at fifteen" (1: 5). Of course, when he wrote this he was little more than halfway between fifteen and fifty, but from behind the wall of anonymity the suggestion that he was farther along in years might have, in the minds of his readers, lent him a character more settled and a voice of greater experience. The fictionality of age and the wisdom assumed to accompany it allowed Brown an authority similar to that which sixteen-year-old Benjamin Franklin had enjoyed over eighty years before in his Mrs. Dogood. Like Franklin, Brown found in anonymity a "way of airing opinions without reference to himself" (Warner 84). Brown was not the trickster Franklin was, however, and did not attempt to hide himself behind the added fictional persona of a woman with a Puritan name.[16]

The passage's second sentence — "I have written much, but take much blame to myself for something which I have written, and take no praise for any thing" — continues the idea of difference between the perspectives of a young author and his more mature self, but it reads almost as a misprint or as a draft version of an incomplete idea. If neither of these is the case, it is possible that Brown might have intentionally left the statement vague in order not to reveal the name of any particular past composition that might lead to his being easily identified. In the paragraph immediately preceding this interesting declaration he makes known to his readers his desire to remain anonymous:

> I shall not ... put [my name] at the bottom of this address. My diffidence, as my friends would call it; and my discretion, as my enemies, if I have any, would term it, hinders me from calling out my name in a crowd. It has heretofore hindered me from making my appearance there, when impelled by the strongest of human considerations, and produces, at this time, an insuperable aversion to naming myself to my readers [1:4].[17]

The novels were known to be his, at least in Philadelphia.[18] Aware that any "notoriety" he might have because of them could "make for me or against me," thus affecting reader response to his new venture, he chose to remain nameless. But he understood that natural curiosity would lead some readers to find him out. He would, therefore, "take no pains to conceal" his identity from "as many as desire to know him," adding partly tongue-in-cheek, "Any body may know it who chuses to ask me or my publisher."

It is this choice of anonymity—not denial of work already performed or "self-hatred"—that seems to be the key to the third sentence in the passage. "I should enjoy a larger share of my own respect, at the present moment," the editor writes, "if nothing had ever flowed from my pen, the production of which could be traced to me." Brown scholars have often interpreted this sentence as a middle-aged conservative's wish that he had not written the literary failures of his radical youth. Steven Watts, for example, writes that in this single statement "Brown evinced extreme bitterness about his failed literary career and attempted to dismiss it altogether" (*Romance* 131). A closer reading, however, suggests that Brown neither wished he had not written nor said that what he had written was worthless; rather, he wished he had not been identified as the author of what he had written. That is, he would have held more respect for himself as a socially, culturally, and politically involved man of letters if his novels had entered the public discourse anonymously. This, it seems, is his mature realization that public knowledge of him—his character, reputation, past work, personal associations, and beliefs—or even a public representation of him as an identifiable—and therefore knowable—individual negatively affected the validity of any public ventures such as the *Literary Magazine*.[19]

Rather than denial or dismissal, this wish to disassociate his name from his writing can be seen in part as Brown's acknowledgement of what Michael Warner calls "the principle of negativity" (42). In the print culture of colonial and republican America, the negation of the individual writer — and reader — in the republic of letters exists, Warner says, as

> a ground rule of argument in a public discourse that defines its norms as abstract and universal, but it is also a political resource available only in this discourse.... [A]lthough the negativity of persons in the public sphere appears in the form of a positive trait — virtue — it is ... in the republican tradition that virtue comes to be defined by the negation of other traits of personhood, in particular as rational and disinterested concern for the public good [42].

But in the increasingly liberal environment of the early nineteenth century, this type of negation, according to Grantland Rice, has not only civic but also economic implications: it "legitimate[s] the orderly production and circulation of private literary goods by rationalizing the evacuation of writers from their texts" (11). More than it promotes republican dialogue in the name of civic virtue, Rice writes in *The Transformation of Authorship in America*, "the recession of the individual writing subject ... facilitates interpersonal economic exchange because it evacuates the idiosyncratically personal, the emotional, and the irrational from the medium of communication" (59). Given the powerful presence of these personal elements in his novels and his acknowledgement in the "Editors' Address" that "an ample subscription" to and "pecuniary profit" from the *Literary Magazine* would be "acceptable," Brown had good reason, in light of Rice's formulation, to be known only as "The Editor." His wish that nothing he had written "could be traced" to him — indeed, this entire curious passage — reveals his understanding of both the civic and economic workings of this principle of negativity in relation to publication.

Brown concludes "The Editors' Address to the Public" with a reminder "that there is not, at present, any other monthly publication in America; and that a plan of this kind, if well conducted, cannot fail of being highly conducive to amusement and instruction."[20] In the whimsical final lines he personifies his miscellany as

> a visitant who calls only once a month; who talks upon every topic; whose company may be dismissed or resumed, and who may be made to prate or to hold his tongue, at pleasure; a companion he will be, possessing one companionable property, in the highest degree, that is to say, a desire to please [1: 6].

Brown's task was to write and collect a variety of useful information to be embodied in his miscellany. Before publication he was in control of the content, tone, and any overt or covert persuasion inherent in his work, but as in the Advertisement to *Wieland* he recognized that the text, once out on the market, fell under the control and was subject to the judgment of those for whom it was intended: the readers.

One letter from "a warm well-wisher," selected for publication when the miscellany was in its most vigorous stage, suggests ways in which Brown could maintain more control over what readers gleaned from his pages. In the April 1805 issue, one "N. W." advised Brown on the "Duties of Editors." After offering his regrets that the *Literary Magazine* "does not seem to have attained a popularity and circulation quite as extensive as ... it merits," N. W. proceeds to ascribe the shortcomings to various aspects of Brown's editorship. "You seem not to know," he writes, "that the mob of readers are glad to have the labour of judging taken off their hands, that they are grateful to those who will take that trouble on themselves." N. W. proposes that Brown preface each selection with his own interpretation of its meaning and value, and regardless of what readers might have thought if a certain piece had come to them "naked and without comment" they will accept Brown's judgment. Furthermore, the editor is advised that, because "the world sets a great value upon every thing *original*," all that appears in the magazine should be claimed as originally composed for it. Who is to know? "The world of books," N. W. suggests, "has never been thoroughly explored by the most enterprising student, ... and the most noted passages, in the most noted books, may be frequently palmed upon the world as original, and either nobody detects the imposture, or the few that do so have no interest in making the detection equally public with the imposition" (3: 301).[21]

An editor was to be imaginative in putting together his miscellany, but it seems Brown's sincerity—his "Quaker honesty and high seriousness" (Clark 245)—would hardly allow him to use his imagination in the service of such gross misrepresentation. To N. W.'s unscrupulous suggestions for improving the reception of the magazine, Brown returns a simple reply: "N. W.'s advice is well meant, but if the editor's integrity would allow him to follow such counsel, he wants, alas! both the wit and the invention that are requisite to make it graceful and becoming" (3: 320). Thus the *Literary Magazine*'s editor publicly refuses to make use of such easily available but underhanded tactics to appropriate more authority to himself.

Both N and W are among the chief letters Brown used singly as signatures, and, as he had earlier in the *Monthly Magazine* sometimes used two letters drawn together from his full name to sign periodical contributions, it is not outside the realm of possibility that Brown himself wrote "Duties of Editors."[22] If he did, the essay partakes of Brown's penchant for the fictional epistle; it is, moreover, a rather amusing subterfuge in that N. W.'s suggestion that the editor publish something not original and claim it as his own is reversed in Brown's publishing something original and claiming it to be written by someone else. The epistolary form, which Brown used in both novels and essays, functions well in the context of Warner's principle of negativity by further removing the sentiments of a given writing from identification with its author. During the life of the *Literary Magazine*, Brown published several seemingly private letters received in his capacity as editor, at least some of which, according to the initials with which they are signed, he wrote himself. While this is certainly manipulating his readership, he seems to have seen no conflict between a casual manipulation and the sincerity with which he carried on his work.[23] Such a practice allowed the magazine a broader repertoire of voices, making it more democratic and dialogic and more economically viable as a true miscellany. Whether Brown wrote "Duties of Editors" or "warm well-wisher" N. W. did, the public benefit of the letter and Brown's response is the same: the interpretation and use of any entertainment and instruction gleaned from the publication would be left to the readers' best judgment, and the editor and his magazine could be trusted not to stoop to underhanded tactics such as plagiarism in order to broaden the readership.

A few months after the appearance of N. W.'s letter, Brown wrote an essay "On Miscellanies," signing it "D." As readers of the September 1805 number were told,

> Those authors who appear sometimes to forget they are men, will be our favourites. He who writes *from* the heart, will write *to* the heart; every one is enabled to decide on his merits, and they will not be referred to learned heads, or a distant day. We are, I think, little interested if an author displays sublimity; but we should be much concerned to know whether he has sincerity.

This essay sheds more light on Brown's refusal of N. W.'s real or concocted suggestions. Rather than tell his American readers what they should understand in the reading of this item or that, as N. W. would have it, Brown allows them to think for themselves, an accomplishment they must aspire to if they hope to reach their potential as individuals and as a people. They are not "referred to learned heads, or a distant day" but to their own reason and understanding. No material for readers' improvement, according to Brown, could be offered in the pages of a miscellany whose editor sought to dupe his audience: "Why, says Boileau, are my verses read by all? It is only because they speak the truth, and that I myself am convinced of the truth they contain" (4: 164). Sincerity was crucial for Brown throughout his career as an author, and he would not — especially, I would argue, in his maturity — sacrifice this virtue at the altar of his own ego.

Nor would this sincerity allow him to lose touch with the workaday world of his readers, as his magazine competition did. In his monograph, *Literary Federalism in the Age of Jefferson*, on the period of Joseph Dennie's editorship of *The Port Folio*, William Dowling traces the steps of "the Federalist retreat from history, a long and complex withdrawal in which Federalism, banished from the civic sphere by a triumphant Jeffersonian ideology, seeks an alternative home in what we now call the public sphere but what the *Port Folio* writers called, in the usual eighteenth-century phrase, the republic of letters" (ix). Dennie and his contributors began their work in opposition to Jefferson, but as the first decade of the nineteenth century progressed, they lost ground to the advances of economic individualism and democratic republicanism. Finding themselves during this period increasingly alienated and isolated from America's changing social and political condition, they discovered in the republic of letters "a last unsuspected source of republican virtue in an otherwise fallen social reality" (84). That is, they saw the classical republican values that seemed to them the only basis of the good society being eroded by the economic and political transformations taking place in America, but they discovered that the republican vision could still exist in — and potentially have an impact on — the American imagination. It is at the moment when Federalism as an actual, vital entity disappears from the nation's daily life that it "reappear[s] as a style or mode of writing," a shift Dowling calls "the transmutation of republican virtue into literary style" (85, 86). He concludes that "*The Port Folio* had counterposed to Jeffersonian democracy a classical republican vision of the new American polity, and then, that battle lost, had struggled to establish literature as a sphere of imaginative reality isolated from the degradation of life in a nation taking as its gospel Jeffersonian democracy and *The Way to Wealth*" (88).

Brown took his *Literary Magazine* in a different direction. He attempted to transform America's imaginative sensibility to keep pace with its civic reality. Neither Federalist republican nor radical democrat, he used his position as editor to steer a middle course through the various ideologies and controversies that characterized the nineteenth century's first decade. It seems as if he saw in a different light the process of democratization that began with the spirit of the Revolutionary War. Rather than retreat into the republic of letters as Dennie and *The Port Folio* did, Brown and his magazine sought to help guide democratization, accepting the liberal individualism that the Federalists feared and at the same time promoting the private and public virtue that was even more necessary to the stability of a democracy than it was to a classical republic. If useful information could improve the individual citizen, there was no need for that citizen to sacrifice an enriched private life for the sake of the public's well-being; Brown's liberal, democratic vision — the legacy of his life in Philadelphia — led him to believe not only that the individual and the community could be enriched together but also that neither need be subordinate to the other.

In "Duty of Periodical Essayists," an essay which appeared in the *Literary Magazine* for October 1806, the writer, one Dr. Drake, says,

> Something more than scholarship is requisite to succeed in this department of public instruction and amusement: the periodical writer must mingle in the world, and note with a penetrating eye the different classes and individuals of mankind, and he must select with discrimination the proper objects of censure and of praise. Even in the present age, when literature is more generally cultivated, and when refinement almost borders on fastidiousness, many petty faults and striking foibles remain to be corrected; our manners still betray peculiarities of character; and a taste for cadence of period and harmony of style, for the luxuries of fiction and the elegancies of critical discussion, now so widely disseminated, presents an ample field for variety and grace [6: 265–66].[24]

The *Literary Magazine* explored for its contemporary readers, among other topics, ideas about the relationship between government and the governed, as well as a new people's tastes in literature and art during the transition between the Enlightenment and the age of romanticism. But Brown refused to abandon the reality of the civic sphere for Dennie's airy republic of letters, continuing to "mingle in the world" and attempting to remain useful to his readers and his country in their quotidian lives.

Thus the task of an editor in Brown's time was more than the selection and ordering of his miscellany's content; Brown and his contemporaries recognized the editor not only as the person across whose desk all submitted materials passed but also as an involved writer, even as the voice, mind, and spirit of the magazine itself. It was in Brown's mind that the plan for the *Literary Magazine* existed, and it is largely in his writing — which makes up roughly half of the miscellany's original offerings — that his ideas and judgments about life in the early United States are revealed.

TWO

The Republic and the Liberal Individual

Although the 1800 transfer of political power from a Federalist to a Republican administration was—considering the bitter ideological struggles of the 1790s—ostensibly peaceful, historian James Roger Sharp says, "As a challenge to the union and the Constitution, it stands second only to the Civil War. The newness of the nation, the fragility of its institutions, and the depth of the hostility and suspicion all contributed to the creation of a volatile situation in which the union's continued existence became highly problematic" (12–13).[1] Jefferson's rise to the presidency did not take place without a long war of words. In speeches, private correspondence, and productions of the press, the Federalists denounced Jeffersonian Republicanism, fearing that its democratic tendencies, its radical potentialities, might eventually lead America along the same bloody course traveled by France after its Revolution. "Democracy," Fisher Ames wrote to Thomas Dwight on 25 January 1804, "is a troubled spirit, fated never to rest, and whose dreams, if it sleeps, present only visions of hell" (337). The feelings on the Republican side were mutual. For his part, Jefferson saw the Federalist rule in Massachusetts and Connecticut as unnatural. In a 1 June 1798 letter to John Taylor, Jefferson, perhaps anticipating the 1800 election, predicted the end of the Federalist regime: "A little patience, and we shall see the reign of witches pass over, their spells dissolved, and the people recovering their true sight, restoring their government to its true principles" (476). Still, this was not a war of words alone, not just a struggle between professional politicians of different ideologies. Although actual civil violence never broke out on any wide scale, "[t]he virulence of party conflict," Jean Matthews has written, "sundered communities, disrupted friendships, and even led to fisticuffs and duels" (7).

The paradox is, of course, that each side saw itself as "republican." Attempts to define the nature of republicanism — and the relationship of a republican government to republican citizens, and vice versa — led to heated debate between Republicans and Federalists during Adams's term as president. In the first decade of the nineteenth century, "republican" was a term on many lips, but, as David Nord has said of its use throughout the 1790s, "its ubiquity was matched by its ambiguity" (115). Depending upon a writer's or speaker's individual politics, Matthews explains, the meaning of "republican" might be rooted in classical republicanism, a tradition in which the government was supported by the civic virtue of citizens who were willing "to subordinate their private desires and convenience to the public good"; or the term could be given meaning by the ideas of liberal republicanism, in which "there was no inherent antagonism between the individual drive for success and communal well-being" (5). Most people could agree that the United States was indeed a republic, but its policies, character, and direction remained in dispute up and down the eastern seaboard, from New England to the South, and west to Tennessee, Kentucky, and Ohio.

The strident nature of this ideological conflict in the early American republic was due, according to Sharp, to the fact that "there was at that time no acceptance of the idea of a loyal opposition, nor was there a tradition of political parties sharing and alternating in power" (282). In England, Sharp says, party conflict could take place under the Crown and within the context of the national ideology the Crown represented. As a result, England could remain relatively untouched by squabbles between various political factions whose ultimate loyalties — above and beyond those to party — were to king and country. But the case was different in the new United States, where "there was no comparable institution ... symbolizing the unity and sovereignty of the country and providing consensual boundaries within which opposition might be expressed or party competition occur. Americans of the 1790s could not make the crucial distinction between a party, which might temporarily hold the power of office, and the government itself" (Sharp 5).

We should not wonder, then, that well into the first decade of the nineteenth century party conflict in the United States continued in a desperate and often vicious tone. From either point of view — Federalist or Republican — the very survival of the republic was at stake. Each side saw the other as threatening the destruction of the Constitution and the nation: Federalists denigrated Republicans as dangerous Jacobins who would lead the United States into an unstable democracy, from which would rise an American Napoleon; Republicans charged Federalists with being monarchists who would finally transform the people from free citizens to the subjects of another king.

Nowhere was the debate between Federalists and Republicans waged with more severity and fervor than in the young country's periodical press. Partisanship tended to govern the editorial policies that guided the nation's magazines and newspapers, but such political biases ultimately went against republican notions of a free press that would make available to citizens the useful knowledge that would educate them and make the nation strong. "Fundamental to ... the information system of a free republic," Richard D. Brown has written in *Knowledge Is Power* (1989), "was the ideal of non-partisan journalism." In his discussion of early nineteenth-century clergyman and scholar William Bentley, Brown suggests that "under the influence of faction" the proper function of "the American press was being subverted.... The spirit of faction was perverting the republican ideal of the press as a vital public service, so that it was becoming [according to Bentley] 'a licentious Press ... an enemy in the bosom of any nation'" (214).

The leading Federalist magazine in the first decade of the nineteenth century was without doubt Joseph Dennie's *Port Folio*.[2] "This is not a time for 'creamy smoothness' in our speculations," Dennie writes in the prospectus which opens the first volume, "nor for lukewarmness in our conduct"; "[o]ne of the primary objects of this undertaking," he says, "is to combat revolutionary doctrine." Speaking in the traditional third-person editorial voice and in the character of his pseudonym "Oliver Oldschool, Esq.," Dennie continues with an anti-democratic invective: the editor, he writes,

> *will not* publish an *impartial* paper, in that style of cold, callous, supine, and criminal indifference, which views, with equal eye, a chieftain, and a follower — a man of sense, and a fool — the philosophy of the Greeks, and the philosophy of the French — a stable government, and the uproar of anarchy.... He will not repeat to "hewers of wood and drawers of water," the Fairy-tales of France, that *all* men are kings and emperors, and nobles, and judges, and statesmen.

Although born in Revolutionary Boston, Dennie was surprisingly pro–British, and this characteristic appears in the prospectus as well:

> To gratify the malignancy of fanatics, he will not *asperse* the government or the church, the laws or the literature of England. Remembering that WE ARE AT PEACE with that power—that the most wholesome portions of our polity are modelled from hers—that we kneel at shrines, and speak a language common to both, he will not flagitiously and foolishly advert to ancient animosities, nor, with rash hand, attempt to hurl the brand of discord between the nations.

Dennie promises his readers that "[h]e will not make his paper 'a *carte-blanche* on which every fool and knave may scribble what he pleases'" and calls only on "men of virtue, influence, genius, learning, and wealth [to] assist his honest endeavours to promote the dissemination of the true, and the beautiful" (n.p.).

Throughout most of the nineteenth century's first decade Dennie and *The Port Folio* waged a literary war against Jefferson's administration, rising democratic republican sentiments, French revolutionary ideas, and American Jacobinism. Federalists were alarmed—but not surprised—by the way in which events had played out over the course of the Revolution in France, where the struggle for democracy had led finally to the military despotism embodied in Napoleon's regime. Jeffersonian sympathy for the abstract democratic ideas that had been briefly realized to disastrous effect in France spurred the *Port Folio* editor and his contributors "to present democracy in its native deformity, by stripping off its assumed mask of republicanism: to rescue that ... venerated name, from the disgrace with which it must otherwise suffer, by its forced and unnatural association with democracy" (qtd. in Dowling 16). In the hands of Jefferson and the democratic republicans, the Federalists believed, the vision of America presented in such literary works as Timothy Dwight's *Greenfield Hill* was quickly being destroyed by liberal and economic individualism, the new market society, and atheism.[3]

The *Connecticut Republican Magazine* (1802) was on the other side of the ideological conflict.[4] This political periodical carried on the title page of its first issue in July 1802 the phrase "Twenty Seventh Year of American Independence," and in the opening item "To the Public," editor Luther Pratt writes that he intends his magazine to be "a practical commentary" on "RATIONAL LIBERTY," fulfilling the wishes of "the friends of EQUAL LIBERTY and JUST GOVERNMENT" (1). He concludes with a celebration of the power of the people:

> To disseminate correct information is our object; possess'd of this, we believe the people capable of judging for themselves; of this truth they

have lately furnished an illustrious example, and instructed those who were BY THEM intrusted with the management of public affairs, that the people were the best judges whether their government was well administered. A change has been effected, not by the blind zeal of a noisy multitude, but by a constitutional expression of public opinion, by
—"Men, high minded men,
"Men, who their duties know,
"But know their rights; and knowing dare maintain" [2].

Using relatively plain language — as opposed to the high-flown diction of Dennie — Pratt acknowledges that the people, in electing Jefferson, have proven themselves worthy of the trust placed in them by the Constitution; but he is careful not to confuse republicanism —"a constitutional expression of public opinion"— with radical, or pure, democracy —"the blind zeal of a noisy multitude" so lately exampled in the excesses of the French Revolution. In this, Pratt adheres to the definitions of these two forms of government generally accepted at that time — that republicanism leads to order, pure democracy to chaos.

Still, the *Connecticut Republican* is an ardent vehicle of democratic republicanism, and it did not allow the calumnies of the Federalist press to go unanswered. Published in its first number is an unsigned list entitled "Political Definitions," which, in language as partisan as Dennie's, presents the democratic republican ideology:

LIBERTY — EQUAL RIGHTS — the right of doing that which doth not injure another, or others. Without this blessing, Man is a miserable and degraded being, incapable of enjoying the sweets of his labor, and of pursuing his own happiness— tyrants and their sycophants detest and dread liberty; it is loved and cherished by the friends of humanity.

A *Representative Democracy*, or *Pure Republic*, is that form of government where the sovereignty resides in the *People*, who delegate periodically certain powers to individuals of the community, to exercise for the common weal. These delegates, or representatives, are accountable to their constituents for their conduct. In this sense, the general, as well as the state governments, are representative democracies [16].

The list then turns to various definitions the magazine deems applicable to democratic republicanism's Federalist opponents:

Old Tories, such as adhered to the "dear mother country," during the revolutionary war.
New Tories, such as subscribe to the doctrine that Republicanism

"means any thing or nothing"—advocates of a standing army, a sedition and alien law, and other acts equally as *beneficial* to the public.

Monarchists,— Beings who resemble men only in outward shape; who seek to bring mankind into bondage, by subjecting them to the arbitrary will of one mortal.— The *Great* Alexander of New-York is a real monarchist.

Aristocrats,— A band of nobles; privileged orders of any kind; any minor part of a community that would gormondize the whole power, and tyrannize over the major: as, for example, the leaders of the "sect" who stile themselves Federalists....

Truth— A thing to which many of the editors and correspondents, of *Federal* news-papers in the United States, pay very little attention [16–17].[5]

None of the decidedly Jeffersonian Republican magazines of the early 1800s survived in the literary marketplace for as long as did Federalist vehicles such as *The Port Folio* and Boston's *Monthly Anthology*, but I would argue that this is due to two things: first, Jefferson was president, and as the party currently holding the upper hand, Republicans felt less need, less desperation, to promote their cause in the republic of letters by supporting such periodicals; second, there were no Republican editors with Dennie's talents and strength of character nor any particular Republican magazines boasting the support and collective learning of a group such as the Anthology Club in Boston. Short-lived as they were, though, the *Connecticut Republican* and related publications spent their brief energies in battling the anti–Jeffersonian press and those Federalist editors and writers whom they defined as "*Agitators*— A Junto who are striving with all their might to destroy the confidence which the people have justly placed in the present Administration of the General Government" (18).

Charles Brockden Brown despised the kind of party wrangling that appeared regularly in daily newspapers and in magazines such as *The Port Folio* and the *Connecticut Republican Magazine*. And yet, despite the claim of political neutrality for his *Literary Magazine*, he was no less concerned than his fellow editors about the future of the nation. But in the world of politics, party was for Brown the great evil; he understood that it was perhaps necessary to some extent, but he seems to have seen it as more often than not carried beyond the point where it could be of any use in either electioneering or policy-making. He remained true to the policy expressed in the "Editors' Address" that he would avoid "the intemperance of party, and ... exclude from his pages, all personal altercation and abuse" (1: 5). Often in the editorial remarks with which he concluded many monthly issues Brown apologizes to one correspondent or another for "that political neutrality to which [the editor] has condemned himself, and which obliges him to decline the introduction of the favours sent him"; his stance on party issues, he claims, puts him "under a moral necessity of silence" (2: 320). Thus, while such words as "American," "national," and "individual" appear often in the *Literary Magazine*, the various party denominations and catchwords of the time do not. The political sentiments Brown expressed — or, as editor, allowed to be expressed — in the miscellany are invested wholly in none of the contemporary party ideologies but seem instead to draw when necessary from any of them whatever was most "just."

The May 1806 number of the *Literary Magazine* includes Brown's "The Character of Atticus,"[6] a sketch of Titus Pomponius Atticus (109–32 BC), who was an *eques* in ancient Rome and a longtime friend and correspondent of Cicero.[7] Brown begins this brief essay with the intriguing announcement that he has "always had a notion that the most perfect character on record is Pomponius Atticus." His admiration, he says, is inspired by the way in which Atticus conducted himself through the political turmoil of ancient Rome: "This extraordinary person, amidst the civil wars of his country, when he saw the designs of all parties equally tended to the subversion of liberty, by constantly preserving the esteem and affection of both the competitors, found means to serve his friends on either side ..." (5: 332).[8] As Brown understood it, Atticus's politically neutral mode of action supported liberty instead of subverting it, and it is possible that Brown hoped his standing editorial policy regarding political subjects would likewise promote the cause of American civil and political liberty in the minds of his readers.

Brown's final judgment of the ancient Roman is perhaps the most laudatory passed on a single character anywhere in the *Literary Magazine*. Atticus, he writes,

> was a sage in *practice*, while most of his illustrious friends were such only in *speculation*. He seems to have seen the bearings and tendencies of the great political currents of his time, with more accuracy than all others. Unlike the restless patriots of his age, he seems to have rightly estimated his own powers of doing good and the capacity of his countrymen to receive it, and to have regulated his conduct accordingly. In fine, no man could be placed in more arduous circumstances, and none ever performed his part with more true wisdom and sagacity [5: 332–33].

Whether or not Brown saw himself in a similar light during the first decade of the nineteenth century cannot be known for certain. But given the "great political currents" running through the early American republic and the "restless patriots" on either side of the period's various controversies, the "worklike" analogy — to borrow from LaCapra — connecting Atticus's days and Brown's becomes apparent: the early years of the 1800s were also a time of "arduous circumstances" in the United States, and individuals of "true wisdom and sagacity" were necessary to the union's survival.

Even as editor of a politically neutral miscellany, Brown managed to address the difficulties with which the young United States was faced, and "The Character of Atticus" provides examples of some important documentary and worklike elements characteristic of the political writing found in the *Literary Magazine*. First, the sketch form was often used — especially in the early volumes of the magazine — to present readers with portraits of important and influential figures, institutions, and places. Second, its subject matter and language encourage readers to see the analogy between the political landscape of Atticus's time and that of their own. And third, it implies that party politics are divisive in nature and a threat to liberty. While maintaining the magazine's nonpartisan stance, as promised in "The Editors' Address to the Public,"[9] Brown often included topics that suggested — either overtly or covertly — analogous or allegorical relationships between the political condition of the United States and that of some place or individual distant in time or space (or both). The political tendency of Brown's journalism seems to be toward clarifying the structure and meaning of America's political life in the context of an uncertain, radically fluctuating transatlantic world, providing American readers a sense of that world and their place in it as a nation and as individuals. Topics dealing directly with politics — especially American politics — are few in the *Literary Magazine*, but, as in "The Character of Atticus," Brown's sense of what was for the United States politically sound or unsound finds unexpected outlets in documentary essays on history and geography, news, foreign or historical political and economic speculations, biographical sketches, anecdotes, and so on. Between the lines of pieces on the French Revolution, forms of government and political economy, American political figures, and other such subjects, Brown struggles to define the American political character and to educate the individual citizens through whom that character was formed.

I. The French Revolution and "The Lessons Which May Still Be Read"

In "Pestilence and Bad Government Compared" (December 1806) Brown examines the difference a particular point of view makes in an individual reader's opinion of an object or event.¹⁰ Three friends — the unnamed narrator, Thomas, and William — are "perusing ... the history of intestine commotions, in one of the ancient republics; one of the colonies of Magna Graecia" (6: 448). This history relates the tale of two factions in a struggle for control of a Greek city-state. When the supposed weaker faction gains power, it begins a reign of terror through four months of nightly assassinations to even the numbers between itself and its adversary. No one knows why certain individuals — and sometimes their families — are being killed, nor do they know when the killings might end. An impenetrable pall of secrecy hangs over the work of the ruling faction's death tribunal until the killings immediately stop after six thousand people have been murdered in midnight visits from the group of executioners.

"Having finished the perusal of this tale," the narrator says, "I could not forbear expatiating to my friends on the enormity of these evils, and thanking the destiny that had reserved us for a milder system of manners." Thomas then wonders if life in America is always better than in that ancient Greek republic and suggests that the faction's killing spree was much like the yellow fever plague that struck Philadelphia in 1793: "'In some respects the resemblance is manifest and exact. In the inscrutability of the causes that produced death; the duration of the calamity; and the proportional numbers of the slain, the cases are alike'" (6: 450). But William sees little similarity in the two events. The 1793 epidemic caused him as a poor young merchant to close his little shop and retreat to the area of Lancaster, where he "'formed an acquaintance with a young lady, who added three hundred pounds a year, to youth, beauty, and virtue ... and now you see me the happiest man in the world. A lovely wife, a plentiful fortune, health, and leisure are the ingredients of my present lot, and for all these am I indebted to the yellow fever'" (6: 451). William does not, of course, name any beneficial circumstances related to the events in Magna Graecia: "If I had been an inhabitant of the Greek colony, I see not how I should have benefited by this state of affairs..." (6: 450). But he is adamant in his assertion that the series of events that led to his greatest happiness in life had their origins in the deadly plague.

Certainly the four-month period of nightly murders in Magna Graecia must have seemed apocalyptic to the citizens of that ancient city-state; so must the 1793 outbreak of yellow fever to the citizens of Philadelphia. But Thomas could have countered the narrator's "thanking the destiny that had reserved us for a milder system of manners" with a contemporary example of horrors more closely related — at least in regards to the human agency involved — to the political tragedy in ancient Greece: the Reign of Terror in France. Likewise, Brown could well have had his three friends perusing the history of that horrific portion of the French Revolution and then comparing it to Philadelphia's ravaging epidemic, both of which reached their heights in the latter half of 1793. There was at the time an actual connection drawn between these two events; as Jay Fliegelman has pointed out, the plague that Brown would later make an integral part of the setting and plot of *Arthur Mervyn* had by some been "tellingly but falsely linked to ships arriving from the revolution-wracked French island of Santa Domingo and by implication to the 'plague' of French Revolutionary ideology" (Introduction xii). Had Brown substituted the political devastation in France for that in the ancient Greek colony, the crux of the essay would have remained much the same, for in the real world of early republican America the French Revolution — like the yellow fever plague in Brown's sketch — was by many considered an apocalyptic event, one that was interpreted in different ways according to particular party ideologies or individual points of view.

Initially it seemed to the people of the United States that the revolution in France was the dawning of a new age of liberty that was spreading — counter to the history of Western empires — from the New World back to the Old. As had been the case with the American Revolution, the conflict in France was between republicanism and monarchy, and if the former prevailed the cause of liberty would be forwarded. Even though Americans had generally applauded the 1789 beginnings of the French struggle, much of their enthusiasm cooled as the revolution progressed, especially with the arrest and eventual execution of King Louis XVI, the rise of Robespierre, and the Terror that followed. Opinions rapidly began to split as the French Revolution moved beyond the achievements of liberty and freedom, beyond victories over monarchy and aristocracy, to what many saw as a dangerous restructuring of society in which ideas of equality appeared on the verge of leveling what some considered to be beneficial social distinctions and wiping out the privileges — and responsibilities — of the natural aristocracy.

The developments in France and the concomitant split in American opinion regarding the growing European crisis — regarding as well the role, if any, the United States should play in the burgeoning conflict between France and England — contributed to the rise of political parties in America during the 1790s. Federalists believed that the French Revolution increasingly characterized itself as brazen anarchy rather than a brave struggle for liberty. According to Richard Buel, Jr.,

> Instead of bringing about a gradual increase of liberty, the French Revolution seemed to [Federalists] to have become a symbol of regressive barbarism threatening civilization, a living proof of the evils inherent in democracy if not in republicanism itself. It seemed to show, not the inevitability of progress following on the unrestricted circulation of opinion, but rather the dire peril of exciting the passions and jealousy of the mob. Many Federalists believed that events in France since 1789 proved the people could be roused to destructive fury against the best government they had ever known by a league of clubs, presses, and societies. And if the French people had been so induced to destroy the Constitution of 1791, even when the monarchy still had ways of influencing public opinion which were lacking in a republic of equal laws, then certainly republics were even more vulnerable [253–54].

To Federalists such as Alexander Hamilton, Joseph Dennie, and Fisher Ames, democracy as it was being practiced in France revealed itself as nothing more than mob rule bent on destroying the institutions of civilization: social distinctions, property (and property rights), religion, and order. In light of their fears of the relationship between such anarchy and democracy—even between anarchy and republicanism—they found it all too easy to visualize America starting down the same path of destruction.[11]

Jefferson, on the other hand, admired the French, and despite the excesses of their revolution he believed that they were advancing the cause of liberty. Federalists were not surprised by this attitude; as Dowling has pointed out, they viewed "Jeffersonianism as a variant of French radical doctrines, an actor in a single cosmic drama being played out on both sides of the Atlantic" (42). But despite the Federalist opinion that the mobs in France were a manifestation of the dangers inherent in democracy, the Jeffersonians "attributed most of the excesses of the French Revolution ... to the ignorance of the people, the proper remedy for which was not coercion but free discussion" (Buel 258). This "free discussion" can be read as "education," and Republicans could support their ideas about the necessary improvement of all citizens in America simply by pointing to the role of ignorance in the catastrophic events in France.

Given that no widespread institution of formal public education existed in Jeffersonian America, "free discussion" of the French Revolution and its causes was in large part disseminated to Americans through the nation's book and periodical presses. Brown had dealt often in his fiction — both directly and indirectly — with the revolution in France. *Ormond*, his second published novel, is filled with references to the struggle. *Wieland* also tests the ideas of the 1789 Revolution but with little direct reference to it. Of *Wieland* Jay Fliegelman writes, "Brown's novel of authority misrepresented and authority imagined is a terrifying post–French Revolutionary account of the fallibility of the human mind and, by extension of democracy itself.... Through the figure of Carwin, *Wieland* powerfully addressed ... fears about the Jacobinization of the impressionable American mind" (Introduction x–xi). I would argue, however, that Brown did not fear democracy as defined by the participation of the people but rather held a deep mistrust of any radical versions of democracy that might attempt to bypass representation or nullify the responsibilities of the natural aristocracy. Although his editorial restrictions prohibited him from dealing directly with American politics in the *Literary Magazine*, he more than once used his roles as editor and author to educate his readers through analogical, even allegorical, essays about republican government in general and the meaning of events in France to America in particular.

In the *Literary Magazine* for March 1805, Brown considers a question raised over the fifteen years since the beginnings of the French Revolution: "Is a Free or Despotic Government Most Friendly to Human Happiness?"[12] While he acknowledges that such a question would have been considered "absurd" and "impudent" after the American Revolution, he recognizes that "the horrors and disasters" that characterized the revolt in France had shown where mistakes in understanding republicanism and its proper formation could lead. The first decade of the nineteenth century found many Americans at least questioning their own historic struggle against despotism, if not altogether desiring to turn back to that form of government as best. In a brief history lesson Brown suggests that the same struggles, just as filled with "horrors and disasters," had taken place in ancient Greece, as well as in ancient Rome and early modern Florence. But the French Revolution had "taken place under our own eyes," leaving Americans with a sense of "grief and detestation [that] has excluded or supplanted every other sentiment" (3: 178). The strong emotions inspired by the horrors in France had blinded Americans to the good intentions with which the chaotic struggle there had begun. In answering the question in his essay's title, Brown attempts to draw aside the curtain of turbulent emotions raised by the violence on the other side of the Atlantic to remind his American readers that the French sought a worthy goal: liberty.

There is a "kind of liberty," Brown suggests, "which is necessarily productive of, or attended with, foreign and intestine wars...."[13] Civil and political freedom are difficult to achieve, and much is staked in a people's attempt to be free to govern themselves. To those who would have the United States return to monarchic or aristocratic rule because, in their world, these seemed safer, more traditional forms of government, Brown points out that the freedom won in their Revolution had been bought at a high price and could not be easily relinquished. He relates the nation's situation to that of gamblers and soldiers: "...persons who are used to a high stake cannot condescend to play for a lower; ... he who is accustomed to contend for his freedom or his life can scarcely find scope for his genius in matters of less moment" (3: 180).

American uprisings such as the Whiskey and Shays's Rebellions, however, as well as the heated emotions that followed the ideological split between Federalists and Republicans, seemed to many uncomfortably symptomatic of French violence. But Brown offers the suggestion that in the new age of political liberty a free people can no longer measure their happiness according to the amount of "tranquility and peace they enjoy." Struggle is inherent in freedom, in improvement and prosperity, and groups or individuals who exercise their freedom naturally conflict, sometimes violently, with others exercising the same: "The trials of ability which men mutually afford to one another in the collisions of free society, are the lessons of a school which Providence has opened for mankind, and are well known to forward instead of impeding their progress in any valuable art, whether commercial or elegant." Thus social and political conflicts must be allowed, Brown argues, "for the sake of the end to be obtained in free government, the safety of the people, and the scope which is given to all the noble faculties of the human mind" (3:180). He cites Greece as the example of what a free people can accomplish in spite of — or because of — the external and internal wars that result from the maintenance and exercise of their freedom. That ancient republic's language, literature, philosophy, and art "remain unequalled," and in Brown's opinion this fact serves as

> the most irrefragable evidence of minds no way sunk by the sense of oppression, or the gloomy prospect of hazard impending from the loss of liberty, or the fear of slavery, to which they were exposed. The ease and alacrity with which they moved on the highest steps of the political, the moral, and intellectual scale, abundantly showed how much they enjoyed that life and freedom of which they were so worthy, and which they so freely risked in the service of their country [3: 179].

Those Americans who would return to monarchy, even those who would simply limit the participation of the people in the republican government, risked arresting the progress of the United States and leaving its potential unrealized.

Only a free government offered such potential, and Brown's democratic republican beliefs led him to claim that the broadest participation of the people was necessary to America's growth, improvement, and prosperity — perhaps even to its survival:

> While those who would engross every power to themselves may gravely tell us, that the public good consists in having matters ordered in the manner they conceive to be right, we may venture to reply, that it consists still more in having proper numbers admitted to a share in the councils of their nation: ... the multitude of council is in itself a greater public advantage than the talents of any single person, however great, can otherwise procure for his country [3: 180].

But the specter of such a democratic ideology, raised by upheavals in France, loomed large in the American mind, and Brown would eventually have to address it for his readers.

His most direct, extended commentary on the French Revolution thus came twenty months later in the *Literary Magazine* for November 1806, almost two years after Napoleon declared himself Emperor of France. While this may seem a late date to be discussing the rise and progress of a conflict that had for some time been more or less settled, the essay "On the Merits of the Founders of the French Revolution" was not reactionary.[14] Brown discusses the progress of the revolt in France as a historian,[15] analyzing it in order to show his readers why the good ideas with which the revolution started ultimately turned to disaster.

The essay begins with a summary of the effect France's failed republican experiment seems to have had on views of political innovation in Brown's own time:

> AMONG the many evils which the French revolution has inflicted on mankind, the most deplorable, perhaps, both in extent and duration, consists in the injury which it has done to the cause of rational freedom, and the discredit in which it has involved the principles of political philosophy. The warnings derived from the misfortunes of that country, and the lessons which may still be read in the tragical consequences of her temerity, are memorable, no doubt, and important; but ... the emotions by which they have been impressed are in this case too violent to let their import and application be properly distinguished. From the miscarriage

of a scheme of frantic innovation, we conceive an unreasonable and undiscriminating dread of all change or reform. The failure of an attempt to make government perfect, reconciles us to imperfections that might easily be removed; and the miserable consequences of treating every thing as prejudice and injustice, which could not be reconciled to a system of fantastic equality, has given strength to prejudices, and sanction to abuses, which were gradually wearing away before the progress of reason and philosophy. The French revolution has thrown us back half a century in the course of political improvement, and driven us to cling once more, with superstitious terror, at the feet of those idols from which we had been nearly reclaimed by the lessons of a milder philosophy [6: 351].

In the foundation and escalation of the French Revolution, Brown believed, were important lessons for American readers about the nature of republicanism and the formation of a representative legislature, lessons that had unfortunately been lost in the frenzy of high emotions generated by the actions — and reactions both in Europe and America — that followed the uprising's promising beginning. Although Brown's restrictive editorial policy on politics again prohibits him from making explicit reference to how the progress of the French Revolution might be relevant to the political situation in the United States, he is clear about what went wrong in France, and his conclusions about representative governments echo through a subtext certainly meant to educate his republican American readers about their own legislative bodies.

Brown follows his introduction with the declaration that "[t]here are two classes of men ... to whom the revolution has done injustice, and who have been made to share in some measure the infamy of its most detestable agents, in consequence of venial errors, and in spite of extraordinary merits." These two groups are "the philosophers or speculatists who inculcated a love of liberty and a desire of reform by their writings and conversation; and the virtuous and moderate, who attempted to *act* on these principles at the opening of the revolution and countenanced or suggested those measures by which the ancient frame of government was finally dissolved." The reputations of the first of these, "the philosophers," fell prey to "consequences which they could not foresee." Their participation in the revolution took place for the most part in the republic of letters, where "[w]hat is written may be corrected; ... [where] a rash and injudicious publication naturally calls forth a host of answers; and where the subject of discussion is such as excites a very powerful interest, the cause of truth is not always least effectually served by her opponents." Here Brown reveals an understanding of writing in the public sphere that agrees with Michael

Warner's recent work in *The Letters of the Republic*. Summarizing an important argument drawn from Jürgen Habermas's *The Structural Transformation of the Public Sphere* (1962) — an argument that will be central to his own thesis — Warner writes that in the new public sphere of print and reading, "political discourse could be separated both from the state and civil society.... It could therefore regulate or criticize both. Because of this autonomy, this space that allowed critical regulation, the bourgeois public sphere played a key role in bringing about both the democratic revolutions of the eighteenth century and the modern nation-states that followed" (x). Thus controversy over reform can in the republic of letters go back and forth between the most bitter opponents without necessarily shedding any real blood. But in the world of action involving "cabinets and legislatures," Brown suggests, the same controversy can erupt into bloody war and chaos (6: 352).

At this point the essay turns to those "virtuous and enlightened men" — the actors — "who abounded in the constituent assembly of France." Their "motives ... were pure," "their patriotism unaffected" and "[their] talents still more indisputable," but they "cannot be acquitted of blamable presumption and inexcusable imprudence" (6: 353). Unlike the philosophers whose revolutionary actions took place largely in the realm of print, these men attempted to translate speculative ideas of reform into reality. Unlike the bloodless battles that can take place in the republic of letters, Brown says, "what is done" — as opposed to "[w]hat is written" — "cannot be recalled," and actions in life may

> have other consequences. They are answered by insurrections, and confuted by conspiracies; a paradox which might have been maintained by an author, without any other loss than that of a little leisure, and ink, and paper, can only be supported by a minister at the expense of the lives and liberties of a nation. It is evident, therefore, that the precipitation of a legislator can never admit of the same excuse with that of a speculative inquirer; that the same confidence in his opinions, which justifies the former in maintaining them to the world, will never justify the other in suspending the happiness of his country on the issue of their truth; and that he, in particular, subjects himself to a tremendous responsibility, who voluntarily takes on himself the new-modelling of an ancient constitution [6: 352–53].

In large part, the remainder of the essay deals with this group of actors, and Brown explains three distinct points "in which they were bound to have foreseen the consequences of their proceedings" (6: 353).

First, "the spirit of exasperation and defiance" with which the revolution began was too strong and "impolitic" to move the cause of liberty forward peacefully. It was all allowed to happen too quickly, and lessons of history were ignored:

> the nation which has recourse to arms for the settlement of its internal affairs, necessarily falls under the iron yoke of a military government in the end, and ... nothing but the most evident necessity can justify the lovers of freedom in forcing it from the hands of their governors. In France, there certainly was no such necessity. The whole weight and strength of the nation was bent on political improvement and reform. There was no possibility of their being ultimately resisted; and the only danger to be apprehended was, that their progress would be too rapid.

Had reason prevailed the "third estate would have *grown* into power, instead of usurping it; and would have gradually compressed the other orders into their proper dimensions, instead of displacing them by a violence that never could be forgiven" (6: 353). A potentially positive revolution — by means of a progressive escalation of "terror," of "proscriptions, insurrections, massacres, and military executions"— ultimately so betrayed France that the nation "fell under the despotic sceptre of a military usurper" (6: 354).[16]

Second, once the new republican government was in power, the revolutionaries mistakenly tried to form a constitution too quickly. With "extreme restlessness and precipitation ... they proceeded to accomplish, in a few weeks, the legislative labours of a century. Their constitution was struck out at a heat, and their measures of reform proposed and adopted like toasts at an anniversary dinner." "In legislating for their country," Brown says, the French revolutionaries

> seem to have forgotten that they were operating on a living and sentient substance, and not on an inert and passive mass, which they might model and compound according to their pleasure or their fancy. Human society is not like a piece of mechanism, which may be safely taken to pieces and put together by the hands of an ordinary artist. It is the work of nature, and not of man; and has received, from the hands of its author, an organization that cannot be destroyed without danger to its existence, and certain properties and powers that cannot be altered or suspended by those who may have been entrusted with its management [6: 354].

Here the contrast with government in the United States is apparent. The American experiment in republicanism had been much longer in the making: the Puritans' abandoning England in the first half of the seventeenth century, their 1689 Boston uprising that deposed royal governor Sir Edmund Andros, the colonists' increasing dissatisfaction and disaffection through the 1760s and 1770s, and finally the Revolution itself and the establishment of the country.

In one form or another, ideas that led to the American Constitution had been considered all through this period, tried in moments of rebellion and practiced on a limited basis far from the immediate reach of the empire. The ideas continued to be explored as the nation first declared itself in writing with the Declaration of Independence, "the paradigm of ... self-recognizing acts of nation-making, the autoreferential rhetorical act that claims to be effectively founding the nation" (Looby 3). The Articles of Confederation drawn up in 1781 became then the first attempt by the United States to bring into existence a written document under which the nation might practice self-government. Like the French Constitution of 1791, the Articles of Confederation — "struck out at a heat" during the thick of America's own Revolutionary War — proved ultimately unsuccessful as a governing document, having more or less failed by 1787, but it served as an important first draft of the Constitution. Finally, because of the frantic pace of their reforms the French had no opportunity to take their governing document before the public, explaining it and arguing for its ideas and legitimacy, an opportunity America had in the form of *The Federalist Papers*.

As France's third short-sighted mistake Brown cites the revolutionary assembly's ignoring the country's natural aristocracy in its attempt to establish a working government after the fall of the monarchy.[17] Men who became popular by the creation of some witty slogan or the performance of some heroic action, but who "had previously no natural or individual influence in the community," were rushed headlong on the tide of their popularity into the legislature. Once their moment of glory had faded they were unable to wield any extensive power in that clamorous assembly.[18] "No representative legislature can ever be respectable or secure," Brown writes, "unless it contain within itself a great portion of those who form the natural aristocracy of the country, and are able, as individuals, to influence the conduct and opinions of the greater part of its inhabitants." The effectiveness of such a representative legislature exists in the "power and weight, and authority of the individuals who compose it." Humans are creatures of custom and "submit to be governed by the united will of those, to whose will, as individuals, the greater part of them have previously been accustomed to submit themselves" (6: 355). A combination of authoritative individuals makes up a sound republican government, not a collection of those "who, by intrigue and boldness, and by professions of uncommon zeal for what were then [in France] the great objects of popular pursuit, had been able to carry the votes of the electors" (6: 357).

At the center of the essay — surrounded by the discussion of all that France did wrong in the course of its unsuccessful experiment with republicanism — stands Brown's description of "the just conception of a free representative legislature" (6: 356). Using the British Parliament as a touchstone but writing with little specific reference to that body, Brown returns to the idea of a natural aristocracy and the more or less balanced relationship that should exist between representatives and their constituents.

Brown's natural aristocracy rises above the general mass of citizens according to "birth, fortune, or talents" (6: 355).[19] It is composed of individuals whom certain geographical regions or segments of the populace hold in a regard predating the representative's membership in the legislature. Therefore, Brown writes,

> an act of parliament is reverenced and obeyed, not solely because the people are impressed with the constitutional veneration for an institution called parliament, but because it has been passed by the authority of those who are recognized as their natural superiors, and by those whose influence, as individuals, the same measures might have been enforced over the greater part of the kingdom.... In such a state of representation, in short, the influence of the representatives is not borrowed from their office, but the influence of the office is supported by that which is personal to its members... [6: 355–56].

Still, success in office depends on more than rank, wealth, and abilities. Representatives must have either a loyalty to their districts and constituents or a healthy fear of losing their positions of power (or, more likely, both).

According to Brown, "the moderation of [the representative legislature's] proceedings is guaranteed by a consciousness of the basis on which [its] authority is founded." Worthy representatives know the boundaries of their influence among the people who elected them to office and take care to keep the workings of the legislature within those limits. In order to avoid the threat of being voted out of office and thus losing their power and influence, such representatives maintain a keen awareness of the balance that exists between their positions and their constituents' concerns, and "the whole assembly proceeds with a due regard to [the people's] opinions and prejudices, and can never do any thing very injurious or very distasteful to the majority." Here Brown explains further his earlier suggestion that the nation is "a living and sentient substance" and the relationship representatives have to that "living" body:

> From the very nature of the authority with which [representatives] are invested, they are in fact consubstantiated with the people for whom they are to legislate. They do not sit loose upon them, like riders on race horses, nor speculate nor project experiments upon their welfare, like operators on a foreign substance. They are the natural organs of a great living body, and are not only warned, by their own feelings, of any injury which they may be tempted to inflict on it, but would become incapable of performing their functions, if they were to proceed far in debilitating the general system [6: 356].

In this way the people have their say. A truly republican government must — to be successful — strike just such a balance between the representatives and the represented; "the lawgivers are not only secure of their places while they can maintain their influence over the people," Brown suggests, "but are withheld from any rash or injurious measure, by the consciousness and feelings of their dependence on [the people's] voluntary deference and submission" (6: 357).

In *The Romance of Real Life* Steven Watts provides an insightful summary of "On the Merits of the Founders of the French Revolution." He focuses on the essay's identification of "what might happen if human passions were left unrestrained" and the fact that "by the early nineteenth century Brown developed a reading of the Revolution that was carefully in line with his broader cultural principles" (160). What lends an unfortunate coloring to Watts's summary of the essay, however, is his overall thesis that by this time Brown was "[n]o longer the brash intellectual maverick" he had been in youth but "a persistent, articulate spokesman for social stability, cultural authority, and self-discipline" (161). What is missing from Watts's analysis, therefore, is the idea that bourgeois self-control does not necessarily imply a maintaining of the status quo. Ideas of self-culture that would play such an important role in the New England Transcendentalist movement a few decades later were already afoot in the nation before they were articulated by Emerson, Fuller, and others. As historian Daniel Walker Howe puts it in *Making the American Self* (1997), many people of the early American republic — Brown included, I argue — understood that "there was more to self-government than self-control; they also believed in self-development" (9).

Brown was indeed more cautious in his middle age, but Watts misses the subtleties of the call for continued governmental innovation and experimentation with which "Merits" begins. The essay warns its readers not so much against passions but against allowing the frightening events of the French Revolution to halt political progress in the American republic: "From the miscarriage of a scheme of frantic innovation," Brown claims, "we conceive an unreasonable and undiscriminating dread of all change or reform." His first-person plural here is typical of the editorial voice he often used, but the "we" also draws American readers into a consensual point of view from which they could see with Brown the errors to avoid in political innovation. Along the way, Brown gives them an object lesson in "the just conception of a free representative legislature." Understood in this context, the entire discussion of the merits of those whose ideas and actions began the upheaval in France represents Brown's attempt to dissolve that "unreasonable and undiscriminating dread" that American citizens, especially Federalists, had conceived by looking at only the most horrific portions of the French struggle. Watts's identification of this essay as a warning that the "nightmarish scene" presented by the French Revolution "was one that ambitious Americans ignored only at their peril" (161) is in part true, but the warning was not intended to stop political progress. To sacrifice desires for improvement in the United States based on the series of catastrophes that befell France, Brown writes, "reconciles us to imperfections that might easily be removed" (6: 351).

Brown thus localizes "On the Merits of the Founders of the French Revolution" for his American audience without overtly breaking his promise regarding politics in "The Editors' Address to the Public." He creates layers of allegory in his essays in order to explore the political life of America through the mirror of foreign politics, thus appearing to remain within his self-proclaimed "limits of a mere historian" of the American political scene. Without mentioning the United States by name, for example, "Merits" powerfully echoes Brown's earlier essay on free and despotic governments and reveals his belief in a representational structure that allows as many people as possible to participate—through natural leaders—in their government:

> The difference between a free government and a tyrannical one consists entirely in the different proportions of the people that are influenced by

> [the government's] *opinion*, or subjugated by *force*. In a large society, opinions can only be re-united by means of representation; and the natural representative is the individual whose example and authority can influence the opinions of the greater part of those in whose behalf he is delegated. This is the natural aristocracy of a civilized nation; and its legislature is then best modelled, when it is in the hands of those who answer to that description [6: 357].

Brown's focus on revolutionary ideology and the ideals of republicanism would certainly have kept the brief past and current organizational structure of the United States close to the surface of his readers' minds, making it impossible, I would argue, that thoughtful subscribers to the *Literary Magazine* in 1806 could have experienced "Merits" without ruminating as much about politics in America as in France.

In an effective purple passage Brown invites his readers to notice what the catastrophic events of the French Revolution had led to in their own fledgling republic:

> When we look round on the wreck and ruin which the whirlwind has scattered over our prospect, we tremble at the rising gale, and shrink even from the wholesome air that stirs the fig leaf on our porch. Terrified and disgusted with the brawls and midnight murders which proceed from inebriety, we are almost inclined to deny ourselves the pleasures of a generous hospitality; and scarcely venture to diffuse the comforts of light or of warmth in our dwellings, when we turn our eyes on the devastation which the flames have committed around us [6: 351].

Just as the "midnight murders" of Philadelphia's 1793 yellow fever inspired different interpretations in "Pestilence and Bad Government Compared," different points of view relating to events in France, points of view obvious in the writings of Hamilton, Adams, Jefferson, Madison, and others, had deepened the division between political parties in the United States and raised serious questions about the ability of a nation to sustain a republican government.

But the sharp edge of French revolutionary ideology cut not only through the upper layer of America's natural aristocracy but also to the heart of American society, and questions about the possible duration of the Constitution and of the republic — questions inspired by memories of the recent failures of the Articles of Confederation and the various French Constitutions — lingered in the minds of the people as well. The period during which Brown produced the *Literary Magazine* came less than twenty years after the 1789 ratification of the American Constitution, a relatively short span of time in the life of a nation (in those days, at least). Had the document and the government founded upon it proven themselves so soon? Or did France's failure predict certain failure for America?

II. Government to Fit the National Character

"On the Merits of the Founders of the French Revolution" reveals Brown's belief that the character of the people determines the shape successful government must take in a nation. For Brown, the factious and licentious nature of the French led to their inability to establish a working revolutionary government. Republicanism seemed to be at odds with the sanguinary French character, and the despotism of Napoleon was perhaps necessary to govern such a nation, especially because there was, in Brown's view, no natural aristocracy to provide the vital link between the people and any sort of representative government they might attempt to establish. But despite Federalist fears of democracy and Republican fears of monarchy, such need not be the case, Brown suggests, in "the wholesome air" of the United States. At various points in the life of the *Literary Magazine*, particularly in the spring of 1805, Brown attempted to allay those fears regarding American republicanism raised in light of events in France. Towards this end he explored for his readers how government of any sort, free or despotic, must finally conform itself to the national character of the governed.

Two essays published in the third volume of the *Literary Magazine*— "Thoughts on the Former and Present State of Holland" (March 1805), by "Viator," and the anonymous "National Liberty and Happiness" (June 1805)—seek to define two types of liberty, political and civil.[20] According to both essays, political liberty and civil liberty are distinct from one another, and neither necessarily relies on the other for its existence.

Political liberty is typically understood as being enjoyed by "those who expressly chuse their governors by periodical elections." But it might be said, Viator suggests, that it is also enjoyed by those who willingly allow themselves to be governed by others. That is, if a given people acquiesce to live under a monarchic or an aristocratic government, then they are as politically free as they want to be: "All government is founded on opinion, and the subjects of the most despotic prince in Europe are not less politically free, are not less completely governed with their own consent, than any of the democratic cantons which once existed in Switzerland" (3: 189).[21]

"CIVIL liberty," Viator writes, "...is the grand purpose for which civil society was formed, and government instituted"; it is the freedom experienced by either citizens or subjects when the government allows them their privileges— the sanctity of their homes, their rights to property, representation, and the like, some of which "even Americans might envy" (3: 188). Even though the taxes in Holland were necessarily high in order to maintain the country against the North Sea, the Dutch republic took care not to overburden the people, especially the lowest members of society, so that their privileges might be protected. In Holland, Viator asserts, there was little reason to believe that even the conquest of the country by Napoleon had affected the civil liberty of the Dutch, the French leader's power there being "chiefly exerted to procure money" and not to govern (3: 189).

In "National Liberty and Happiness," Brown's anonymous correspondent describes more particularly the transactions that take place between a national government and a people who enjoy civil liberty: "In my opinion, to constitute civil liberty, there must be equal laws, and those impartially executed; justice must be promptly, equitably, and cheaply dispensed; and the nation at large should be entitled to express its sense of public measures, and to confine the exertions of political power within the sphere of public good." The writer then surprisingly points "to Prussia, in the reign ... of the great Frederick" as an example of such civil liberty. Although the government of Prussia was a monarchy, Frederick's laws were "short, determinate, and easily understood." His legal system was so efficient that "there scarcely occur, in the lapse of thirty years, three instances of legal oppression." Furthermore, he willingly allowed the people — or their representatives— a voice in the conduct of public business: "Frederick acknowledged with pleasure the states of each province: they met regularly at stated times in national assemblies; he consulted them on matters of general legislation; listened patiently to their advice; committed to them the administration of their internal government, and entrusted them with the collection of taxes." Such actions by a king, the writer says curiously, "represent not the image of military despotism, but rather breathe the genuine spirit of *just* monarchy, which of all governments promises perhaps the greatest share of public happiness" (3: 434). Prussia under Frederick was prosperous. In the course of forty years both its population and revenues tripled, agriculture and manufacturing improved, and the country, rising "from obscurity and contempt ... to the highest rank of national renown," provided its people a life characterized by "an extraordinary balance in favour of public happiness."

Understood in this context, the Prussians enjoyed both political and civil liberties suited to their collective character. Their privileges were protected, and they experienced the greatest happiness and freedom because they did not suffer under the burden of having to take a direct part in the running of the country.[22] Politically, they accepted the rule of a wise and virtuous king and were happy and prosperous, "collectively and individually," within what Americans would have seen as the strict confines of despotic rule. The writer says, however, that even such lives of subjection provide a "history ... which might serve to revive the obsolete virtue of patriotism, and to teach the true duties of citizens to those who have long branded the Prussians as slaves" (3: 435).

Brown was no monarchist, but certainly the suggestion that political or civil liberty and monarchy could coexist in a single nation must have raised many eyebrows among his readers. The *Literary Magazine*'s American audience, still trying to come to terms with its own relatively new liberties, surely had difficulty understanding how a people living under any single ruler or ruling group could be considered either civilly or politically free. The focus of these essays, however, is neither on Frederick's "*just monarchy*" in Prussia nor the shifting political climate in Holland but on the character of the people in those nations. According to the writer of "National Liberty and Happiness," "The different forms ... of just government ... must be relative to the national character; and opinion, which governs all things, will render that system good in one country, which would be bad in another." In short, no comparisons could be made between different peoples and different governments; that Frederick's monarchy succeeded in Prussia, for example, did not mean that exact duplicates of his government and policies would succeed in, say, Spain. The implication for Brown's American readers lay just below the surface of this idea. That is, the miserable failure of democratic republicanism in France should mean little to the United States because the national character of the French differed from that of the Americans. Only if the people changed, only if their opinion of the leadership turned, would there be any real threat to America's current liberties and popular government.

Such changes in the overall political character of America were unlikely by the beginning of the nineteenth century. The anonymous writer of "On the American Constitution" (March 1805), probably Brown, suggests that

Americans—unlike the Dutch, the Prussians, and the French—had for almost two centuries enjoyed a certain measure of both civil and political liberty. Owing to the physical nature of their country and its population, as well as their physical separation from the imperial center, the people "had long been accustomed to live under a popular government." By the time they perceived that King George III was attempting to exercise a tyrannical power over them, Americans had become "a people ... resolved to be free" (3: 190). They resolved to live under neither a monarch nor a military despot as the majority of people in Europe did; they believed they knew what was best for themselves—or at least what they most wanted for themselves—politically and economically. In this, their common experience since the days of Jamestown, Plymouth, and the first settlement of Boston provided them with a clear understanding of those freedoms for which they fought during the American Revolution.

According to the writer, this understanding of freedom marks the decisive difference between the political characters of the Americans and the French in their respective revolutions, revolutions often viewed at the time as mirror images of each other. Political and civil liberties were, the essay offers in explanation of the far different outcomes of these revolutions, familiar to Americans. For the rebelling colonists "had been educated amid the enjoyment of freedom," and "to them, therefore, liberty was not a stranger, known only by distant report, with whose features they were not sufficiently acquainted to distinguish her from the impostor licentiousness, that so often assumes her name, and counterfeits her pretensions." They were a people characterized by a "love of liberty [that was] attempered with that of order and decency, and accompanied with the virtues of integrity, moderation, and sobriety" (3: 190). The French, unfortunately, had no similar experience with and understanding of freedom, and thus, as Brown shows in "Merits," they were ultimately unable to make the necessary distinctions between liberty and licentiousness.

The national character of America was exemplified by its leaders, exactly the natural aristocracy Brown says France lacked in its attempt to form a representative government. This group of well known men—Washington, Adams, Jefferson, Madison, Hamilton, Jay, Franklin, and others—"understood the nature of liberty, and were zealous in her cause" (3: 190). For a time their political agendas cohered, matching that of the majority of the people they represented, and they formed "the best republican government hitherto known" (3: 192). And even though these same individuals would later lay the foundations of the factions that would inspire fearful comparisons between their Revolution and that of the French, in the crucial struggle for freedom they ultimately accomplished what the French could not: they established a Constitution that could withstand the blows of their own political battles. The writer suggests that, before party passions took hold of them, these were men "who, while they despised the political and ecclesiastical prejudices, which are fostered in the countries of Europe, knew the necessity of obedience to laws, and of a regard for religion and virtue, both in principle and practice; and who were not fettered by that intimate political connection with foreign princes, which is always dangerous to the independence of republics." The writer of "On the American Constitution" follows this laudatory description by identifying such characteristics as the key the French never found in their own struggle; thus "[a]n attentive view of the history of the American revolution, will point out the causes why that of France has not been attended with more salutary consequences" (3: 190). The United States succeeded in establishing a republic which fit the national character of the people, and in this the Americans and their leaders fulfilled, as Brown's nonpartisan magazine puts it, "the great ends of government; which was ordained by Providence, not to gratify the ambition of princes, the pride of nobles, and the vanity of ministers, but to promote the wealth, the peace, and the happiness of the whole" (3: 192).

III. Party Passions and the Politics of the Individual

As Brown suggested in his important March 1805 issue of the *Literary Magazine*—in "Is a Free or Despotic Government Most Friendly to Human Happiness?"—it is typical of a free people in a free political climate to collide in sometimes violent ways. Those freedoms that formed America's national character in turn inspired the people to form individualized notions of what was better or worse in public policy: "The forms of legislature, which imply numerous assemblies," Brown writes, "have been often censured as exposing men to all the inconveniences of faction and party division; but, if these inconveniences are to be dreaded, they nevertheless may be fairly hazarded" for the benefits they offer a free people (3: 180). The rise of parties troubled Brown, and it was party conflict, not necessarily politics and government, that he intended to avoid with his strict editorial policy regarding political topics. The same leaders who had seen the nation through its revolution and the founding of its government — America's natural aristocracy — also led the way in this characteristic division into parties as well. Although their accomplishments before the ideological rupture between Federalists and Republicans secured for them an honorable place in American history, Brown's anti-party political sentiments caused him to shade his sketches of them with a touch of regret that party passions divided their powers and made them something less than what they might have been, not only as a group but also as individuals. Their well known splits — between Hamilton and Madison, for example — had repercussions in the quotidian lives of citizens, forcing them to take up the banners of various parties and involving them in the conflicts which party passions seem naturally to instigate. Even though Brown recognized this as necessary in a free society, unfortunate as such a necessity might be, he used his *Literary Magazine* in subtle ways to hint at the debilitating effects of party involvement and to suggest ways in which individuals might participate in parties without diluting their personal strengths and dividing their families, their communities, or their nation.

In a headnote to the July 1804 issue of the *Literary Magazine*, Brown introduced a new series that would feature "portraits of all eminent and illustrious men" in America. This was something of an overstatement, as only six such biographical "portraits" appeared over the next few numbers. But all six subjects fit the description: George Washington, John Adams, Thomas Jefferson, Alexander Hamilton, Benjamin Franklin, and John Jay. These brief sketches lend a stronger nationalistic bias to the issues in which they appear and reveal Brown's understanding of the duties of "eminent and illustrious men" not only to fulfill their responsibilities as the nation's natural aristocracy but also to record their own lives for the benefit of all.[23] Although he claims that "[j]ustice obviously demands that [in presenting these portraits the editor] should pay no regard to party animosities and divisions" (2: 243), his beliefs regarding the damaging effects of such parties are only thinly veiled by the supposedly neutral texts.

The first of these six essays naturally focuses on Washington, who, Brown's headnote says, "will hardly fail of being acceptable to all" (2: 243). "On the Life of Washington, Now Publishing" (July 1804) is different from the biographical sketches that follow in the series in being actually a letter-review "To the Editor, &c." of the first installment of John Marshall's intended three-volume biography of Washington, which, perhaps because of reviews such as this, was eventually extended to five volumes. The reviewer, Brown writing as "Curioso,"[24] suggests that "great praise may yet be justly the writer's due" (2: 245),[25] but he finds the plan of the work faulty. Washington, having "a just regard for posthumous fame; and knowing, likewise, that no collection of documents, relative to a single person would reflect so much light upon the history of his native country," was known to have "taken care to arrange his papers in exact order, and thus to facilitate the task of their publication" (2: 244). Brown had expected that a copious selection of these papers would be used to reveal Washington's character, as well as to shed light on "the magnitude, variety, splendour, or duration of the parts" he had "acted on the theatre of human life" (2: 245). Instead he finds "in the volume just published, *one third* of the projected work entirely devoted to a general history of North America, anterior to the revolution!"

Marshall's *Life of George Washington* (1804–1807) had been anticipated as a major step towards establishing legitimacy for the young United States. Given the many verse eulogies that appeared after Washington's death, a number of which Brown had reviewed in the *Monthly Magazine*, Americans knew the world does not often see individuals of the fame and character of a Washington, and that America had produced him seemed an early indication of the promise the nation's future held. Washington was "eminent and illustrious" in his new country, certainly, but, with the exception of Franklin, he was the first American to be known and admired on an international scale as well. Brown had hoped that the work would not only present its subject in a manner that would satisfy "the demands and the expectations of the world" but also exercise "influence on our literary reputation ... among the learned of all nations" (2: 244, 243). Ideally, Washington's biography should have become — along with Franklin's *Autobiography*— part of the foundation for a secular American hagiography;[26] in turn, given Washington's widespread renown, Marshall's book should have earned culture in the United States the respect that proponents of a national literature craved. Brown sees the work as falling short of both ideals; disappointed himself, he fears that readers throughout "both the new world and the old" will be as well (2: 245).

Although no mention is made of the Federalism of either Washington or Marshall, Brown's belief that party affiliations divide and weaken all in which they play a part may have had some influence on his decision to write and publish this review. Chief Justice Marshall was a Federalist historian and his history was written in the light of Federalist ideology (Kamrath 54); his concentration on "a general history of the United States," in which "the Washington papers are merely designed to furnish the materials of this history" (2: 246), participates in Federalism's downplaying of individuals for the greater good of the national political body. Brown suggests that Washington would have seen the project differently: "In his eyes, it was the duty of a good and great man not only to make his life serviceable to mankind, but to extract a public advantage from his death; and how can any man more eminently contribute to the public good than to leave a benevolent example to posterity?" The better plan for Washington's biographer to have adopted for "diffusing and perpetuating the knowledge of these precious remains"— Washington's papers— would have been one in which the leader's individual mind was displayed through his own words. With democratic confidence in the understanding of individual readers, Brown concludes, "Thus would all the world have been enabled to judge of Washington and his transactions, *at first hand*, to cull and select for themselves, and deduce their own theories and inferences."[27]

Washington was beyond being affected by Marshall's biography or by Brown's opinion of it when the review appeared in the *Literary Magazine*, but the subject of the next biographical sketch I discuss was not only still living when he was profiled but also near the middle of his tenure as president. The unsigned "Thomas Jefferson" opens the September 1804 issue with this disclaimer:

> The biography of such a man as Thomas Jefferson can only be drawn up by his own hand, and a true judgment of his merits can only be formed by future generations. When the animosities of the present age have been laid asleep by time, his character and actions may rise to the view of their native and proper colours, and the meed of blame or praise will be conferred on him, in the degree to which he is justly entitled to it [2: 413].

True to this opening the sketch of Jefferson provides only minimal biographical information: that he came from an affluent Virginia family, that he had studied law and played an important role in the Revolution and in the formation of the Constitution. The writer, probably Brown, then expresses his "fervent wish" that Jefferson "exercise [his pen] in recording the events of his own life," saying,

> We are not always proper judges of our *relative* merit, nor can we see ourselves *as others see us*; but since a man is best acquainted with his own motives to action, and since the most important information relative to any one is connected with the light in which he views himself, it seems to be the duty of every eminent person to be his own biographer. Independently of these claims to curiosity which the history of Mr. Jefferson

possesses for its own sake, his life has been too intimately connected with the history of his country, not to be particularly worthy of being recorded by his own hand [4: 414].[28]

The strength of the sketch is its comment on the divisive nature of party passions, and Jefferson, well known both then and now as a focus of these, provides a perfect example. According to the essay, America's "civil liberty" is what initially opens the door to voters' passions for the party line:[29]

> In consequence of living in a country, where civil liberty is enjoyed with fewer curbs and restraints than were ever before known; where the honours and riches of the state are open to unbounded competition; where the voluntary suffrages of mankind are the only passport to political power, and their suffrages are influenced by the esteem which individuals may be able to acquire for their wisdom and virtue, the intellectual and moral characters of the candidates for public favour become objects of universal and rigid scrutiny: and such is the influence of the passions, that the same man, and the same conduct, is the worst or best, the brightest or darkest, according to the medium through which the gazer examines it.

Because free voters viewed Jefferson through the "medium" of party, his public and private characters and actions were understood largely in relation to an individual's political ideology. This is what William Chambers has called the "we-they perspectives of parties," which on either side stressed "the virtues of 'our' leaders and policies and symbols and the evil of 'theirs'" (25). The *Literary Magazine* suggests that such partisanship flew in the face of Enlightenment ideals of reason and good sense and made "competitors ... into monsters and demons, and ... champions into angels and divinities" (2: 413).

Brown's editorial avoidance of "the intemperance of party" must be based on the ideas of party politics expressed in "Thomas Jefferson." The sketch's author seems both sincerely concerned about the damage partisanship inflicts on an individual such as Jefferson and honestly puzzled by the influence — positive and negative — of his subject's person and ideology. He wrestles with the problem of understanding Jefferson's importance to the United States. Undoubtedly, the political "animosities of the present age" made Jefferson difficult to profile for a supposedly neutral magazine. For Brown, to attempt to investigate "the character and conduct of this eminent personage" within the spatial and ideological bounds of the miscellany "would be highly absurd.... It would be equally impossible to escape the indignation of his friends or enemies, ... or to destroy that bias in the writer's own mind, which, whether favourable or unpropitious to the person in view, is necessarily adverse and destructive to candour and truth" (2: 414).[30] Because party passions were so pervasive in the early American republic, the writer can present universally accepted "truth" about Jefferson as a key American figure only by presenting him in the most sketchy manner. In the end, the final sentence of the brief essay immediately following the Jefferson sketch — a note on "Milton's Religion"— might be applied to explain some of the puzzlement inspired by Thomas Jefferson: "It is much easier to say what he was not, than what he was" (2: 414).

The writer of the "Alexander Hamilton" sketch (October 1804) encountered no such problems in saying who and what Hamilton was. The essay praises Hamilton both as an eloquent statesman and a man skilled in military art, but it exhibits a palpable regret that he wrote so little about his life as to leave "a veil of impenetrable obscurity" over his background and training.[31] Hamilton's military and political career are described as paralleled only by examples drawn from the glory days of Rome, when the great men "laid down the sword, after their exploits were finished ... [and] took up the pen to record them, or rose in the senate or the forum to defend them, and in all these provinces displayed the same genius and skill" (2: 491). His accomplishments in law are noted and admired; so is his adept handling of those "complicated forms of administration, and the infinitely various relations of a trading country, and a manifold revenue" (2: 492), referring, of course, to Hamilton's economic program established during Washington's administration, a program which Jefferson found himself unable to dismantle or abolish completely. "All the world acknowledges," the writer says, "that, in America, the most eloquent orator, and the most skilful and perspicuous political writer, was Hamilton."

But by the time this sketch appeared, Hamilton had already died in the duel with Aaron Burr. The duel itself is not directly mentioned in the sketch, being referred to only as "an untimely accident" and a "mysterious fate" (2: 492). Despite the laudatory tone of the Hamilton sketch, opinions of the statesman held by the *Literary Magazine*'s regular readers must have been to some degree tainted by an essay on the "Death of Hamilton," which had appeared two months before in the August 1804 number.[32] Although this earlier essay calls Hamilton's death "one of the most memorable and disastrous events that ever occurred," it deals harshly with the species of "*honour*" that would lead a man into "the *folly* of duelling." Had

Hamilton refused Burr's challenge, he would have won applause from his friends and stood as an example against dueling; by accepting it he instead gave his example in support of this "inhuman and pernicious practice." Ill-concealed sarcasm colors the recognition that Hamilton's honor created an "obligation" that "was too strong for the duty which he owed his family, his friends, his country, mankind at large, and himself" (2: 337). At its conclusion the article throws a negative light on the mind of this Federalist and leader of the nation: "Alas! that men are not uniformly good: that the greatest minds are sometimes enslaved by the most deplorable errors; the grossest illusions" (2: 338).

With this portrayal in mind, readers must have come to the end of the later "Alexander Hamilton" sketch with some questions about the truth of Hamilton's qualities. But party politics, not foolhardy dueling, taints the biographical notice:

> As a member of a free community, he was of course enrolled in one of those parties in which such a community can never fail to be divided. Hence, while all admire his genius and his knowledge, and the purity of his motives, a part only acknowledge the force of his reasonings, the truth of his opinions, and the wisdom of his conduct.

Hamilton should have been an American leader, the writer says, during "the storms of the state" that were bound to rage in the early decades of the nineteenth century. But according to the *Literary Magazine*, his dying in a duel had left him not only a great public loss but also a lesser man in the memory of his fellow citizens and their posterity. His position as a party man among the Federalists, moreover, had divided and weakened his influence. "A mysterious fate has drawn away his genius and intelligence to another sphere," the essay concludes, "and who shall venture to call in question the rectitude of this decree?" (2: 492).[33]

As the Jefferson and Hamilton sketches suggest, "a free community ... can never fail to be divided" by party passions. Those who would be leaders must necessarily concern themselves with one political party or another in order to win "public favour." But what of the everyday citizen who votes for a particular candidate? "In a country where freedom of discussion on public topics is permitted," says the author of "On Embracing a Party in Politics," an essay Brown selected for the same September 1804 issue in which the Jefferson sketch appears, "no man capable of raising his views beyond mere personal interest can pass through life without some time or other engaging in party" (2: 445). But the nature of party, necessary as it may be to the progress of a free society, is to divide both the leaders and the people, to weaken or destroy the influence of that natural aristocracy which must concern itself with the government and welfare of the nation. This idea emerges as a key concept in "Embracing a Party": "As the essence of all party is division, its natural effect is to narrow our ideas, and fix our attention on parts rather than on wholes" (2: 448). Such being the case, caution is suggested when entering into the unavoidable party affiliation. The form such caution takes in the free individual must be an awareness "of the difference between *taking a part*, and becoming a *party-man*" (2: 446).

To begin with the latter, to be a "*party-man*" is to have "such an attachment to party as influences the whole character, and gives tone and colour to a man's conduct through life. It is the ruling passion; and like all other passions scorns the controul of good sense and moderation." The author suggests that such an obsession obviously manifests itself in the life of one who gives in to a passion for partisan politics: "To point out to you a single person under the full dominion of it, would be sufficiently to warn you of its baneful efficacy in poisoning the comforts of life, and debasing the moral character" (2: 446). Such participation in party is identified as "*prudential*" or based on self-interest, a mode of participation in which, the author says, "you ... manage the business of party so as to suffer the least and gain the most in your pecuniary concerns" (2: 445). In *Making the American Self*, Daniel Walker Howe explores and reaffirms this connection between prudence and self-interest in early American life and politics. "In the prevailing model of faculty psychology," Howe writes, "...there were two faculties of the will acknowledged as rational: conscience (the moral sense) and prudence (the sense of self-preservation). Conscience was a guide to virtue; prudence a guide to self-interest" (12). Furthermore, certain passions—those of "avarice and ambition," for example—may easily be grouped under the heading of rational self-interest "rather than sensitive powers" (Howe 66). Understood in this context, the call by the writer of "Embracing a Party" is to individual participation in the moral cause of liberty—"*taking a part*"—and not in the self-interested cause of license—"becoming a *party-man*."

In "*taking a part*" in party, on the other hand, an individual maintains "only such occasional or subordinate interference in party affairs, as is consistent not only with due attention to one's private concerns, but with a preservation of the ordinary intercourses of society and civility between neighbors and fellow citizens, though of opposite opinions" (2: 446). This notion that private concerns come first echoes an earlier *Literary Magazine* item entitled "Domestic Politics" (May 1804), another of Brown's own essays in the form of a letter "To the Editor, &c."[34] The letter suggests that private life is the basis for a man's conduct in public life:

> Although, in a free country, it may be thought a slavish maxim, that men in private life should pay no regard to public affairs, but leave them to those who are appointed to conduct them; yet I am persuaded that this maxim, or rather advice, properly understood, would produce the happiest effects. In order, therefore, that it may not be misunderstood, I would make this small amendment: "Mind your own affairs *first*, and what time you find can be spared from them, bestow it on the public concerns, and bring your private virtues and your private experience into the public stock" [2: 93].

What an individual learns in private life is the difference between a monarchy and a republic, the ways and means of governing, and the regulation of finances. Beginning at home, a man learns to manage a household that is peaceful, stable, and financially secure, and the private virtues that create this domestic environment are the same that should be exercised in any public office.[35] If this is not the case, then the politician "who has not been 'faithful over a few things,' will require to be carefully watched when he is 'ruler over many'" (2: 95).

The suggestion that private virtue may be made to serve the public good is central to "Embracing a Party." The individual who would proceed with a cautious participation in partisan politics must, as the writer does, "consider party in that light in which a sense of the true dignity of character, and a regard for the public good, require that it should be considered" (2: 446). This is true as much for the representative drawn from among the nation's natural aristocracy as for the individual members of any local or regional constituency, and it implies that individuals with Howe's strong faculty of "conscience (the moral sense)" need not divide their private and public characters. To control "credulity" while participating in public business and avoid falling prey to party "exaggeration" helps steer those who would "*take a part*" away from the pitfall of simply being "engaged by the names of the leaders, and the banners under which they march" (2: 448–49): "One of the best correctives of this tendency is a strong conviction that men are always men, liable to all the variety of motive suited to their nature ... that complete folly and knavery are almost as rare as their opposites ... and that wonders of all kinds are great improbabilities"

(2: 448). Sounding much the same as the rare voices we sometimes hear in our own political battles two hundred years later, the author says, "if we are to contend at all, let it be about principles rather than persons, and with the spirit of men, rather than of children. It is true philosophy alone which can elevate the mind above all that is low and debasing; and opposite as the characters of philosophy and party have usually appeared, I despair not of their union in one breast" (2: 449).

"On Embracing a Party in Politics"—like the sketches of "eminent and illustrious men" appearing in the magazine through the latter half of 1804—derives its power from a focus on the individual rather than the family, community, or class, something relatively new in the public sphere of the early United States. The choice to participate in partisan politics, as well as the choice to affiliate with a particular party, was at its root an individual decision made based on an individual's character and interests. In *The Politics of Individualism: Parties and the American Character in the Jacksonian Era* (1989), Lawrence Frederick Kohl explores the nature and role of individualism in the United States during the 1820s and 1830s; in presenting background material for his study, Kohl suggests that almost from its beginning early in the seventeenth century "America had been moving from a world of community, hierarchy, and deference to a world of individualism, equality, and self-reliance. But since the Revolution, these changes had been rapidly accelerating" (4). Likewise, Howe says that those "decades following the American Revolution and the establishment of the Constitution witnessed an extraordinarily rich and varied experimentation by the people of the new nation with new, voluntarily chosen identities" (108). It was during those years between the 1770s and the 1830s that "a new type of man emerged in America" through a liberalizing process of social and political change that "extricat[ed] ... the individual from the tight web of human relationships which characterized traditional societies" (Kohl 7, 8).

Brown's years as editor of the *Literary Magazine* stand almost at the center of the period of transformation Kohl specifically identifies, and Brown, I argue, used his miscellany as a means by which to participate in the nascent shift from a community-centered to an individual-centered America. His essay "On Habituating Ourselves to an Individual Pursuit" (March 1806),[36] for example, claims that it is through focusing on a single "master passion" that individuals improve themselves and thus make themselves happy (5: 177). As the pursuit of happiness was named as one of the inalienable rights in the Declaration of Independence, it remained closely associated with the individual and the private as the shift away from the communal and public progressed. At its root the struggle for happiness is between "dissatisfaction and pleasure," and Brown proposes to "invent a scheme, by which at once we repel *ennui*, and acquire and augment pleasure." In the same way that "the blind, who have a finer tact, and the jeweller, who has a finer sight" have improved these senses "by practice," all individuals can, through "[i]ntense devotion to an object," find "means of deriving more numerous and keener pleasures from that object" (5: 176). But this is not simply a plan for the scholar, artist, learned elite, and skilled artisan. It is also for the farmer and "mean trader," whose "happiness" in their fields or in keeping their books "may be as satisfactory as that of the astronomer and the poet": "Nature, an impartial mother, renders felicity as perfect in the school-boy who lashes his top, as in the astronomer who regulates his star. The thing contained can only be equal to the container; a full glass is as full as a full bottle; and a human soul may be as satisfied, in the lowest of human beings, as in the highest." Brown ascribes to this "scheme" advantages for both public and private life: "In superior minds [a master passion] is a sovereign that exiles others, and in inferior minds it enfeebles pernicious propensities. It may render us useful to our fellow citizens, and, what is of great consequence, it imparts the most perfect independence to the individual" (5: 177).

Rather than subordinate the happiness of the individual to the good of society, as the classical republican tradition required, Brown implies that the good society will follow naturally the happiness of the individual. He builds on the idea of possessive individualism as it was theorized by Hobbes and Locke in the seventeenth century.[37] One of the primary elements of this theory is that we are free only insofar as we are independent. For Brown such independence results from having that one "master passion" which gives life a "unity of design [that], with a centripetal force, draws together all the rays of our existence, and the more forcibly it draws, the more perfect is human felicity" (5: 177). He directly connects this happiness to independence, both of which come from a mind occupied by an individual — and independently chosen — pursuit.

Brown seems to have found it increasingly evident that few if any physical, mental, or spiritual elements in a modernizing world could be reliably understood and interpreted by groups rather than individuals. His suggestion that readers pursue their singular interest was in part made in the hope of providing them a sanctuary from the world's — and perhaps especially America's — "terrible whirlwind of ideas" (5: 177). But it was also a recognition of reality. Despite classical republican theory "the people" was inescapably composed of individuals, and not all of these could be divided into and categorized as easily identifiable groups. Thus Brown took up in an October 1806 essay the old saying "Many Men, Many Minds":[38]

> MANY men, many minds, says the proverb. This is true in every sense, in relation to all subjects, moral, political, and religious, and even in our judgment of sensible objects. No two men feel or see the same external, visible, or tangible objects in the same light. So different, indeed, are the impressions made on the senses of different men by the same objects, that we are sometimes irresistibly impelled to say that some men possess a sense intrinsically different from those of other men [6: 245].

Together with an acceptance of individual pursuits and individual identity, Brown would have his readers understand that no two of them could be exactly alike. They may all read his miscellany for different reasons and put it down with different thoughts of what they read, but if they were all improving then their individual paths to self-improvement would in some way and at some point converge to the benefit of the nation.

Certainly these ideas, democratic as they are, would have troubled those adherents of classical republicanism who believed that a unified, virtuous community must exist for the republic to survive. To allow private life, with its different virtues and dangerous vices, a place in the formation of the national character was a step toward the destruction typified by the French Revolution. Brown, however, saw such notions of liberal individualism not as dividing families, communities, and the nation but, if guided into the right channels, as improving these entities from the ground up:

> The true lesson to be learned from the *many minds of many men* is not sloth, despair, and incredulity, but, first, an invincible charity and forbearance towards the holders of adverse opinions and repugnant systems; and, secondly, an inflexible resolution to pursue truth for its own sake, to keep the mind ever open to conviction, ever accessible to argument; meanwhile, steadily maintaining and practising the opinion which, for whatever reason, appears, at present, to have most of truth, to be nearest certainty [6: 246].

Although Brown's approach to fiction is generally linked in the American literary tradition to that of Hawthorne and Poe, in such speculative essays as "On Habituating Ourselves to an Individual Pursuit" and "Many Men,

Many Minds" he sounds more like a forerunner of Emerson, Thoreau, and Fuller in encouraging the development of individual units who then strive together towards unity. He suggests that there is a truth discoverable by individuals and that traditional wisdom — even the wisdom of yesterday, as Emerson says in "Self-Reliance"— should always remain open to question, revision, or negation.

Brown's aim to help establish a national character based on individualism was inherently political, for the strength of the nation and its government lay in addressing the needs of the individual citizen; Brown's selection "On the American Constitution," for example, says in regards to the Articles of Confederation that the first attempt at a unifying political document for the United States failed, for one reason, because it did not address the needs of the individuals who collectively made up "a people who were resolved to be free" (3: 190). Although he studiously maintained the *Literary Magazine*'s neutral political stance, allowing as editor and making as writer no overt attacks on American individuals involved in politics, two strong political sentiments regarding the political individual emerge implicitly from Brown's editing and writing for the miscellany: first, a sentiment of nonpartisanship based on the idea that party passions too easily robbed the political individual of personal autonomy and weakened the foundations of a free society; second, a sentiment of liberal individualism, which he encouraged — along with the individual's judicious and limited participation in public life — as both the beginnings of true government by the people and the ends of true government for the people.

IV. Towards an American Culture

When Rip Van Winkle returned home after his twenty-year sleep in the mountain woods, he found his formerly quiet village "busy" and "bustling," with a "disputatious tone about it." Behind this transformation of the place was a transformation of its inhabitants: "The very character of the people seemed changed." The first question Rip heard in this new world was put to him by one of "the tavern politicians," who "inquired 'on which side he voted?'" The second question from another "busy little fellow" asked him to reveal "'Whether he was a Federal or a Democrat?'" Rip, who came to the tavern only to find his family and friends, did not know how to answer these questions. His old identity was gone, and he could not understand the new identities offered in the questions the people asked. Only when he found out that his former domestic despot, Dame Van Winkle, was dead, only after "the company broke up, and returned to the more important concerns of the election," was Rip Van Winkle able to loaf and loiter "with impunity," to form his individual character according to his own wishes and not those of a tyrant, either domestic or political. Being "no politician," he found that the politics surrounding him in his new life "made but little impression on him" (Irving 43–47). He had a singular story, and with no one to tell him how to tell it, he told it and revised it and told it again until it suited him.

As Washington Irving seems to have intended, "Rip Van Winkle" portrays a change in the character of the United States during the course of the Revolution and the following struggle to establish a working republican government. For my purposes, Rip's avoidance of political entanglements seems integral to his freedom to create — or recreate — for himself a life not dictated by any outside influences but defined according to his own individual character.

A British travel writer, excerpts of whose work Brown presented in the *Literary Magazine* for July 1804, says, "Arts and sciences are low in the United States, although they seem to be emerging from the gulph of politics, which have hitherto swallowed up every other pursuit. No person, who has visited them, can doubt their genius being adequate to works of art and literature, if rouzed from its torpidity" (2: 255). Politics in the "busy, bustling, disputatious" young country certainly overshadowed cultural attempts towards the shift from a colonial to a national mindset in the early American republic. Despite this overshadowing, however, there certainly existed some interest in transforming the national character and culture in an effort to make it as distinctively American as the nation's politics seemed to be. But this transformation could not be easily realized.[39]

Americans found it difficult to achieve independence from forms of cultural expression diffused from the Old World. Besides the impediment of an almost overpowering national interest in politics, cultural development in the United States faced such obstacles as the widespread, easy availability of traditional British cultural forms — books, magazines, fashion, manners, and the like — and the limited availability of an education that would nationalize, or decolonize, the American people. In the literary world, for example, reading material available to Americans in the late eighteenth and early nineteenth centuries was overwhelmingly European in origin. Great Britain alone exported a tremendous number of books to the British West Indies and North America during the eighteenth century; of the more than 211,000 books London reportedly exported to the New World between 1701 and 1780, over seventy percent were destined for what is now the east coast of the United States, from New England to Florida (Amory 514). Cathy Davidson notes that in 1804 one circulating library in New York "could include only some forty American titles in a list of almost fifteen hundred works" (11).[40] Hugh Amory and David D. Hall concur, adding that even though more books were being published in America during the first decades of the republic, the percentage of books by American authors did not increase substantially: "the texts of choice for reprinting were British" (481). As Edward Hartley says of Americans in *Clara Howard*, "...our notions are the offspring, more of the books we read, than of any other of our external circumstances. Our books are almost wholly the productions of Europe, and the prejudices which infect us, are derived chiefly from this source" (53).

Because American "prejudices" sprang from British sources, America's reading practices reinforced the imitation of British manners and fashion. Not only were the reading materials issuing from foreign merchant vessels and native presses "almost wholly the productions of Europe," but they were also read in the United States by a people who were more comfortable with established British culture and ideas than with an inchoate American perspective. Understood in this context, American readers imbibed from their reading of British materials something of an intellectual infection, as Brown's Hartley suggests, that prejudiced them against their own country's political and cultural life. Brown recognized this and began attempts to remedy the situation in the first issue of the *Literary Magazine* (October 1803). "When the works of our countrymen discover talents and information," he writes, "the feelings of every scholar and of every patriot should wish to see them meet proportionable encouragement, instead of being ranked below European productions of inferior merit" (1: 44).[41] In July 1804, Brown stepped up his efforts to promote American books to American readers:

> THE Editor of the Literary Magazine believing that a monthly list of new publications will be acceptable to his subscribers, as a general reference in the selection of books to purchase, and as exhibiting a tolerably correct view of the prevailing taste for reading, and progress of literature in the United States, has determined to appropriate two or three pages in each number to that purpose, and invites authors and publishers to communicate notices of works printed, in the press, or about to be put to

press, and they will always be faithfully inserted, free of expence. (2: 318–19)

Brown's first installment in this department — although listing only books published by Americans such as his own publisher John Conrad, Hugh Maxwell, Thomas Dobson, and others — is woefully short of works written by Americans and intended largely for the American market.[42] But as installments of the list continued to appear in the *Literary Magazine* this situation changed, and the items noticed became almost wholly of American origin, both in writing and publishing.

Yet even wholly American productions during this time were largely derivative of the forms popular in eighteenth-century England — the miscellanies, books of poetry and sentimental novels (although Brown rarely seemed to have opportunity to list either of these, suggesting that few were being published), Addisonian or Johnsonian essays, and so on. Given the barrage of familiar British forms adapted by American writers, along with the large number of British reprints and imports, American readers could not help but read with a colonial mentality. For many years before and after the Revolution, those authors in the United States who attempted to explore their native political and cultural situation within the confines of British and European literary genres experienced resistance both from readers accustomed to content that better fit the forms and from their own political leaders. Comfortable with British arts and manners, for example, adherents of classical republicanism — a group largely composed of Federalists — discouraged cultural experimentation in order to quell the revolutionary spirit of a people who had recently taken up arms to fight for independence. For these proponents of the cultural status quo, it was not important that a book, a poem, or any other expression of culture be American but only that it serve a denationalized public good. This idea, together with the young nation's preoccupation with politics, bound the imaginations of individual artists and thinkers in the United States with a chain that was difficult to break. How were readers to experience the pleasures and peculiarities of their Americanness — both politically and culturally — while reading almost exclusively British or European works? How were cultural expressions in the United States to assume their own indigenous character and quality if they were largely imitations of works diffused by the same foreign source?

Evident in almost all the political journalism Brown presented in the *Literary Magazine* is a call for self-government based upon a democratic republicanism that could promote the happiness and development of the American individual as a distinct entity. At the same time, in the face of slowly increasing democratization and acceptance of liberal republicanism and liberal individualism, the influence of the republic of letters as a characteristic of republican print ideology began to fade as "the political system and publication became specialized in a mutual separation" (Warner 176); thus by the middle of the nineteenth century, Henry David Thoreau could claim in "Life Without Principle," "Now that the republic — the *res-publica*— has been settled, it is time to look after the *res-privata*— the private state..." (369).

But Brown's day saw the republic not yet settled and the move toward the type of individualism for which Thoreau would eventually become an icon just beginning to emerge as the natural extension of Jeffersonian ideology. The concomitant of Brown's political sense of democratic republicanism was a sense of an incipient nationalism based on the idea of the nation's being constructed of autonomous individuals, a sense which in miscellaneous pieces — appearing side by side with his political essays— became further and more clearly formulated in relation to an indigenous American culture throughout the life of the *Literary Magazine*.

Three

The Mockingbird, the Mirror, and the Makings of an American Character and Culture

For the June 1805 issue of the *Literary Magazine* Charles Brockden Brown chose a curious essay on birds from an anonymous American correspondent apparently living abroad, probably in England. "The Nightingale and Mock-Bird" compares these two singers, the former a European species, the latter — the common mockingbird — a North American. "We Americans who have never passed the ocean," the writer begins, "and many of us, indeed, who have crossed it, are utter strangers to the nightingale, except in description." Then, in acknowledgment of the pervasive British influence in American reading practices, the essay continues: "In this way, indeed, there are few objects more familiar to us; since, in all the descriptive poets of the old world, from Virgil to Cowper, the nightingale is a perpetual theme of panegyric; and hence we have naturally imbibed a most profound veneration for this chief of natural musicians" (3: 417).[1]

One reason the nightingale stands out above other songbirds is simply that it sings at night, when the rest of the world is relatively quiet.[2] Indeed, the nightingale's reputation is further qualified, according to Brown's correspondent, by the necessity of its being caged in order to perform at its best, "because those [in the wild] which we hear in the spring are so rank, that they seldom sing any thing but short and loud jerks."[3] Even in a condition of captivity, however, some nightingales are unable to live up to their counterparts in poetry, "for some of them are so vastly inferior that bird-fanciers will not keep them, branding them with the name of Frenchmen" (3: 418). But when the nightingale's song is sung to perfection it is—in literature, at least—incomparable.

The writer then pauses: "I have often considered whether the nightingale may not have a very formidable competitor in the American mocking-bird...." This latter bird's talents are then presented in an increasingly exaggerated description:

> I have ... chanced to hear the mock-bird in great perfection. In the course of a minute he imitated the wood-lark, chaffinch, black-bird, thrush, and swallow. He was able, too, to bark like a dog, so that the bird seems to imitate blindly, and without choice. He performed, too, in a rich mellow whistle, a simple Scots air, in adagio time, of seventy-six notes. This pipe comes nearest to the nightingale of any bird I ever met with [3: 419].

The progression of this description makes it difficult to read without calling to mind Edgar Allan Poe's criticism of that "species of hyper-patriotic triumph" with which his countrymen tended to inflate the reputations of things American, especially "the *pioneers* of American literature" (404). Surely a bird that could whistle a seventy-six-note adagio rendition of even the simplest melody would far outperform "the various *bars*" heard in the nightingale's song (3: 418).[4] Although the two birds never inhabited the same woods, the natural abilities of the American mockingbird seemingly require some exaggeration so that it can compete with its more famous English—or European—cousin.

"The Nightingale and Mock-Bird" invites, I argue, an allegorical reading that connects—through the two feathered songsters—the cultures of the Old World and the New. To understand the singing of the caged bird, the nightingale, as an allegorical representation of England is to hear in its voice the various but related beauties of Chaucer, Spencer, Shakespeare, Milton, Pope, Goldsmith, Johnson, Cowper, and Smith. These authors represent what might be perceived as a more or less homogenous cultural voice spanning, by Brown's time, over four hundred years of English life and letters. But were these authors also caged? Certainly a substantial portion of the literary tradition within which each of them wrote was to some extent shaped—and restricted—by various Old World realities: traditional or classical literary genres, limited geographical space, an imperial culture, a national religion, a monarchical government, and, in the case of Charlotte Smith, gender boundaries. Furthermore, the song of the nightingale is identified with the night in much the same way that the works of the great authors in the English tradition were identified, according to American revolutionary ideas, with an empire and a culture darkened by the corruptions of luxury and effeminacy. Due to connections such as language and history Americans nevertheless "naturally imbibed a most profound veneration" for the literature and culture of imperial Great Britain, but they expected soon to outshine the ex-mother country's cultural life because they considered their own purer and freer.[5]

There is great potential, Brown's correspondent suggests, in the mockingbird to rival, if not surpass, the nightingale, but there is also a serious flaw which keeps that potential from being realized: the mockingbird is too much of a mimic and listens too indiscriminately to the world around it. "I have little doubt this bird would be fully equal to the song of the nightingale in its whole compass," the writer concludes, "but then from the attention which this feathered mimic pays to any casual and disagreeable noise, these capital notes would always be debased by a bad mixture" (3: 419).

To find in this portrayal of the mockingbird an allegorical representation of America is to hear the clashing voices of which life in the United States was composed — Federalists and Republicans, Puritans and deists, merchants and farmers, artists and mechanics, Northerners and Southerners, people of the eastern cities and of the western frontier, women and men, and so on.[6] Life in the United States was also affected by substantial immigration from the Old World; the nation early developed a marked cultural pluralism as a result of the steady influx of English, Irish, Scottish, German, Dutch, and French immigrants, all bringing with them their own national mores and characteristics. But the clash of voices and the imitation of others in the cultural life of the United States does not inevitably lead to the "bad mixture" of which the writer of "The Nightingale and Mock-bird" speaks. The central concern is the mockingbird's— the American's— imitating "blindly, and without choice."

Any form of mimicry, results in something less than the original imitated. In a postcolonial society such as the early American republic, mimicry serves to disrupt the formation of character on both individual and national levels. Homi K. Bhabha refers to this disruption as the "*ambivalence* of mimicry (almost the same, *but not quite*)" which "becomes transformed into an uncertainty which fixes the colonial subject as a 'partial' presence" (87). Understood in this context, contests between various American factions and the mimicry of both imported and immigrant cultures certainly worked to retard the completion of indigenous elements in the American character and culture.

Edward Watts suggests that republicanism itself was responsible for America's mimicking the Old World and thus that "colonialism survived in the early republic" in the guise of republicanism (9). He therefore draws a line between republicanism and democracy, creating two mutually exclusive groups. America's leaders were members of the elite, Watts argues, and political struggles in the new republic were basically disagreements between men of power whose ideological differences, if often argued with heat, were relatively slight. The republican literary tradition — exemplified by such works as Dennie's *Port Folio* and Ames's essay "American Literature" — "conceived of reading and writing as ways to convert the public from their revolutionary democratic ideals to an embrace of the authority of the republican elite. They perceived literacy and literary exchange as vehicles for transforming and stabilizing the public" (E. Watts 12). By perpetuating British ideas, fashions, and literary forms, republican leaders participated in a process of "redcoating," a form of cultural "mimicry" in English-speaking, postcolonial societies that "aims to restabilize the community by recreating the only standards of legitimacy the populace had ever known: that of the colonizers" (13). In other words, republican leaders in the early years of the United States intended that the cultural changes brought about by the passing of power from the British crown to the American elite remain, according to Watts, largely superficial.[7]

Watts's argument regarding cultural mimicry is certainly valuable to a discussion of American literature in the first decades after the Revolution, but it requires, I would argue, some important modifications. Citing the recent work of historians such as Joyce Appleby and Gordon Wood as his precedents, Watts says, "*Republicanism* ... subsumes Federalist/Antifederalist party distinctions and has been applied to the common ideological grounding of both parties: the concept of disinterested public leadership" (11). Still, Watts's blanket use of "republican" to cover both Federalist and Jeffersonian ideologies seems somewhat suspect.

There was, for example, a vast chasm between the ideologies of such political magazine editors as the *Port Folio*'s Joseph Dennie, a Federalist, and the *Connecticut Republican Magazine*'s Luther Pratt, a Jeffersonian Republican. As has been seen, Dennie produced his magazine for an elite readership and was overtly critical of any suggestion that the masses could participate positively in — or even understand — the government of the United States. Pratt, on the other hand, promoted the idea that the voice of the people — of the voters, at least — was paramount in the new nation, and he applauded their understanding in electing Jefferson president in 1800. While these two editors may both have seen themselves performing similar roles in support of "disinterested public leadership," their notions of what constituted the "public" and "leadership" are too distinct to be reconciled within a monological understanding of republicanism.

Watts's specific identification of monovocal mimicry and recolonization with republicanism and of polyvocal originality and decolonization with democracy is problematic as well. Republicanism and democracy are not inherently polar opposites. An act of recolonization is not necessarily one that can be identified with Watts's republican group of a learned and politically conservative elite only; one *Literary Magazine* author wrote in "National Liberty and Happiness" that "despotism or tyranny is an abuse, whether it be exercised by one or ten thousand" (3: 435). Nor is democracy — the "ten thousand" — always and inevitably decolonizing; the French Revolution began, for instance, as a democratic movement and ultimately led to Napoleon.

Furthermore, republicanism is not inherently monovocal. The Federalist and Jeffersonian authors that filled early America's public periodical press identified themselves— when they identified themselves at all — by a multitude of pseudonyms, making the magazine appear, at least, to be anything but monovocal. Warner's principle of negativity is maintained through anonymous and pseudonymous participation, but it would seem that this aspect of republican print ideology is neither in complete agreement with Watts's monovocal republicanism nor at complete odds with polyvocal democracy. Public discourse in the miscellanies of republican America — and in the republic of letters in general —could not be heard as a single voice in a single ideal reader's mind. Each successive anonymous or pseudonymous piece in a magazine or newspaper could take on a different voice in the minds of its readers, and each individual reader — because of particular differences in gender, background, social status, ideology, and so on —could hear in the same text a voice different from that heard by fellow readers in the public sphere. Thus the early American miscellany — especially when it claimed to be of general interest — had to be polyvocal in order to appeal to and address the polyglot nature of the United States.[8] Yet if a certain amount of monovocalism resides within the content of—instead of in the contributors to— a periodical, the case of Dennie and Pratt shows that republican voices expressing this content could vary widely. Both of these editors believed themselves republicans as much as did John Adams and Thomas Jefferson; but if they and their magazines are actually to be subsumed under the same ideological banner — along with the multitude of anonymous and pseudonymous authors who inhabited the public sphere — then their differences certainly seem to indicate that republicanism can easily become polyvocal.

Even if intentional cultural mimicry, then, must be more specifically identified with Anglophiles such as Dennie instead of republicanism in general, Watts remains correct about the ultimate intention of those who promoted it: "to restabilize the community by recreating the only standards of legitimacy the populace had ever known: that of the colonizers." Such imitation left the United States neither English nor American, incomplete, as Bhabha suggests, and uncertain. Culturally, then, America would remain — as long as its mimicry of the ex-mother country continued — a more or less empty national space waiting to be filled with its native contents, whatever those might prove to be.

Brown, despite his arduous efforts in the cause of an American literature, recognized the "sterile" and imitative state of culture in his native country. In the 1801 preface to the *American Review*, for example, he had written,

> We are united by language, manners, and taste, by the bonds of peace and commercial intercourse, with an enlightened nation, the centre of whose arts and population may be considered as much *our* centre, as much the fountain whence *we* draw light and knowledge, through books, as that of the inhabitants of Wales and Cumberland. In relation to the British capital, as the centre of English literature, arts, and science, the situation of *New* and *Old-York* may be regarded as the same. It is only the gradual influence of time, that by increasing our numbers, and furnishing a ready market for the works of domestic hands and heads, that will, at length, generate and continue a race of artists and authors purely indigenous, and who may vie with those of Europe [iv].

Given the settler colony status from which the United States was created, some imitation and mimicry of the former imperial center were inevitable, and part of Brown's overall plan for the *Literary Magazine* seems to have been to help readers come to an understanding of how to avoid being influenced — like the "mock-bird" — by every "casual and disagreeable noise" heard in the national and international public spheres. Readers were provided information and instruction regarding American and transatlantic culture so that they might adopt — or adapt — those cultural elements most worthy of imitation. They could then create the balance of their own and the national characters. Nationalism, of course, was not available to Americans of the early republic in the more commodified form it would take on by the middle of the nineteenth century; the incipient sentiment of nationalism, however, was available, and the *Literary Magazine* sought to develop that trace of Americanness in both individual readers and the nation. Indeed, by the end of the first decade of the nineteenth century, the ambiguity over the meaning of "America" and "American" was beginning to pass, but the transition from cultural ambiguity and mimicry toward "a ready market for the works of domestic hands and heads" would remain a movement vital to the nature of the national character and culture of the United States long after the death of the magazine in late 1807 and of its editor in early 1810.

I. "The American Character"

Brown, posing as another anonymous correspondent of the *Literary Magazine*, submitted for the July 1804 issue a brief note "To the Editor, &c."[9] accompanied by an article — also presented anonymously — "taken from a popular and celebrated foreign publication." In prefatory remarks to the excerpt, "The American Character," Brown describes the value of a nation's being aware of the image of itself that exists in the minds of foreign peoples:

> AS it is extremely useful to a man to know the opinion of others concerning himself, so there is somewhat of the same advantage in knowing how we are regarded as a whole community, by other nations. There is, no doubt, the same prejudice or bias in our own favor, in the comparisons we form between our own nation and others, as those that take place between ourselves and other individuals; and it by no means follows, that we are not entitled to censure, merely because we indignantly reject it: but, whether we admit or deny the justice of the censure, it is always useful to hear it. If it fails to enlighten ourselves, on the important subject of our own character, it at least affords us some information as to the character of the observer.

Recognizing that "blunders committed by European travellers in America" are common, Brown proposes to highlight in italics those "blunders" found in the excerpt he presents to the *Literary Magazine* and suggests that readers identify for themselves whatever errors are beyond his own experience.

The excerpted portion of "The American Character" opens by suggesting that the United States is little more than a geographic construct inhabited by a broad range of neonative and Euro-American cultural groups,[10] a range continually broadening with the arrival of foreign immigrants:

> The inhabitants of the several states differ as much from each other, in their customs, manners, and genius, as they are distinguishable from their ancestors. It is impossible to assign any general character to them, not only on account of the difference of climate, but because the continual influx of a vast number of foreigners, who import their early and habitual inclinations, and never entirely lose them but with their lives, will require the smoothing hand of three or four generations before the peculiarities of each are worn off, and rounded to any thing like an approximation of manners [2: 252].[11]

Despite the confusing, fluid nature of the American situation, the writer stumbles ahead and briefly attempts the "impossible": to define the general "characteristics of a native American," which "consist of a deliberate, and almost repulsive, gravity, a cool, phlegmatic manner, and a dry, desultory, monotonous tone of speech. This substance is evidently affected by the leaven of so many heterogeneous, fluctuating particles, and is, altogether, a strange and almost indescribable compound" (2: 253).

Embroiled already in contradiction, the essay turns upon itself again as it continues with a region-by-region catalogue of the obviously varying American character. The description of the United States and its people takes its organization from the discipline of geography and moves, as though following a map, from the northernmost New England states south to Georgia and then west to the newer states of Vermont, Kentucky, and Tennessee.

In the northern regions of America the people of New Hampshire, Massachusetts, Rhode Island, and Connecticut "retain ... their primitive manners." They are known as being "brave, enterprizing, and industrious," as having savvy business minds. According to the writer, the great majority of immigrants coming into New England are "English and Scots," and it is perhaps for this reason that the area's inhabitants continue to imitate, in such cultural areas as fashion, the English styles.[12] Although New York receives a wider variety of immigrants—not only English and Scottish but also Irish, German, Dutch, and French—its "manners and dress," too, "are very nearly English." In Pennsylvania, where fashion "is a medley of the English, German, and quaker styles" (2: 253–54), the immigrants come largely from Great Britain and Germany.[13]

"Here a line seems to be drawn betwixt the northern and southern states," the writer says, "as the difference is immediately perceptible. Whether from the effects of climate, or the toleration of slavery, (perhaps a mixture of each) industry declines, and the white man becomes a vegetable."[14] In his discussion of the American South, the essayist does not continue his habit of noting what European people most often emigrate to what states, and throughout the description of those original states below the Mason-Dixon line, Brown makes no italicized identification of errors. Except for North Carolina, "which has emerged very little from its original state of barbarity," the southern states are described as luxurious and indolent. In Maryland, "what in other parts is termed an agriculturist, assumes ... the pompous style of a planter." This character is

> inappetent, restless, and uneasy, for want of every kind of exercise, [and] his time is spent in gaming, carousing, or sleeping.... Horse-racing, cock-fighting, and billiards, are the chief games, which are followed up so closely, that when the money is gone, it is very common to hear a Negro staked against a few barrels of rice on a game of billiards.

The Virginia planter "excels" the Maryland in this sort of behavior, refusing "even that degree of exercise, which monarchs have not thought themselves disgraced by: I mean that of amusing themselves in a flower-garden."[15] South Carolina and Georgia are the same, "only that the latter is the least rich and populous" (2: 254).

American expansionism is noted by the excerpt's inclusion of Vermont, Kentucky, and Tennessee. But according to this foreign author, these places do not seem to represent a promising prospect for America's future. His judgment of these new states, which Brown disagrees with by italicizing it, is that they are "daily receiving *the refuse of all the rest. The inhabitants are almost as unpolished as the Indian natives they have dispossessed*" (2: 254). The italics suggest that Brown and his readers may have perceived the leading pioneers of the westward push as having the strength of character that would eventually come alive in Cooper's Natty Bumppo, even if British eyes could not yet see it.

Such negative foreign attitudes towards American expansionism might also have held implications for the character of the people and settlements long established along the eastern seaboard as well. If foreigners saw those moving westward out of the original colonies as the *"refuse"* of the more refined states initially founded by British settlers, then it was only a short step in logic to identify the implied best of the nation in Boston, New York, Philadelphia, Charleston, and other America cultural centers as likewise the *"refuse"* of the former mother country. Certainly Brown would point this out as an error to his readers in order to prevent the American character from being sullied by such implications. If America was to be considered a viable political and cultural entity, it had to be so on an international scale, not only self-sufficient in its own lands but also able to compete intellectually, socially, culturally, and politically with the nations of the Old World. The former imperial center's view of American expansion as degeneracy-in-progress represented a threat that could undermine the viability of the United States.

The foreign author concludes his geographically constructed analysis of early nineteenth-century America with a comparison between it and twelfth-century England:

> From this analytical sketch it must be apparent the Americans can possess no other national character than what our common ancestors might be supposed to have had immediately after the succeeding irruptions of the Saxons, Danes, Romans, and Normans; and, in all probability, never will, as there is no less a difference between the northern and southern states, than betwixt the Hebrides and the West Indies [2: 254].

It should be remembered here that earlier this British essayist said that it might take "three or four generations" for the edges of difference evident within the population of the United States to be "rounded to any thing like an approximation of manners," but that "sooner or later" all the "different habitudes ... give way to the general mass of American customs, which long usage and republican genius have established" (2: 252–53).[16] And so in his prediction that there probably "never will" be broad cultural characteristics common to the American people, the writer contradicts himself once again.[17]

"Useful information and rational amusement being his objects," Brown says in his "Editors' Address to the Public," "[the editor] will not scruple to collect materials from all quarters." He promises to "ransack the newest foreign publications, and extract from them whatever can serve his purpose" (1: 5). But what did Brown expect his *Literary Magazine* subscribers to take away from their reading of this contradictory essay on "The American Character"? The works of foreign authors "enable us to know what ideas are formed of us by strangers," he says, reiterating his suggestion at the beginning of the headnote that this is an "advantage" to both an individual and a people (2: 252). What I would argue is more important for his readers, however, is Brown's understanding of the power of print. Although an author is but a single human being, subject to all the influences and prejudices of past experience and present circumstances, "the mass of mankind are only his readers; they look with his eyes, and take the fashion of opinions he dictates." Brown recognizes the authority willingly invested in published authors by unsuspecting readers. The influence of an individual who publishes is perpetuated and extended by every reader who interacts with his work in the republic of letters; thus through publication the ideas and judgments the author offers are legitimized in the public sphere.

Brown argues with the foreign author by italicizing "blunders" in the sketch, pointing out to his readers the importance of thinking clearly and critically when dealing with such a powerful medium as print. He then invites them — by both suggestion and example — to do the same. But what is striking by the end of "The American Character" is that Brown has italicized relatively few mistakes about America as a place and Americans as a people. Moreover, those "blunders" he identifies — that the people of New England are overly inquisitive, that the people of New Jersey are mostly Quakers, that a person caught passing through Connecticut on a Sunday "*is seized, led to a place of worship, and seated between his guards during divine service, with the eyes of the congregation upon him, much to his and their edification, no doubt*" (2: 255) — seem to have a rather limited impact on the description as a whole. Brown's editorial silence on matters of seemingly greater import — the nation's imitative culture and regional division, for example — tends to support the idea of the American character's being largely an artificial construct inflected by the varying degrees of cultural influence exercised by its colonial past, as well as by place and its concomitants: local custom, institutions, education, politics, and so on.

Indeed, Brown's editorial practices, influenced as they were by his increasing acceptance of the ideology of liberal individualism (exemplified in the miscellany by essays such as "On Habituating Ourselves to an Individual Pursuit" and "Many Men, Many Minds"), promote the idea that no two citizens — or regions — of the United States seemed able to typify the nation's cultural identity. In an essay called "American Manners" (April 1805), another of Brown's anonymous correspondents sets out to correct some errors made both by foreign writers and natives:

> AN American who pays any attention to foreign literature has perpetual occasion for surprise at the representations which he meets with of his own country, not only among foreigners, but among those who are natives of America. The grand error of the last is the propensity to confound the United States in general, with some particular state or district. They seem entirely unmindful that the United States are no more than a league of several nations as dissimilar to each other as any two nations of Europe. In climate, we have, of course, all the varieties between the south of Spain and the north of England; but in our manners and habits, social and political, we are, in many particulars, as unlike each other as the Provencals and Livonians [3: 291–92].[18]

Coming as it does from the pen of an American author and from the pages of an American magazine, this essay seems less critical than "The American Character." The differences between groups and regions were a reality in the sparsely populated United States, but so was its union. As Anderson says in *Imagined Communities*, "the members of even the smallest nation will never know most of their fellow-members, meet them, or even hear of them, yet in the minds of each lives the image of their communion" (6). The condition of the United States in the first decade of the nineteenth century — a vast land dotted with only a handful of cities and relatively few towns, villages, and farms— made it even more unlikely than in "the smallest nation" that individuals would meet a broad range of their fellow citizens.

How, then, were Americans to know what was thought or expected of them in regards to the formation of a national character and culture? How were they to know what distant fellow citizens were like in order to stop confounding "the United States in general" with their own "particular state or district"? Much of the burden of carrying this information to the people fell to America's burgeoning periodical press, which was, in some corners at least, involved in its own struggle to break away from its colonial past and still colonized present in order to define its own character as a medium.

It is probably due to the somewhat hazy notions of what America and the American were that relatively superficial representations of the country and its people appeared in the periodical press prior to 1800. Dennie's *Port Folio* and Boston's *Monthly Anthology* could, for the most part, have been as easily written by British journalists as American, the attitude of the former being so often pro British and the content of the latter including little specifically American material. Most other magazines in the early republic, especially the miscellanies, usually offered items with only vaguely drawn images of their native country: sketches of political figures, tales set nowhere in particular, and poetry that might as well have come from Europe, so little does it reflect American sensibilities. As William Free has pointed out regarding *The Columbian Magazine* (1786–1792), much of the "belletristic material" in that earlier miscellany "has no identifiable reference to American life. Images, characters, and settings either are generalized beyond individuality or are European." Free suggests that, for belle lettres at least, "conventions of the borrowed English genres hampered American writers seeking to portray their own country" (114):

> The periodical essay, the novel or short tale of manners, odes, elegies and *vers de société* with their suggestion of an established social order and a continuous tradition of manners and morals proved an awkward vehicle for national ideals of a republican society — unlimited growth and progress, maximum individual liberty, and freedom from the limitations of social tradition or past order [113].

In the real world outside the republic of letters relatively few took time to consider how they might contribute to the creation of an indigenous American character. There were, moreover, real obstacles in the way of making America's cultural life distinct from that of Great Britain. Politics overshadowed culture. The population was scattered across large areas, and political centers were often removed from the cultural and artistic, as in the 1800 removal of the national capital from metropolitan Philadelphia to the backwater of the District of Columbia. Libraries were few and more often than not poorly supplied with scholarly works. College professors were often forced to spend the majority of their energies on fundamental teaching, leaving them little time for more scholarly activities. The Puritan work ethic combined with a rapidly expanding liberal economy encouraged individuals of talent to go into fields of endeavor more profitable than the arts. British and European works filled the bookshops, crowding out the few native productions that found publication. Old World systems of literary apprenticeship and patronage were, on the whole, nonexistent. And the list of obstacles goes on.[19]

The people of the United States were certainly rough in many ways and imitative of British and European elegance in others. It was Brown's task as an editor to apply, as the author of "The American Character" says, the "smoothing hand" to the rough edges and to guide imitation into channels that would eventually "give way" to a "general mass of American customs." In order to accomplish this task, the content of Brown's magazine had to be localized and seen as under local control. Americans could write essays such as "American Manners" for the miscellany without editorial intervention, but an essay such as "The American Character" required mediation from Brown or his correspondents.

The pages of the *Literary Magazine* are filled with American places, people, and subjects. These localized the content. Brown's readers could have experienced no confusion — such as readers of the *Columbian Magazine* or *Port Folio* often could have — over whether or not his was an American publication. Certainly there is much in the miscellany that imitates the British examples of the genre and much that is about the Old World, but Brown often presented his American audience with reading materials that provided not a window on England and Europe but a mirror reflecting an increasingly clearer image of themselves and their country.

II. The Mirror of Travel

In his discussion of American literature and British forms, Free identifies the regimented genres of "geography, biography, and history" as most "congenial to American subject matter." To this list I would add travel literature, which stands as a genre unto itself, a link between the relatively empirical geography and biography and the more creative personal essay and fiction. It was a genre Americans took advantage of in a variety of ways throughout the eighteenth century and into the nineteenth. Travelers, surveyors, statesmen, ethnographers, naturalists, farmers, and even those who were captives of Native American tribes often wrote their travels in an attempt to capture some aspect or other of the American experience. In this discussion, however, I limit myself to works written by British travelers in America in an effort to understand how Brown and his readers might have used travel literature by visitors from the former imperial center not in an attempt to embody American experience in writing but as a mirror in which to see themselves as they were seen by their closest counterparts in a transatlantic culture.

The world known to Europe had been expanding since the end of the Middle Ages, and in an "enlightened" western culture that valued order, travel literature fascinated people with the strangeness, the anomalies, that lay beyond their ken (Micklus 361). The idea of America was born, of course, in the literature of travel written by such men as Columbus and

John Smith, and later, when in the early nineteenth century the new American nation was an already large and still expanding country, narratives of travels in the United States provided American readers valuable information about foreign perceptions of themselves and the land and ways of life of distant people who were their "imagined" fellow citizens. Thus it was, at least in part, that the American nation itself was made real to readers through the travel literature available in the republic of letters.

The nature of the genre, according to Robert Micklus, might explain both why it was enjoyed by its readers and why it has been until recently largely ignored by literary critics: on the one hand, Micklus suggests, it was popular with its audience because "the sheer factuality of travel accounts ... was ideally suited to an age that valued empirical observation as the means to understanding truth" (362); on the other hand, it has been ignored by many modern literary critics because "it consists"—for the most part—"of closet performances intended only for private audiences, ... provides merely a factual account of real events rather than the creative fruits of an author's imagination, and ... is often composed at such scattered intervals that it cannot possibly possess the unity and coherence we expect from serious literature" (360).

Early publishers paid well for travel narratives; in eighteenth-century England, Henry Fielding received one thousand pounds for the manuscript of *Tom Jones*, but John Hawkesworth was paid six thousand for his 1773 *Account of the Voyages ... in the Southern Hemisphere* (Micklus 361). In America, magazine editors such as Charles Brockden Brown requested that acquaintances and correspondents away on trips submit accounts of their travels for publication; for example, while John Blair Linn—brother of Brown's future wife Elizabeth—journeyed to Boston in the summer of 1804, Brown wrote to him, "I am highly pleased to hear that you have kept something like a journal in your absence. I long to see it. I wish you would transmit it to me immediately by post, and give me leave to make immediate use of it in the Magazine now in the press."[20]

In Brown's *Literary Magazine*—as well as in many other periodicals and books—the literature of travel provided a site for the intermingling and contesting of ideologies, cultures, and individuals. Mary Louise Pratt calls this site the "contact zone": "the space of colonial encounters, the space in which peoples geographically and historically separated come into contact with each other" (6). Travel literature could suggest to its readers their relationship to some foreign Other, show them — as if in a mirror — how they were perceived by that Other, and strengthen their sense of communion with distant fellow citizens. Examples of the genre were never a regular feature in the *Literary Magazine*, but throughout the miscellany's eight volumes Brown made use of travel narratives often enough to allow his readers to step into Pratt's "contact zone" as it existed in the republic of letters and view from there images both of themselves and of the world beyond.[21]

For example, in "An Emigrant in America" (December 1806), an anonymous correspondent of the *Literary Magazine* wrote, "There cannot be a more extreme contrast to any country that has been long under cultivation, or a scene more totally new to a native of Great Britain, than the boundless forests of America. An emigrant set down in such a scene feels almost the helplessness of a child" (6: 411). England was a cultivated land, physically as well as socially, and the rough quality of America was a shock to the system of many emigrants and travelers who had left home and crossed the Atlantic either to speculate on a new life or simply to experience the New World. Almost two hundred years after Bradford and Winthrop, America remained a "howling wilderness" to this "new settler" (6: 412). The metaphorical child that the new arrival became when faced with the American landscape could suffer the same difficulties an actual child might face in the woods: the fear of solitude, the threat of becoming lost, bewilderment, starvation. Unlike the Puritan groups associated with Bradford and Winthrop, however, the "enlightened" Europeans settling in America — permanently or temporarily — in the early part of the nineteenth century did not turn so much to God for protection and guidance as to the natives: "So many instances are quoted of the ill success of Europeans, when placed at once in the heart of the wild woods, that I have heard several gentlemen, of the highest abilities and experience in the United States, pronounce an unqualified opinion, that a new settlement could not be formed without a basis of native Americans." These natives were not Smith's or Bradford's but the early republic's Euro-American incarnations of Pocahontas and Squanto: the "practiced *woodsman* [who] can find his way through the trackless forest" (6: 412).

The writer of "An Emigrant" kept the essay factual, one of the primary requirements of eighteenth-century travel writing. "Readers and critics expected travel writers to adhere to certain conventions and forms," Richard Wisneski writes (4):

> Writers were not to talk about themselves.... [They] had to describe cities and towns, the customs and manners of the people they encountered,

the landscape, trade and commerce.... Their texts were in many ways constructs. If travel writers wanted to manipulate what they described to present their own agenda or messages to their audience, they had to do so under the confines of these constructs [5–6].

Following the conventions prescribed for the period's travel literature, the writer of "An Emigrant" describes as a matter of fact the difficulties individuals from Great Britain would face in leaving home for the United States. The resulting picture is an interesting mixture of an Englishman's anxiety over hardships and his admiration for "native Americans" who had learned to live with, even to conquer, the land's harsh conditions. Because Brown's editorial policy often constructed the *Literary Magazine* as a mirror made of text, American readers could see reflected in this article the realities of their thinly populated new nation, but there was also in it an image of themselves in which they could take some measure of pride. Their forebears had come into an even wilder land, had settled it and survived. By the first decade of the nineteenth century, Brown's readers, descendants of those hardy colonists, could claim as their own — and, as Myra Jehlen suggests, identify with — a place that often frightened and confounded contemporary visitors from the former imperial center.

Jehlen's *American Incarnation* (1986) helps to explain some of the difficulty an immigrant faced in the early United States. The notion of liberal individualism had thrived in Europe during the long eighteenth century, thanks in part to the philosophical writings of Hobbes, Locke, and Rousseau. But there it had remained a rather abstract ideal, more or less embattled in reality. In one sense the same was true in America: here "notions of individual autonomy defended by natural inalienable rights, of the sanctity of private property, as it fulfills individual self-possession, and of representative government as an ideal social order implied by such self-possessive individualism ... bespoke another liberal nation, not a new world" (Jehlen 3). But if this was the entire case, why would the writer of "An Emigrant" claim that in America "[h]e has a new set of ideas to acquire: the knowledge which all his previous experience has accumulated can seldom be applied; his ignorance as to the circumstances of his new situation meets him on every occasion" (6: 411–12)? Because of the overpowering impact of nature in the New World, liberal individualism was extended to its natural end, its "culminating stage that was substantially different from its intermediate European form" (Jehlen 3). The wild continent forced a change in the concept of liberal individualism; transformed by the land, the abstract theory became concrete necessity. "America was an avatar of the world prior to feudalism," Jehlen writes, "and, in the sense that it still awaited its primal molding, it was anterior to the old world's division.... American civilization remained at one with [nature] and embodied nature's laws organically.... The European immigrant who became an American saw himself not as entering a better society but as leaving society altogether" (5). Those who would emigrate from Great Britain must prepare themselves well for this shock that their sensibilities would receive in America. Their ideas that liberal individualism was part of natural law, that it was the manifestation in the human sphere of the immutable laws of nature, would collide with a new reality on the American continent, where civilization did not parallel — and yet remain separate from — nature but was built out of nature and remained, to adapt Emerson's phrase from *Nature*, "part or particle" of it (13).

Contrary to his usual practice when publishing pieces about America from the pens of British or European authors, Brown presented "An Emigrant in America" to his readers without editorial comment, perhaps because he felt it to be instructive and agreed with — or at least was not stirred to argument by — its content and sentiments. More typical is the attitude and approach apparent in "An Account of Parkinson's Tour in America" (March 1806).[22] Presenting the narrative of his travels — and travails — in the United States during the last years of the eighteenth century, Richard Parkinson's work set out "to undeceive those who have been taught to consider America, either as a place of refuge from poverty, or as a scene of speculation." In contrast to the author of "An Emigrant," Parkinson does not adhere to the rules governing travel writing. The excerpts from his volumes that appear in "An Account" carry complaints about how physical and social conditions in America conspired against his personal schemes to profit from agricultural speculation in the New World. Parkinson's arrogance and his message that coming to America is not worth a British man's time and expense are not subtly embedded within travel literature's conventions but seem to be the narrative's focal points.

Parkinson came to the United States in 1798. An acquaintance, John Sinclair, had received from George Washington an offer to let sections of his holdings in Virginia to British farmers. Figuring to make a quick fortune in cultivating "the *promised land*," Parkinson "pitched on a farm of twelve hundred acres, at twenty-two shillings (about five dollars) an acre of rent" (5: 220).[23] He bought cattle, pigs, dogs, and several fine horses in England and loaded them with his family onto a ship for a twelve-week voyage across the Atlantic. After arriving in Norfolk in mid November, with substantially less livestock than he originally had, he made a difficult trip to Mount Vernon; it was "a voyage generally of eleven hours," Brown writes, "but which ... bad luck protracted to nine days" (5: 221). Parkinson was disappointed in Washington's land but apparently settled his family and livestock there anyway. Over the next two years and more he used the farm as a base for his travels. From the beginning, American "weather, the land, roads, markets, landlord, parson, justices, servants, and neighbors," Brown writes, "all come in for a share of [Parkinson's] abuse: and so cautiously is every consolatory topic avoided, that we are at a loss how, in the midst of all sorts of calamity and vexation, he could either have paid his rent, or preserved his reason" (5: 219).

Parkinson's overly passionate grumbling becomes an easy target for ridicule, and Brown — with a light touch of such ridicule in mind — immediately draws his readers together through the use of a first-person plural point of view: "A TOUR in the United States has lately been published in Europe, written by Richard Parkinson, a practical farmer, who lately spent three years among us." The use of "us" in this opening sentence invites the magazine's American readers into an imagined community of which Parkinson is not a part; in addition to this, the first-person plural suggests that Brown is aware of his former settler colony's continuing need to develop what Bill Ashcroft and his colleagues have called "an alternative, differentiated identity" (9), an identity with which they can respond from the margins of America to the former imperial center of Great Britain. Brown's second sentence then manipulates the community of readers he has just formed as he prejudices its perception against Parkinson with the suggestion that "[i]f a native reader derives no instruction from the wisdom of this, he will at least be amused with its follies and mistakes" (5: 219).[24] The voice of the essay — once this community of readers and its attitude towards Parkinson and his work are established — remains largely in Brown's summary, not in Parkinson's narrative. For example, by not allowing Parkinson a recital of the woes that stretched his journey from Norfolk to Mount Vernon from the usual eleven hours to a full nine days, woes that might have inspired some sympathy in readers' minds, Brown's summary presents the simple fact and then moves on, undercutting Parkinson's authority by leaving the reader to wonder at the farmer's ineptness. Thus in contrast to the conventions of book reviewing in early American periodicals, which tend to provide long excerpts from the work under review with relatively few reviewer comments, Brown — through extensive summary, argument, counterargument, and other rhetorical ploys—wrests control of the selected portions of *A Tour in America* from its author.

But before dealing with the story of Parkinson's experiences in the New World, Brown deals with Parkinson himself. *A Tour in America* is, Brown says, Parkinson's playing to the English court, a distasteful practice in the eyes of an American audience: the work is "fostered, it is probable, by a willingness to court the prevailing partialities of Englishmen, and diversified by an occasional appeal to the feelings which find favour within the circle of courts" (5: 220). The clear implication is that Parkinson's animosity toward the United States is a reflection of Great Britain's; the clear suggestion is that readers should be on their guard. Brown then calls into question not only the usefulness of the work but also the author's ability to write effectively. Parkinson's "style"—an element of composition with which Brown was always concerned in his reviews—"is as coarse and vulgar as might be expected from a mere practical farmer; talking without ceremony, and for the most part in ill humour, on every thing that befel him or came in his way during his last lease."[25] Then, having dealt thus tersely with the author's style, Brown notes what he considers Parkinson's limited analytical abilities:

> Such a man has only one mode of discussing whatever you propose to him; the method of averment and instance. He suddenly comes down with a broad, positive, blundering assertion, and backs it with "the very thing that happened to himself," or the story of his neighbor *such a one*, which, being *fact* must decide the matter. There is, indeed, always abundance of inconsistency in the statements of these lovers of plain fact; and it requires but little attention to their stories to refute them on their own ground [5: 219].

At this point Brown briefly turns to his readers, chastising them for being too often unwilling to expend the "little attention" necessary for such simple refutations. Until readers begin to practice close reading, Brown suggests, authors such as Parkinson

> are absolute masters of the argument; and when they embody their conversations for public use, it is wonderful how implicitly they are followed by the multitude, always abhorrent of just theory or general principle, prone to the observation of insulated occurrences, and unwilling, through timidity, to depart from particular examples, though often beguiled by indolence into the most dangerous applications of them [5: 219].

To "embody ... conversations for public use" is, of course, to publish them, and by the early years of the nineteenth century, American readers accepted "publication ... as a condition of legitimacy" (Warner 67). The tendency in the still intellectually colonized America was to grant greater authority to publications by authors from the former imperial center than to those by native authors, and Brown — acknowledging the power of print as he also does in the headnote to "The American Character"— seems to have understood that unthinking, unquestioning readers would allow the simple act of publication to lead them blindly into "dangerous applications" of what British authors such as Parkinson presented them with in print. So it was Brown's task as an editor to control Parkinson and guide readers' experience of this blatantly imperialist author.

Once "An Account" begins to deal with the text of *A Tour in America*, Parkinson's voice is allowed center stage only when the British farmer's prejudice against the United States has most obviously affected his judgment of the new nation's land and people. Within these sections— where the readers of Brown's miscellany come face to face, so to speak, with Parkinson — Americans find their land portrayed as barren, their laboring class as insolent and lazy, their markets as difficult to reach, their agricultural economics—from producer to consumer — as overpopulated with middle men, their weather as frightening, their "'chief teachers'"—"'Tom Paine, doctor [Joseph] Priestley, and others of the same description'"— as more cunning than educated or moral (5: 226).

In all of this, Parkinson's method of understanding and judging the land and people of the United States is through comparing them with those of England.[26] Brown rejects this comparison as at least unfair, if not altogether invalid, and most often ascribes Parkinson's misinformation and mistakes to faulty reasoning and ulterior motives (that is, his playing to the court). The English enjoyed a land that had long been under cultivation; what parts were useful for the farmer had long been cleared and settled, and in so relatively small a country, markets were easily accessible. Parkinson's plan of "rearing prize cattle" was one whose time had not yet come in America (5: 220); had Parkinson given any thought, Brown suggests, to conditions in the United States— where land and market opportunities were too different, in general too primitive, to support the kind of speculation he attempted — he would have understood both that his hopes were premature and that there could be no fair comparisons made between agricultural practices in England and America. Of the British farmer's purpose in writing —"to prove that there is *no land* in America worth cultivating, and *no enjoyment of life* to be procured"²⁷— Brown writes, "There is little ground for fearing or hoping that the land of the United States will be cleared and cultivated by British capital or industry, while their own wastes, both in Europe and America, are left under heath and forest" (5: 219). In other words, America need not be worried about Parkinson's opinions, be these right or wrong. Brown thus makes it plain that Parkinson's harsh judgments ultimately mean little to American readers, and the chief benefit of reading *A Tour in America* then becomes that of seeing images of Americans and their homeland as they appeared reflected in British eyes.

Brown concludes that Parkinson "has confounded the qualities of the soil with the stages of cultivation and the progress of society" (5: 225). Understood in this context, Parkinson's disappointments were not simply based on physical conditions in America, and Brown does not shy away from elaborating on this for his readers:

> It is very clear, from his own statements, that his opinion of the soil was mingled with his disgust at the manners and customs of the country, and that the want of those comforts to which he had been habituated in England was the chief cause of his discontent with the farms of America.... The grievances which form the theme of these volumes is the necessary consequence of the recent settlement of America, its scanty population, and limited capital [5: 221].

"American liberty and equality" were the chief reasons Parkinson believed himself unable to find good help in carrying out his schemes. The great country gentlemen in England were the masters of their lands and the people who worked them; in America, Parkinson writes, "'...I have been obliged to clean my own boots and shoes when I have had four servants in the house.... I should term such very bad management in England; but the idea of liberty and equality [in the United States] destroys all the rights of the master, and every man does as he likes.'" No white man in America called another white man "master," and Parkinson is often confused when he is unable to distinguish who works for whom.²⁸ Brown counters that this interpretation is "folly," that the seeming equality is not a negative result of American freedom. It is instead a situation arising from the youthful condition of the country: "...as numbers increase in America, the evil complained of will wear out; that while the government remains sufficiently strong to secure the rights of property, and the monopoly of the labouring classes continues to decrease; these, like all other dealers in articles of growing supply, will become more and more courteous to their employers" (5: 222). Still, in the end Brown uses "employers" instead of "masters," indicating that even when America progresses to the point where working relationships are clearer to the British they will not mirror the strong master-servant division to which Parkinson and his fellow countrymen were accustomed.

Brown's strict mediation of the contact zone where Parkinson and American readers of the *Literary Magazine* meet allows the latter not only to see their image as it existed in the mind and press of Great Britain but also to see obvious misrepresentations addressed by a native author in a native publication. Parkinson was on the same social level in England as many of the Americans about whom he wrote, but the picture he created of them was of an uncouth people who lacked education and paid too little attention to "'divine worship'" (5: 226). They lived in a land that "'appears ... to be a most proper place for the use to which it was first appropriated, namely, the reception of convicts'" (5: 224). Although Brown allows such a picture to appear in Parkinson's own words, he undermines it throughout the essay by subverting Parkinson's authority, questioning his abilities as a writer, and challenging his judgments. Readers knew that American culture — in both town and country — was not equal to British culture, and in "An Account" Brown offers no opinion on whether or not it should be. He allows America its own character — vague though it was at the time — without comparing it to the ex-mother country and suggests that it is too early for the nation to have achieved the level of cultural refinement he, his readers, and much of the transatlantic world ultimately expected.[29]

III. Education and "Enlightenment" in America

Just as Parkinson blames excessive liberty for the lack of polite deference in social relationships in America, so the foreign author Brown presents in "The American Character" blames a "love of liberty" for the "want of education" that prevented the young United States from fulfilling its cultural promise:

> The American is naturally grave, deliberate, and temperate; enterprising, ingenious, and if not scientific, it is owing more to a want of education, than a want of genius. The love of liberty, and impatience of controul, break out at a very early period of their youth. Children are

> too gay, and too delighted with the prospect before them, to be naturally inclined to study; they are for enjoying life, when they should be learning how to enjoy it. Some degree of restraint upon them is therefore necessary for their welfare; but if the reins of parental authority sit loosely upon a boy, no wonder if he quits the thorny path of science, before he has gathered any of its sweets, for that of pleasure [2: 256–57].

That Brown allows this passage to stand without italics indicates that he did not consider such an idea to be one of the foreign author's "blunders" and that he agreed to some extent with this judgment of education — or the lack of it — in America.

Early on in the new nation, education became an important item on the agendas of both Federalists and Republicans. In his first inaugural address on 4 March 1801, Thomas Jefferson sought to close the political breach caused by his ascent to the presidency. The speech was a call for unity in "[a] rising nation, spread over a wide and fruitful land, traversing all the seas with the rich productions of their industry, engaged in commerce with nations who feel power and forget right, advancing rapidly to destinies beyond the reach of mortal eye" (290). Stability on "this distant and peaceful shore" was his primary concern (291). Reason, not the power and injustice that many believed reigned in Britain and Europe, provided the foundation of such stability, and the president told his listeners to "bear in mind this sacred principle, that though the will of the majority is in all cases to prevail, that will, to be rightful, must be reasonable." And to support advancement of the citizenry's ability to reason well, Jefferson identified "the diffusion of information" as one of "the essential principles of our government ... which ought to shape its administration" (294, 293).

This idea that the national body be ruled by reason and not its diverse passions remained a theme throughout Jefferson's time in the presidency. In the first of his annual messages to Congress, he noted "an augmentation of revenue arising from consumption" that led him to believe that some of the taxes with which the people were burdened could be lifted; among these the postage on periodicals could be adjusted "to facilitate the progress of information" (301). The "improving of our reason," Jefferson said in his second inaugural address, "and obeying its mandates" is one duty of a republican people; likewise, in his 3 December 1805 message to Congress, he implied that the "maintaining of the authority of reason, the only umpire between just nations," is one duty of a republican government (319, 323).

By the time Jefferson gave his sixth annual message to Congress on 2 December 1806, "the diffusion of information" was referred to as education. And because education was so important to the health of the republic, Jefferson proposed that it become a public institution:

> Education is here placed among the articles of public care, not that it would be proposed to take its ordinary branches out of the hands of private enterprise, which manages so much better all the concerns to which it is equal; but a public institution can alone supply those sciences which, though rarely called for, are yet necessary to complete the circle, all the parts of which contribute to the improvement of the country, and some of them to its preservation [326].

This idea was not new, of course. In *A Plan for the Establishment of Public Schools and the Diffusion of Knowledge in Pennsylvania* ... (1786), Brown's fellow Philadelphian Benjamin Rush, himself a man of letters and a signer of the Declaration of Independence, says that

> it is ... possible to convert men into republican machines. This must be done if we expect them to perform their parts properly in the great machine of the government of the state. That republic is sophisticated with monarchy or aristocracy that does not revolve upon the wills of the people, and these must be fitted to each other by means of education before they can be made to produce regularity and unison in government [qtd. in Warner 129].[30]

"All revolutions," Jean Matthews writes, "are concerned with education since the rising generation must be socialized into the new ideology." This is true not only for major revolutions such as that of 1776 but also for minor ones such as Jefferson's self-proclaimed "Revolution of 1800." The financial setback of the 1807 embargo, however, effectively prevented the president from putting a plan for public education into action, but still the important point was made: education was vital to the stability and progress of the American republic.

Brown seconded the need for broader availability of education in America. To be viable on an international level, he believed, the United States must move toward the establishment of a nationally institutionalized education system for its youth. He turns "to the bleak hills of Scotland" for an example of the goal America might set for itself in its attempt to nurture "knowledge and genuine refinement." In a brief essay on "Education in Scotland" (October 1805),[31] Brown presents readers of the *Literary*

Magazine with Scotland's enviable situation in which "the establishments for public education ... seem to excel those of all other nations, not only in their methods of instruction, but in their number and diffusion." In a country with a population of less than a million and a half, "twelve hundred schools" instruct "fifty thousand children continually" and "four universities" boast more than "two thousand" students. These public establishments are supplemented in serving Scotland's educational needs by academies, pulpits, "private preceptors," mothers, and apprenticeships (4: 266). In Scotland, Brown says,

> we must recollect that ... there is upon average, a church, a religious pastor, and a public school for every twelve hundred and fifty persons, or every two hundred families; that one third of the youth, at a teachable age, are pupils of these schools; and that the higher branches of instruction, at the universities, are regularly dispensed to at least one in *twelve* or *fifteen* of all the young men of the nation.

But such was not the case in the United States: "If the state of Pennsylvania were merely on a par with Scotland, ... it ought to possess six hundred public schools, the same number of churches and religious instructors, twenty-five thousand pupils, and a state college, to which the state alone should furnish one thousand students. Widely and lamentably different from this, however, is our real condition" (4: 267).

Brown largely avoided the controversy over educational reform carried on by Noah Webster, Benjamin Rush, John Sylvester John Gardiner, David Daggett, and others.[32] Only one issue in particular inspired him to comment: the debate over the value of youth studying classical authors in Greek and Latin. Typically the controversy divided more or less along political lines. For the most part Federalists conducted the defense of classical learning in the new American republic, defending study of the ancients as the core of a citizen's education and intellect. To do away with Greek and Latin might make education beyond reading, writing, and arithmetic easier, perhaps less boring, but the Federalists could not envision these results as having anything but a negative effect. The classics, they argued, would keep citizens conscious of the lessons of the past — of America's connection with the historical republics of Greece and Rome[33] — so that the nation was not set adrift in the present world where revolution had become a serious threat to government. Furthermore, a study of the classics taught the proper conduct of republican citizens.

That almost any advanced education American students received required a heavy dose of classical languages and literature was exactly the problem for Jeffersonians. Classical learning, they suggested, was not the most important component of the useful information necessary to develop an educated citizenry, Rush's "republican machines." Students should attend to more practical matters—their own language, their understanding of liberty, American law and policies, American government and society, geography, and public education. Furthermore, requiring study of the classics was an exclusionary act that limited successful participation in advanced education to those only who had an interest in or aptitude for ancient languages and arts. Education needed to be available to all, not just the elite, if the nation were to have a truly well informed citizenry.

Brown took neither side in the political aspect of the controversy. Instead, he approached the issue in response to a religious debate regarding the possibility of classical learning's having an anti–Christian tendency, a debate that took place in the *Literary Magazine* and under his editorship.

In "Has Classical Learning an Anti-Christian Tendency?" (June 1805), an anonymous correspondent defended the study of the classics against those who claimed that reading works from a culture based on a pagan religion represented a threat to the reader's Christian beliefs. Had the last ancient empire of Rome fallen with its pagan deities still in tact, the writer suggests, this threat to Christianity might have been real. But the empire became Christianized before it fell, so even the Romans no longer believed in their former gods. This allowed humans to take an interest in the classical world "without any danger of adoring, those objects of primitive superstition"; "...those marble gods ... were now regarded, not as objects of religious veneration, but merely as specimens of human art" (3: 427). By the beginning of the nineteenth century, a classical education had long been fashionable. "To be conversant with the history, literature, and *religion* of a nation that was not christian," Brown's correspondent writes, "...is deemed, not only ornamental in the citizen, but necessary to the preacher of truth" (3: 428). Perhaps somewhat valid arguments against classical learning existed, but that "built upon the supposed danger there is of the student's conversion to the religion of the Athenian populace ... is surely the most groundless and absurd."

Two months later a response to this essay, "On the Anti-Christian Tendency of Classical Learning" (August 1805), argues the opposite side of the issue. Young students being introduced to the classics—usually by means of ancient Greek and Roman mythology—do not know, the anonymous author claims, that Ovid wrote fiction;[34] and even if they do know, "Truth and fiction produce similar effects on the mind. One affects the reason, the other affects the imagination; and both influence men's conduct" (4: 137). If the moral writings of the ancients influence conduct, then this opponent of classical learning suggests that readers may easily imbibe a dose of pagan religion along with republican morals, as he identifies an intimate connection between morality and religion. Perhaps the strongest part of this argument against classical learning is based on the example of differences between the genders. Near the end of the essay, the author quotes from Hannah More's *Strictures on the Modern System of Female Education* (first published in 1800), in which More writes that women, generally without opportunities for a classical education,

> though struggling with the same natural corruptions [as men], have commonly less knowledge to unknow, and fewer schemes to unlearn; they have not to shake off the pride of systems, and to disencumber their minds from the shackles of favourite theories; they do not bring from the porch or the academy (pagan schools) any "oppositions of science," to obstruct their reception of those pure doctrines taught on the Mount [4: 141].

The piety of men, on the other hand, because of their broader educational opportunities and their generally larger sphere of social interaction, suffers from being mixed "with so much heterogenous matter": "Their very spirits are imbued all the week with the impure follies of a depraved mythology; and it is well if even on Sundays they get to hear of the 'true God, and Jesus Christ whom he has sent.'"

Brown entered this debate pseudonymously the following month with "Classical Learning No Anti-Christian Tendency" (September 1805).[35] He judges between the two essays and finds for the first. Neither previous writer had exactly defined the ideas they were arguing for or against, so Brown takes the definition upon himself: "What I mean by an *anti-christian* tendency in classical learning, is merely its tendency to inspire a *belief* in the truth of the *adventures* and *attributes* of heathen divinities." Christian truth, he suggests, impressed as it almost always is before the student learned Greek and Latin, is incompatible with those supposed pagan truths offered by such ancients as Homer and Ovid. There is no need for teachers to warn their young scholars that the classical myths are fiction because, according to Brown, children grown beyond infancy understand this intuitively. Furthermore, an objection to the classics on the basis of its anti–Christian tendency assumes "that a classical education only can introduce us to a knowledge of these fables, and next, that it introduces us to the knowledge of nothing else" (4: 186). In answer to the first of these assumptions he identifies the obvious truth missed by his two correspondents: that English translations of ancient mythology are just as likely to influence young readers as versions in the original language. In answer to the second assumption he points out that Greek and Latin works are not confined to pagan mythology; the Septuagint, gospels, and epistles—"the primitive records of christianity itself" (4: 187)—are written in the languages of ancient Greece and Rome, as are the ancient works that argued for Christianity and ultimately defeated paganism in the Roman world.

While Brown's support of classical learning seems to align him with those Federalists who insisted that such an education represented an important element in the intellectual life of a republican leader, his identification of the benefits obtained by reading the classics again reveals him as a proponent of an emerging liberal individualism. A thorough education—one including the range of classical writing from mythology to the founding documents of Christianity—endowed the individual with an independence and a liberality of thought. Paganism in the modern world— "among civilized Europeans," at least—was "exploded" (4: 191). Thus in education the ancient texts began as the student's teachers of languages, but ultimately became not a possible agent of that student's conversion to paganism but instead moved to a subordinate role in support of the mature individual's character: "When I insist upon the impossibility of a man of liberal education, in a christian country, believing in paganism, I reason not from the inherent nonsense of the pagan system, but from the irresistible influence of education and example" (4: 190). Understood in this context, it seems apparent that only those Greeks and Romans of the lower classes, those who lacked the "education and example" available to their natural aristocracy, adhered to the pagan mythology as an actual religion:

> Even in the flourishing ages of Rome and Greece, ... the popular religion was for the most part the religion of the vulgar and ignorant. The philosophers trampled on these tenets in their closets, and ridiculed them in their lessons, though no doubt, through the influence of popular example and early impressions [from childhood], they gave an occasional and superstitious assent to them... [4: 191].

The texts that survived from the days of Greece and Rome and had been handed down through the ages were written largely by a few "enlightened" philosophers, not by the "vulgar and ignorant" believers. "The natural effect of the study of the sages, orators, and historians of Athens, is directly opposite to pagan superstition," Brown writes, and if readers religiously revered the creative works of poets such as Homer and Ovid, they were adopting "for sacred truths, chimeras which the poets had employed as mere instruments of refined entertainment." The ancient texts themselves, therefore, creative or otherwise, should pose no real threat to the happiness of a modern individual with a liberal education.

But in reality few Americans boasted such an education. The United States was a literate nation, but its people were largely Bible and newspaper readers. Brown's recognition of educational shortcomings in America — as revealed in "Education in Scotland," for example — led him to question the widespread eighteenth-century notion of "enlightenment."

"Can the *public* be denominated *enlightened*?" (4: 113). Brown poses this question in the August 1805 issue of the *Literary Magazine*, in an essay called "On 'the Enlightened Public' and 'the Age of Reason.'"[36] The question is rhetorical, for Brown believed that the existence of almost any philosophy or ideology was necessarily temporary due to the dynamic nature of the human mind and human society. "A progressive state" seemed apparent in both the moral and natural worlds, and in individuals as well as nations, "[b]ut it is not with the human head, as with the human heart." Sounding just as he historically and intellectually was, something of an heir to Benjamin Franklin and something of a forerunner to Emerson, Brown says,

> The perfection of any virtue is obtainable, but perhaps never that of knowledge; the actions of a hero are perfect, but the works of a scholar may in time be found erroneous; Alexander is still our hero, but Aristotle has ceased to be our preceptor. Virtue is similar and permanent, for an action of benevolence, or heroism, can never change its nature; but a system of philosophy, or a school of taste, must be annihilated by new philosophies and new tastes [4: 111].

Thus it was in Brown's time, as he seems to have felt at some level, that classical republicanism began to give way to— to "be annihilated by"— liberal individualism, the Age of Reason to the Age of Romanticism, and so on.

Even though the Enlightenment appeared to be real in the lives of American and European elite at the beginning of the nineteenth century, Brown believed it to be in some ways a deception perpetrated by the republic of letters. Print culture was far-reaching, and the leading thinkers of the day published for a readership of lesser lights who tended to congregate in important centers—London, Paris, Madrid, Philadelphia, and so on. That the intellectual elite of these and other centers began to think similarly about nature and human life was, for Brown, no widespread, spontaneous awakening to new universal truths but the result of a relatively small number of authors who wrote works that were widely read:

> the art of printing has imparted stability to our intellectual structures, in what depends on the mechanical preservation. A singular spectacle has, therefore, been exhibited; and it is sometimes urged by those who contemplate, with pleasing astonishment, the actual progress of the human mind, as a proof of the immutability of truth, that in the present day, every enlightened individual, whether he resides at Paris, at Madrid, or at London, now thinks alike; no variation of climate, no remoteness of place, not even national prejudices, more variable and more remote than either, destroy that unanimity of opinion, which they feel on certain topics essential to human welfare.
>
> This appears to be a specious argument in favour of the enlightened public. But we should recollect, that this unanimity of opinion, which so frequently excites surprise, proceeds from their deriving their ideas from the same sources; at Paris, at Madrid, and at London, the same authors are read, and, therefore, the same opinions are formed [4:112].

Brown recognized the reality of the Enlightenment as being starkly different from the picture of it created by those deceived by the print phenomenon: "He who thinks, will perceive in every enlightened nation, three kinds of people; an inconsiderable number instructed by reason, and glowing with humanity; a countless multitude, barbarous and ignorant, intolerant and inhospitable; and a vacillating people with some reason and humanity, but with great prejudices, at once the half-echoes of philosophy, and the adherents of popular opinion" (4: 112–13).

The education and potential enlightenment of the "countless multitude" appears to have weighed heavily on Brown's mind from at least June to September 1805, more than a year before President Jefferson proposed that education become an item of "public care." Perhaps his particular concern at this time was prompted by an item he included in the May 1805 issue, "Report of the Committee Relative to the Establishment of Schools Throughout the State of Pennsylvania, in Such a Manner That the Poor May Be Taught Gratis."[37] This article consists of two parts: first Brown's reaction to the report in general and then the committee's resolutions. To begin with the latter, these resolutions describe the selection of and powers invested in an educational board for each county. They establish a group of "three trustees" to hire and oversee "a suitable person to teach the English or German language (as the case may be) grammatically, write a fair hand, and arithmetic, on the most approved plan."[38] Furthermore, the resolutions define who is to be educated under the plan: "All the youth under fourteen years of age, may, at the county expence, be taught reading, writing, and plain arithmetic; their further progress shall be at the proper expence of those who send them" (3: 386).

Brown seems to have approved of these resolutions, but apparently there were at least two assumptions in the report, the whole of which is not reprinted in the article, with which he took issue. The first assumption is "that few, if any, will object to contribute *a small portion of their wealth* towards aiding their more indigent neighbors to have their children thus educated" in reading, writing, and arithmetic. Had the Enlightenment, according to Brown's understanding of it, been a reality throughout all classes of people and opinion consistent across all geographic and cultural boundaries, this assumption of benevolence might have been safely made.[39] But those local individuals with wealth enough to support the education of their poorer neighbors' children more often than not would be included in Brown's category of unenlightened, "vacillating people with some reason and humanity, but with great prejudices." Thus Brown democratically suggests that "[to] encourage the promotion of literature generally, the children of all our citizens ought to be taught at the public expence. In this way, no invidious [*sic*] distinctions of *rich and poor* would be exhibited, nor would the feelings of any be unnecessarily wounded" (3: 385).

The second assumption with which Brown takes issue is the implication that to learn the basics of reading, writing, and arithmetic was enough in "qualifying [students], in some measure, to be *useful members of society*, and thereby laying the surest foundation for the continuance of our *civil and religious liberties*, and perpetuating our *happy form of government*" (3: 386).[40] Basic reading, writing, and arithmetic, I would argue, were not enough for Brown. Students must learn to think. He suggests, as Emerson would three decades later, that the mode of education in which rote memorization played the most important part did little to educate individuals.

In "On the Difference Between Learning and Knowledge" (September 1805),[41] Brown identifies reading as the means to both learning and knowledge, but he associates learning largely with memory, knowledge with reflection. Learning consists of reading, study, and rote memorization. But that individual who has become learned only by rote is able to offer little to society. Such "erudition is a gross lust of the mind; ... it is passion without fruition" (4: 180). If the details of a course of study — no matter how broad or deep in contemporary science and literature, as well as in the classics — are only remembered, the study is ultimately worthless. In his address on the American Scholar, Emerson identifies an individual educated in this way as "a mere thinker, or still worse, the parrot of other men's thinking" (*Oration* 5); similarly, Brown says, "Many are familiar with the Latin and the Grecian compositions, whom the Latins and the Greeks, full of taste and sensibility, would never have admitted into their society" (4: 179). Individuals who simply remember what they read contribute nothing to the progress of national culture; indeed, they are likely to be culturally, socially, and politically passive rather than active, perpetuating cultural imitation and the status quo.

Thus, only those who reflect and reason upon whatever they discover through study have the opportunity to become enlightened. "For my part," Brown writes, "I consider as knowledge, that only which a man knows by reflection." Knowledge, then, consists of more thoughtful reading, a broad and active intelligence, and imagination. But knowledge constituted in this way is useful only inasmuch as it benefits the individual and society in the present. The educated individual with the ability to reflect, then, is one "who is anxious to familiarise himself to his own times, and is conversant with whatever relates to his own *century*, who has little by rote, and a great deal *by thinking*" (4: 178).[42] According to Brown, "time ... may make an *erudit*, but genius only can form a *philosopher*" (4: 177).

IV. "THE ART OF READING" AND THE AMERICAN WOMAN

Reading is key to both learning and knowledge, but what, how, and why one reads makes the difference between the useless and the useful in relation to liberal society. "Since writing is justly denominated an art, reading may surely claim the same distinction. To adorn ideas with elegance is an act of the mind superior to that of receiving them, and is the province of genius; but to receive them with a happy discrimination is a task not less useful, and can only be the effect of a just taste." So says Brown in the opening paragraph of his "Remarks on Reading" (March 1806).[43]

Just as he divides scholars into two categories—those who seek learning and those who seek knowledge—so in this essay he divides readers along similar lines. Most readers read passively, and few read actively; or, to use Brown's terms, a difference exists between those who read for "perceptions" and those who read for "ideas" (5: 163).

The "art of reading" is based on this distinction "between perceptions and ideas." To read for perceptions is simply to receive impressions from the words of a text, impressions of real or fictional characters, settings, motivations, actions, and so on. Reading that yields only perceptions, while it may be pleasurable, is, according to Brown, taking the easy way through and out of a text. A reader who reads in this way "quits his author in a pleasing distraction, but of the pleasures of reading, nothing remains but a tumultuous sensation. He has only delighted himself with the brilliant colouring, and the mingled shadows of a variety of objects..." (5: 163). This reader is associated with that scholar who values only "learning," whose voluminous reading remains only a vast collection of facts gotten by rote, impressive to the unthinking but devoid of any usefulness to humankind.

By contrast, the individual who actively reads for ideas "will not only have the ideas of the author at command, and strongly imbibe his manner, but will have enriched his own mind by a new accession of matter, and find a new train of thought awakened and in action." As is true for the scholar who values "knowledge" over "learning," "reflection" is key for this type of reader: "it is only when these objects [the varied impressions gained from reading] exist in the mind, and are there treasured up and arranged as materials for reflection, that they become ideas." But this type of reading is not easy, and often readers capable of reading for ideas indulge themselves by reading for simple perceptions and then "complain that their memory is defective, and their studies fruitless" (5: 163); the truth is, Brown says, that in such moments they are avoiding "the laborious task of forming ideas" (5: 163–64).

With the spirit of a Utopian in the republic of letters, Brown aims at the formation of a model reading community in America, a collective of translocalized individuals who read for ideas, understanding that this species of reading is often—like the work of the seeker after knowledge—intensive rather than extensive: "Ideas are therefore labours," he claims. The issue, of course, was not whether the *Literary Magazine*'s American readership was literate but instead how it might be made up of better readers. Brown recognizes in this essay that a reader's skills could be improved with technique and practice, just like the skills of a poet, painter, or musician.[44] Literacy is a process that does not end with one's ability to read the words of a text and sign one's name on the dotted line.[45] Reading skills could be developed along a continuum such as that progressing from mechanic to artisan to artist; the further an individual progresses—that is, the more deeply her or his reading is influenced by improving taste and attended with reflection—the more literature affords that individual independence of both action and thought. As Cathy N. Davidson argues, "True literateness ... ideally entails increased autonomy" (69).

A text provides an author and a reader a definite and defined location for an intellectual exchange, a specific address where the two can meet in the republic of letters. For better or for worse, the author and publisher have done their work in initiating the exchange, but in the ideal situation the reader does not simply receive what is offered but must likewise contribute to the meeting if a true exchange is to take place:

> ...readers must not imagine that all the pleasures of composition depend on the author; for there is something which a reader himself must bring to the book, that the book may please. There is a literary appetite which the author can no more impart, than the most skilful cook can give appetite to the guests.... Every man must come [to the text] prepared as well as he can [5: 165].

To explain further the process of exchange that ideally takes place between the author and reader, Brown switches the metaphor from the culinary to the sportive: "There is something in composition like the game of shuttlecock, where, if the reader does not quickly rebound the feathered cork to the author, the game is destroyed, and the whole spirit of the work becomes extinct" (5: 166). Brown's use of "composition" to include both writer and reader emphasizes the notion of exchange taking place in the republic of letters. In writing intended for publication, no step in the process leading to the literary transaction between author and reader takes place without each of these entities being present to one degree or another. Although in discourse written for public consumption authors may write with no particular reader or type of reader in mind, they still write to be read, to communicate; they are, moreover, as Davidson points out, "themselves readers of the work that they are writing" (4). Likewise, although a reader in the act of reading may "hear" in the mind's ear the voice of such a work as her or his own—or at least as one of her or his own making—the words originate with that unseen author on the other side of the text.

"A professional student," Brown writes of that reader who is devoted to such literary exchange, that reader who reads for ideas, "should divide his readings into a *uniform* reading which is useful, and into a *diversified* reading which is pleasant" (5: 166). The former type of reading might be considered professional studies and the latter recreational. For Brown as an editor and author, the miscellany provided readers with opportunities for both types. "Miscellanies ought to be multifarious and concise," he writes in "On Miscellanies" (September 1805);[46] by way of example, he suggests, "Montaigne approves of Plutarch and Seneca, because their loose papers were suited to his temper, and knowledge was acquired without tedious study" (4: 166). In a busy American life, those who were inclined to self-improvement but found little time for study could turn to the "airy and concise page" of a miscellany for "lively anecdote" and "profound observation" (4: 167), thereby entertaining and improving themselves with both recreational and professional reading.[47]

Brown's *Literary Magazine* apparently reached on a monthly basis some six hundred subscribers, and it probably reached a much greater number of readers as it passed among the family and friends of those individuals who subscribed. By comparison, the number of copies printed in the first run of a new American novel of the time ranged from three hundred to fifteen hundred copies (Davidson 17), so, barring notable exceptions such as Susanna Rowson's *Charlotte Temple* (1791), Brown's miscellany possibly reached as many American readers as the novels with which it competed in the literary marketplace. The *Literary Magazine*, however, neither stirred up a continuous cloud of controversy nor drew condemnation from a range of critics as did the novel. But as works such as Davidson's *Revolution and the Word* attest, the rise of the novel — the rise of novel-reading — was the most important event in the literary history of the early American republic. Brown joined his own voice with many others in the republic of letters in an attempt both to analyze this phenomenon as it was happening and to judge the novel's value for American readers.

As a former novelist himself, Brown was perhaps better qualified to understand the rising genre than many other editors. Throughout the eight volumes of the *Literary Magazine* he discusses British novelists, writes sketches of novels available on the market, and parodies the Gothic conventions that increasingly characterized the genre.[48] In "On the Cause of the Popularity of Novels" (July 1807),[49] Brown suggests that novel-reading was so widespread, especially "among young readers," because of "the tameness and insipidity of common life and common events" (7: 410); from the drudgery of daily routine readers "fly for relief ... to the composition called *novels*" (7: 411). Such works are able to take the emotions and situations of quotidian life and romanticize them in a way that allows a restless mind to escape for a time from the monotonous round of days.[50] Brown's good readers seek out the instruction or useful knowledge in such fictions, but they are by far the minority among novel readers. Those who seek only to escape — by far the majority — are unlikely to be willing to invest their energy in such intensive reading.

A more striking problem Brown notices is that, as published authors increasingly manipulated more or less believable situations and characters into almost every variation possible, "the common adventures of novels were becoming as insipid as the progress of real life." Novelists began to move away from portraying events that, however much romanticized, could instruct as well as entertain. The new trend was "to enliven these narratives by a certain proportion of murders, ghosts, clanking chains, dead bodies, skeletons, old castles, and damp dungeons."[51] Brown tentatively finds such fiction acceptable, especially if the trips readers take to these "regions of fiction" are simply for amusement and the vehicle is among "the most classical productions of [the Gothic] description." But he is suspicious of the many imitators of, say, Ann Radcliffe, for it is in escaping to these lesser authors that readers "shall often be deluded by estimates of human life and happiness that are calculated upon false foundations" (7: 412).

Most of Brown's contemporaries criticized the novel for promoting a bad, even dangerous system of morals to the innocent reader. But this assumes a passive reader who approaches the text with an unsuspecting fascination for its allure; the novel and novelist thus become, for most critics, the active agents in this view of the author-text-reader exchange. Brown, I argue, rightly focuses on the reader and her or his motives for taking up the book. To read well written tales full of murders is not to the reader's disadvantage if the reading is, as he says, for amusement only. The active mind that reads for ideas will leave a book if there are no ideas to be found in it; moreover, the good reader — although necessarily influenced by the content of the text and, by extension, the mind of the author — is largely in control of the reading situation once the book is out of the hands of author and publisher. Understood in this context, Brown seems to have had an innate understanding of the role of the reader in the republic of letters.

In regards to novel-reading — for either instruction or amusement — as an escape from the dull routine of life, Brown concludes that "he to whom real life appears dull, must himself be a man of dull capacity" (7: 412). While males were generally seen as actively involved in life, dull or not, in the early American republic, they are not of the gender typically identified with novel-reading in the period. As Davidson points out regarding the sentimental novel, "the implied readers" of such novels were often "the 'Daughters of Columbia,' who are, implicitly or explicitly, young, white, of good New England stock, and for the most part unmarried" (112). In "Popularity of Novels" Brown confirms this identification of the main class of novel readers; his focus in the following passage, however, is not the sentimental but the gothic novel:

> ...surely it is no wonder if our timid females are pushed from their stools in reading the "horrid, barbarous, and bloody murders" that are now served up for their *amusement*.
> *Amusement!* did I say? — Yes, certainly for their *amusement*. This is the most favourable conjecture, for surely it never could have entered into the brain of any writer of [the Gothic] description that our lovely females wanted *instruction* how to commit or avoid murders. Amusement it therefore must be, and certainly is amusement of a very singular kind, such as appears to me to be very incompatible with tenderness of frame, or purity of mind. What should we think, if a lady, who had the command of an extensive library, should ransack the indexes, and reject every page but that which contained an account of a murder? [7: 412].

Brown's sarcasm is clear. Fiction for amusement and instruction should not cause female readers to be "pushed from their stools" in excitement, shock, or terror. In a more serious tone than he uses in discussing the sentimental novel, he finally questions the attraction of Gothic novels — "Why are works entirely composed of murders considered as most certain of being perused?" — but wisely leaves the answer to his readers, many of whom, it may be conjectured, were young women.

In an Addisonian essay titled "Novel-Reading" — the first section of "A Students Diary......Number V" (March 1804), a semi-regular feature during the early years of the *Literary Magazine*[52] — Brown creates a dialogic situation in which his narrator and a Miss D discuss the efficacy of reading novels:

> I HAVE just been reading a dissertation upon novel-reading, in which the writer says a great many grave and weighty things on the subject, and

finally winds up by asserting, that supposing the whole stock of the Novelist's library to amount to one thousand, five hundred of these are void of all judgment, genius and taste, composed without knowledge of the world, or skill in composition; and of the remainder, four hundred and ninety-nine are calculated only to corrupt and deprave the morals. While engaged in pondering on this very comprehensive declaration, who should enter the apartment but Miss D..... on a visit to my sister [1: 403].

Miss D's feeling for fiction is enthusiastic. While she concedes that there is an extremely rare "profligate novel" and that, taking the genre as a whole, there is a "greater number which are trivial or insipid" than are good, she says a good novel that is "a just and powerful picture of human life in which the connection between vice and misery, and between felicity and virtue is vividly portrayed, is the most solid and useful reading that a moral and social being (exclusive of particular cases and professional engagements) can read" (1: 404, 405).

The narrator agrees: "I cannot but say ... that my fancy has received more delight, my heart more humanity, and my understanding more instruction from a few novels I could name, than from any other works...." But he also cautions the young woman against rash judgments regarding the number of profligate novels: "I could name half a dozen French and English, in a trice, that deserves this character...." Apart from the American editor's jab at the lack of moral worth in literary productions of the Old World, the narrator makes two other important comments during his conversation with Miss D. First, he seems to know the author of this "dissertation upon novel-reading" and reveals to Miss D that "he has little leisure for that kind of reading which the world, in general, has agreed to call mere pastime or amusement, and his taste leads him far away from such a library as yours" (1: 404). I suspect that this is yet another jab, this time made by Brown the former novelist and aimed at those critics of the novel who condemn the genre — Brown's entries included — without reading widely enough or understanding its potential for the amusement and instruction of readers. Second, the suggestion is twice made — once by Miss D and once by the narrator — that it is easy to find someone to help a reader choose the most entertaining and beneficial reading material; "...guides to a right choice are always to be found," the narrator says as the essay ends (1: 405). It is not difficult to imagine that Brown is offering himself to the American reader as just such a guide, not only to the choosing of the most beneficial novels but also to "the art of reading" itself.

According to Brown, Miss D "has an ample fortune, a lively curiosity, studious temper, and, though young and handsome, no lover. She has therefore abundant leisure, and all the means of reading at command. Novels are her favourite performances, and she has collected such a number of these as would enable her to supply the whole stock of a circulating library" (1: 403). Brown admired the qualities of "lively curiosity" and "studious temper" as they appear in either gender, but Miss D's portrait is not typical of the portraits of females in the *Literary Magazine*. The young woman who passionately defends the novels she loves to read is perhaps more fictionalized, perhaps more idealized, than other women who inhabit the pages of the miscellany.

Miss *****, the focus of "Female Learning"—included in an earlier installment of "A Students Diary" (January 1804)—seems the polar opposite of Miss D. "I have been listening, tonight," the Addisonian narrator of "Female Learning" begins, "to a very ingenious defence of *unlearned women*, by Miss *****." The narrator had lent this young woman a book, with which he expected to find her enthralled at their next meeting. Instead, she is at her needlework. She is thus employed, however, of her own choice, not of necessity as wife or mother. A sense of autonomy characterizes her actions: "It seems she had taken up the book," the narrator says, "and after reading a few pages with little interest, had laid it aside for the needle, which pleased her much better."[53] Miss ***** is a virtuous "Daughter of Columbia," a future "Republican Mother," to use Linda Kerber's terms.[54] Similar to Milton's Eve, who walks away from Raphael's story of the Creation and the war in heaven, "not, as not with such discourse / Delighted, or not capable her ear / Of what was high," Miss ***** does not seem to lay the book aside because it is beyond her understanding. In Eden, Eve prefers to wait and hear Adam tell the story in the context of their domestic, conjugal relationship; in early republican America, Miss ***** makes her choice between luxurious learning and dutiful, virtuous action—domestic action—and "congratulates herself on finding pleasure in that to which propriety enjoins her to attend" (1: 245; Milton 363).

"Rarely in the literature of the early Republic," Kerber writes, "do we find any objection to the notion that women belong in the home; what emerges is the argument that the Revolution had enlarged the significance of what women did in their homes" (*Toward* 38). Brown's women—even *Alcuin*'s Mrs. Carter, the most outspoken of them—are comfortable in the domestic sphere so long as they are allowed their independence and are recognized as equals. The education they want is "primarily to enable [them] to function more effectively within their traditional sphere, and only secondarily to ... emerge from" that sphere (Kerber, *Toward* 37). Miss ***** prefers needlework to books not because education and literature are not worthy pursuits; instead, she wisely recognizes — and seems to convince the narrator of "Female Learning" — that for an individual, female or male, to strike a balance between literary pursuits and domestic or social duty is impossible. Because an excessive attachment to literature negates the individual citizen's impetus to balance, Miss ***** finds it better to devote her time to those useful pursuits she most enjoys. As neither wife nor mother at this point, her attention to domestic duty answers to the demands of neither husband nor children. Needlework is thus her individual and independent choice.[55] Brown's narrator, apparently of a bookish character himself, begins to see how an attachment to literature as strong as Miss D's in "Novel-Reading" prepares a woman less for a "useful, happy, and respectable" life than an adherence to those arts that will eventually be most important in her "traditional sphere," the management of a household: "I never saw a man or woman," he says,

> smitten with a passion for books, whose happiness and usefulness were not somewhat injured by it; but the injury is much greater and more palpable in women than in men. The domestic sphere being appropriated to the female, her inattention and unskilfulness produces the most injury; whereas *her* prudence and economy may obviate many inconvenient and disgusting effects of a studious disposition in the master of a family [1: 245].

Understood in this context, Miss *****'s choice to be an "*unlearned*" woman prepares her for the "Republican Mother's life," in which she will dedicate herself to individual virtue and duty; along with like-minded young women in early America, she will eventually both inculcate and inspire the same dedication in her sons and husband whose sphere is the political and social world (Kerber, *Toward* 58).

While Brown's narrator in "Female Learning" seems convinced of the impossibility of maintaining, in regards to literary pursuits and domestic duties, "the balance immoveable between the opposite demands of the kitchen, the drawing room, the nursery, and the library" (1: 246), Brown as editor and author continued to promote the efficacy of women's reading. The myth of the female's mental inferiority had, for Brown and others, long been debunked. In the context of a democratic republic, then, reading becomes a duty for women because of the role it plays in forming — and informing — the well-rounded individual.

In "Madelina. *A Female Portrait*" (April 1805),[56] Brown's narrator responds to the prompting of a "lively, volatile girl, to draw her character" (3: 269). Refusing to attempt such a sketch directly, he instead creates a portrait of an idealized female character and invites Madelina to compare herself to it. Next to an amiable personality, reading and the cultivation of woman's intellect appear to be most important:

> She cultivates her mind, by regular and close attention to every profitable study. She has leisure, and the greatest part of it is spent in reading. She deems this an amusement indeed, but also a duty. She indulges, without scruple, that inclination, which leads her to works of taste, fancy, and domestic morality, because she regards these as the regulators, sweeteners, and embellishers of life; but while these are her favourite pursuits, she by no means despises or shuns the more rugged paths of history or science.
> Still, however, she is no bookworm, no recluse, no pedant. She meditates and reasons for herself, and her studious hours are betrayed, not by mere literary talk, by anecdotes of authors, and criticisms on their works, by hard words, and formal quotations, but by a certain dignity of thought and refinement of language, which nothing but familiar converse with books can give, and which diffuse themselves through all her conversation [3: 270].

When finished with the sketch, he catechizes Madelina to guide her self-evaluation: "Are you studious? Do you spend a certain proportion of each day in reading? Were the reflections of any five minutes of your life suggested by any thing you met with in a book? Are any of the terms or ideas, which occur in your conversation, derived from this source?" (3: 271).

The reading of judiciously chosen literature, which, beyond basic literacy, was one of the most worthwhile components of a female's education, not only improved her heart, mind, and conversation but also supported the American woman in her role as the stabilizing force in the culture of the early United States. "On the Influence of Women" (June 1806)[57] theorizes that, instead of simply being limiting, woman's "stationary situation in society," her position in the domestic sphere, provides her an opportunity to "excel men in what is termed a knowledge of the world" (5: 403). Her reading consists of "works of imagination and taste," and these works, combined with the opportunity for steady observation of human life, have made the "heart ... the great province of woman" (5: 404). Unlike men, "the wandering and active sex," women do not diffuse their power through far-reaching social, political, and economic aspirations and connections.

Nor is their education one "of memory and reason; their logic consists not of arguments, but of sentiments" drawn from the small circle of their empire and their reading.[58]

Brown then provides examples of how women have been the prime movers in the "secret history" of the male-dominated worlds of politics and religion. In regards to politics he writes, "Ancient and contemporary history will ever abound with multifarious instances" of women at work behind the scenes of a successful government; "the saying of Themistocles is noted: That child, said he, pointing to his son, governs all Greece: for he governs his mother; his mother governs me; I govern the Athenians; and the Athenians govern Greece" (5: 405). It is the same in regards to religion: "Let the fair sex be converted, and the religion is established; a woman at least can win her husband, a mistress the prime minister, a queen the sovereign" (5: 406).

At bottom, woman's "stationary situation" allows her "knowledge of the world." This knowledge, in part, allows her to govern the heart of that man — merchant, mechanic, artisan, artist, minister, or politician — who seems to hold power in the family, the community, or the nation. Life in the domestic sphere allows her leisure for literature. Her moral stability, her usefulness, her understanding of her empire, her ability "to detect and to manage the secret foibles of men" (5: 404) — all this, for Brown, characterizes American woman and comes from her position in the culture, her nature, and good reading.

V. Art in America?

The character and culture of a nation are, perhaps, most clearly revealed in its art, both visual and literary. The foreign author Brown presents in "The American Character" provides an overview of the arts and sciences in the United States and declares those he mentions — theater, painting, invention, music, and architecture — "below mediocrity" and "tiresome" (2: 255, 256).[59] Among the peoples of Europe and the citizenry of early America, those who thought seriously about art were surprised — and more than a little disappointed — that art in the new United States was indeed at such a low ebb. In regards to the fine arts of painting, sculpture, and architecture, one writer in the *Literary Magazine* says, "It is a paradox ... that a civilized, peaceful, free, industrious, and opulent nation, of four or five millions of persons, sprung from one of the most enlightened nations of the globe, and maintaining incessant intercourse with every part of Europe, should have so few monuments of these arts among them, either in public or private collections" (3: 181). This writer's "Plan for the Improvement and Diffusion of the Arts, Adapted to the United States" (May 1805) called for the establishment of an endowment which would found galleries to house copies of the best artistic productions of antiquity and of contemporary Europe. As works of proven art became readily available for viewing in America — the plan also provides details for constructing the galleries in a way that would allow works to be viewed in the best light, at the best height, and so on — more works of native making were likely to appear from the nation's nascent artists.

Some of this work was already underway. Only three months after "Plan for the Improvement and Diffusion of the Arts" appeared in the *Literary Magazine*, Brown published his own review of the "Pennsylvania Academy of Fine Arts" (August 1805).[60] The Academy was the work of a group "of gentlemen in Philadelphia"; money had been raised, the building designed "by an amateur of great taste," and a sizeable "supply of the best models ... engaged from France and Italy" (4: 129). "Whatever justice there may be in the contempt with which the literary and scientific spirit of America is regarded by Europeans," Brown writes in a spirit of "zeal for liberal pursuits" and in contrast to both the foreign and native critics, "we are surely remarkably distinguished for our genius for the arts. Notwithstanding the want of examples, and incitements, America has hitherto produced the greatest painters of the age..." (4: 130).[61] As a citizen of the United States known only by the pseudonym "R.," Brown promises the gentlemen involved in establishing the Pennsylvania Academy that, while he "has not the honour to be enrolled in this fraternity," he "will always ... diligently second their efforts, and sincerely rejoice in their success."

Other individuals were even more optimistic about current conditions of creativity in the United States, especially in regards to the literary arts. Roberts Vaux, for example, in his 10 January 1807 Anniversary Address to the American Literary Association,[62] briefly surveys the history of America from Columbus through the Revolution. The speech is strongly colored by Vaux's nationalism:

> THE records of antiquity, and the history of modern times, united with our own observation on man, contribute to confirm the opinion, that, among numbers of distinguished and honourable characteristics of his nature, there is one pre-eminently conspicuous virtue, which, amid all

the adverse occurrences that checker his way through this world, and frequently rend from their base the strongest affections and most deep-rooted prejudices, remains unshaken: this is love of country [7: 323].

This nationalistic fervor leads Vaux to associate with Bacon and Newton the names of Franklin and Rittenhouse, "philosophers that America is proud to call her sons" (7: 325); with Gibbon and Hume, Ramsey and Belknap, "under whose pens have swelled the pages of historic truth"; with Raphael, West, "whose pencil moves ... under the patronage of an European monarch"; and, somewhat embarrassingly from our vantage point, with Milton and Pope, Humphreys and Dwight, "bards of our own soil" (7: 326). Problems do exist in America, Vaux says, in the slave trade and in the attempts of Thomas Paine and others "to undermine the fair fabric of religious and moral excellence" (7: 330), but he challenges his auditors—and readers—to "advance with redoubled ardour, and prosecute with renewed vigour the various duties that devolve on us as members of this association. Let our attainments in science, and advancement in literature confirm our *piety*, fortify our *justice*, and cherish our love of *mercy*" (7: 332).

"Our country is generally considered as a youthful, or rather, in some respects, an infantile country," Brown writes in his review of the Pennsylvania Academy of the Fine Arts, "whose imbecile and growing state requires corporal nutriment and exercise, rather than intellectual..." (4: 129). He knew firsthand that the intellectual commodity of literary art, at least, was not encouraged in the United States. In July 1806 Brown included in the *Literary Magazine* a brief essay entitled "Why the Arts Are Discouraged in America."[63] No cultural or constitutional reason existed to cause the arts to be neglected. The land and weather were not overly harsh, and the free government seemed congenial to artistic pursuits. The people were strong-willed, and a vast majority were literate, at least to some degree; most people worked hard and were flourishing. Brown finally identifies the discouragement of the arts as a result of the nation's newness:

> A people must secure a provision of absolute necessaries, before they think of conveniences; and must enjoy conveniences before they can indulge in the agreeable arts of life.... The Americans began with log-houses, and are now in the progress to brick and stone, convenience and elegance; their attentions observe the like progress, and expand with the ability of attainment. When agriculture, with its attendant arts, and

> commerce, have rendered them comfortable in all respects, they will then naturally aspire to and encourage works of ingenuity and polite arts; which, though as yet unsuitable and beyond their views, will then evince their prosperity instead of their decay [6: 77].

According to Richard Brodhead, "Writing always takes place within some completely concrete cultural situation.... A work of writing comes to its particular form of existence in interaction with the network of relations that surround it: in any actual instance, writing orients itself in or against some understanding of what writing is, does, and is good for that is culturally composed and derived" (8). Understood in this context, Brown's writing existed within a cultural situation that was still in its early developmental stage. This may explain — at least in regards to his novels— why his fiction seems to the modern reader inchoate and fragmented. Brown's work as a journalist and editor was situated in, and given meaning by, a particular "culture of letters" (Brodhead 9), which was still trying to define itself in relation to its indigenous cultural and political setting and the larger transatlantic world. As Brown suggests in "Why the Arts Are Discouraged in America," the nation was not ready, especially in an economic sense, to accept or support art for art's sake. But the cultural situation of republican America demanded that the people be well informed, and there was no more pervasive vehicle for "useful information" than periodical literature. Thus his work as a journalist and author in the first decade of the nineteenth century was given purpose by the social, political, and literary context in which it appeared.

In "Remarks on Reading," Brown says that "writing is justly denominated an art." It was his art. His brief but explosive career as a novelist had been disappointing financially, but given the wealth of material he wrote after the publication of his final novel, it cannot be said that he gave up on literature. That the early nineteenth century accepted as literary the entire range of writing allowed him to remain a literary man throughout his relatively brief adult life. And because writing was so important— because reading was so important— Brown continued to explore the elements and effects of writing and reading in the *Literary Magazine*, to explore these directly through his essays and indirectly through fragments of fiction.

Four

Fragments of Fiction

Magazine fiction in Charles Brockden Brown's day was not what it was in Edgar Allan Poe's. Far from being the complex, powerful, and more or less coherent genre that began to fill American miscellanies after the success of Irving's *Sketch-Book* tales, magazine fiction in Jeffersonian America took many different forms—anecdotes, dialogues, epistles, literary fragments, and so on.[1] Some tales were brief imitations "in the manner of" some popular British or European author;[2] others were little more than pieces pirated from British periodicals, sometimes with changes made to adapt them to the American scene. Practically all were presented for the sake of their morals rather than as works of literary art. As James L. Machor says, the cultural "work of a novel or short story" from Brown's time "was tantamount to the morality of its exposition and message..."; the assumption, Machor continues, was "that readers were learners" (329). Eugene Current-Garcia concurs: in short magazine fiction during the early decades of the United States "the theme alone—or more specifically, the *moral*, explicitly stated first and last—*was* the story" (11).

Brown's first periodical, *The Monthly Magazine, and American Review*, offered a substantial amount of its editor's fiction between 1799 and 1800, including several fragments, sketches, and short stories, as well as the serialization of his unfinished novel *Memoirs of Stephen Calvert*.[3] But the *Literary Magazine* published for its audience far fewer examples of this kind of work. At least part of the reason for this seems to be that little imaginative literature of note was issuing from the American press between 1803 and 1807. To borrow a phrase from Current-Garcia, it was a "period of belletristic drought" (3), and the *Literary Magazine*—indeed, the latter half of Brown's career—bears witness to this fact. For example, of the twenty-one items Brown included in "Notices of American Writers and Publications" (August 1804), only the eighth deals with belles lettres:

> We have but little opportunity of noticing original poetical performances. The muse seems at present to slumber in a country eminently calculated to awaken her exertions. We have skies, which give us the varied and kind returns of seasons; we have winds, which one would think would blow the spark of genius into flame; we have waters, which should allure to their banks the vagrant foot of enthusiasm; and we have mountains, which furnish us with all that is grand and elevating in prospect. Why then slumbers the poetical muses of America? We could indeed give a list of poets, whose works are entitled to a considerable portion of praise; but we complain of the smallness of their number, and we wish to see some effort which shall go beyond any that has yet appeared [2: 345].

Brown understood poetry — works of the imagination as distinct from those of philosophy or reason — to be an art form including both verse and prose. Because Aristotle's *Poetics* and other works that followed it stressed "imitation" as the defining characteristic of poetry — of all the "imitative arts" — Brown suggests that "this definition must evidently comprehend all verbal delineations of nature, whether in verse or prose. A prose comedy is at least as perfect an imitation of nature as a tragedy in verse; and a well written novel is as accurate a copy of nature as an epic poem" (2: 583).[4]

No apparent barrier stood in the way of the creation of literary art in the early United States. The American landscape and climate, as well as the nation's form of government and the freedom it allowed the people, should, it was thought, inspire many native writers. According to Brown, however, little poetry of merit — either in verse or prose — appeared in America during the first decade of the nineteenth century. He provides further detail on this dearth of imaginative writing in the new country in his December 1803 review of Winthrop Sergeant's "Boston ... A Poem":[5]

> THIS poem ... is a very brief descant on the discouragements which genius meets with in America; of the frailty and inelegance of our architecture, in that mode of building which exposes our towns, and particularly Boston, to the ravages of fire; on the broils and animosities of party, and on the absurdities of fashion and dress, manners, amusements, music and poetry. On each of these topics, the poet expatiates briefly, but with considerable spirit and elegance....
>
> On the whole, there is much strength of imagery, and spirited versification in this little performance. Should the writer continue to pursue the same path, we doubt whether his own case would not prove

an exception to the charge so often made against America, of being insensible and inattentive to genius of its own growth.... Thus the insensibility to poetical and literary merit, so far as this insensibility is real, ought to entitle us to condolence and compassion, rather than to chiding and rebuke, since to want this faculty, is to want a source of very great pleasure; and since no man is enabled to acquire it by reproach and ridicule [1: 190–91].

The "chiding and rebuke," "reproach and ridicule," came from both Americans and Europeans. Although Brown regretted the reaction of the former and more or less expected the reaction of the latter, he seems to have accepted the situation with the understanding that in order for American writing to earn respect from either group it would have to compete with the writing of the former imperial center, which constituted the majority of belles lettres read by the British and his fellow Americans. Along with this fact of America's postcolonial and imitative culture came a problem not easily overcome: in attempting to compete at the publisher's and bookseller's shops with the works of England's Shakespeare, Milton, Pope, and Cowper, the native literary productions of the United States—especially in poetry as Brown understood it—faced significant difficulties arising from the new nation's cultural, literary, and financial realities: the colonial habits of American readers, the perceived lack of quality in American writing (in relation to the productions of the traditionally read English authors), the absence of an international copyright, and so on.

As a writer of verse, Brown was little more than a poetaster, and there were in the young American republic no native writers of verse consistently able to rival the great bards of the former mother country. But the realm of prose fiction seemed to offer to American writing some opportunity for distinction. The eighteenth-century masters—Richardson, Fielding, Goldsmith, and Sterne—were dead (although still widely read). The early nineteenth century had yet to yield any fiction from Scott, Austen, Irving, or Cooper. But no one was taking advantage of this apparent opportunity. Brown, the leading producer of American fiction at the turn of the century, was creating little work in the genre while editor of the *Literary Magazine*. Certainly native fiction was being published; Brown's own publisher John Conrad printed an edition of Brackenridge's *Modern Chivalry* in 1804, and the sentimental fragment, whether of British or American origin, was still a staple in American magazines and newspapers. But nothing produced during the middle years of the nineteenth century's first decade is widely known today. If there was in fact an opportunity for American writers of fiction to distinguish themselves in the international public sphere of that time, it was an opportunity missed.

Of the few pieces of fiction published in the *Literary Magazine*, most are Brown's.[6] And most are fragments. Mukhtar Ali Isani has written that the literary fragment was a popular American genre during the latter years of the eighteenth century. Although his claim that it was "generally of native origin" has been rightly questioned (17),[7] Isani's essay still provides a good summary of the genre's characteristics, whether the origins of most of his examples are American or not. For example, like a miniature classical epic, the fragment typically begins *in medias res*; pieces were sometimes two paragraphs or less in length and usually did not run beyond one thousand words. Most adopted a first-person narrative voice and remained a monologue as often as not (18). Like the novels of the time, fragments exhibited elements of the sentimental and the Gothic; as Isani says, "'A turn among the tombs'"—typical in both sentimental and Gothic fiction, although for different reasons—"is a common exercise" in these brief tales (19).

"By 1800," Current-Garcia claims in *The American Short Story Before 1850*, "between 400 and 500 short tales of one sort or another had appeared in American magazines. Many of these were mere fragments..." (3). Isani identifies 1800 as an important date to the fragment as well, but for him it is the date by which the form "had already become static" and had begun to lose popularity as "editors and readers demanded greater sophistication and variety" (26). But Isani's conclusion, I would argue, is too simple. The fragment served as one strand in the evolution of the American short story and, rather than dying out, continued to be a presence as the genre developed into maturity.[8]

Brown's most typical contribution to the fragment genre in the *Literary Magazine* is "New Year's Day. A Fragment" (January 1805).[9] In keeping with the form's characteristics, the sketch is composed of ten paragraphs and some eight hundred words, and a first-person narrator delivers the details as a monologue. Strong sentimental elements—remembrance of the days of youth, the death of friends, a fortunate marriage, a moral—color the brief tale, and dramatic ellipsis points at beginning and end indicate that "New Year's Day" is only part of a larger story.

The narrator begins by reflecting on the singular effect New Year's Day has on the life of an individual:

> ....WHEN we reach a new year's day, we reach an eminence in the journey of life, where we are naturally prompted to pause, from which we

have an opportunity of seeing a large portion of the road we have passed, and are powerfully induced to cast our view forward in search of futurity. Each one who has attained this height looks back and looks forward on a scene, and with emotions, peculiar to himself. What are my emotions? what is the scene which I have passed, and what the prospects which futurity discloses to *my* anxious view?

This speaker is thirty-four years old, roughly the same age as Brown.[10] Reminiscences of friends who met death before him come to his mind. The first he remembers as his "earliest and infantile playmate, with whom I used to *play horses*, and con the *ABC* together." This individual held great promise due to his family situation and the education he was given. But he "trod the paths of idleness and dissipation" to a "hospital for lunatics" and was ultimately "consigned to a nameless grave" (3: 22). The second he remembers as a friend "whose moral habits were as blameless as his studious propensities were laudable." This young man was crippled, but he took up medicine as a profession — like Brown's good friend Elihu Hubbard Smith. The arduous work, however, brought on his death "before his twentieth year": "[m]any times, during our intercourse, had he occasion to sit beside my sick bed, and often did he predict that ere the next sun should rise, I should draw my last breath. Yet it was my lot to follow *him* to his grave" (3: 23).

Of himself the narrator says, "I have been most unfortunate in possessing a character, and imbibing habits, which merit nothing but poverty and ignominy; which have invariably and incessantly committed to hazard life, health, fame, and competence." And yet he is the one who lives and prospers. To the sentimental fragment conventions of a captured moment within a larger story, the remembrance of youth, and the "'turn among the tombs,'" Brown adds a marriage, unmerited in the narrator's view but happy nonetheless:[11] "All that surpassed my hopes, and far outstripped my deserts, has showered itself down upon me; and this anniversary [New Year's Day] has risen with more felicities to my view, than any former one: felicities which want nothing but stability and long continuance to make full the cup of my desires........" (3: 23).

The use to which Brown puts these sentimental conventions, however, differs widely from their use in the typical moral fragment. Despite morbid memories of friends believed to have been worthier of success and happiness than he, the narrator does not die weeping over their graves at the end of his tale but is instead both successful and happy. His story reflects the rise of liberal individualism. No longer is the good life seen as the outward revelation of an inward justification, as in Puritan theology; nor is success the result of or reward for republican merit. The narrator has had neither the social and educational opportunity of his first friend nor the talents of his second, yet the life he has led has brought the fulfillment of all his individual "desires" and "every good that fancy could image" (3: 23). In the liberalizing society of the early nineteenth century, self-interest thus becomes more openly accepted as integral to individual success; furthermore, as Brown's America became increasingly characterized by a merchant economy, self-interest became a viable, if still often questionable, motive to action. As is typical of the genre, Brown's fragment has a moral, but the moral itself—that the self-interested individual is responsible for her or his own life—is atypical. A tension exists, therefore, between the neoclassical form of the tale and its incipient romantic message. The moral rises above the story's eighteenth-century sentimentalism and, like the narrator from his eminence in the opening paragraph, looks forward to nineteenth-century romanticism.

In its formal characteristics, then, if not in its moral, "New Year's Day" easily fits the fragment genre so well adapted to the magazines of the early United States. But the two major works of fiction Brown published in the *Literary Magazine*—"Somnambulism"[12] and "Memoirs of Carwin the Biloquist"[13]—push the genre even farther along the line of development toward modern short fiction and novelistic fragments. Indeed, they break out of the formal confines of the genre and as longer fictions offer deeper explorations of changing life in America, truer reflections of the fragmentation taking place in the early republic, and thus greater rewards to the diligent American reader. In discussing Brown's approach to fiction, Warner Berthoff suggests that the fiction's "appeal to exacting readers in the early nineteenth century was due ... to the intellectual forcefulness, the steadiness and purposiveness of thought"—as opposed to plot or technique—"that Brown's method served to release" ("'Lesson'" 46). Understood in this context, "Memoirs of Carwin" and "Somnambulism," like the more traditional "New Year's Day," forcefully explore—albeit in more depth and detail—the fragmentation of America's liberalizing society during the Jefferson years, the concomitant rise of self-interest and romantic notions of individuality, and the explosive potential in the conflict between the eighteenth century's ideology of reason and the nineteenth century's ideology—and practice—of imagination.

I. "Somnambulism. A Fragment."

Like *Wieland* and *Edgar Huntly*, "Somnambulism" is set on the American frontier between civilization and the wilderness.[14] And as is the case with the novels, the fragment's setting and action reaffirm Brown's ability to use this frontier as a space for creating an American Gothic and exploring ideas about an American life in transition. Within this setting, Brown utilizes some rather typical Gothic conventions— darkness of night, a young woman in danger, an unknown presence, and the like — to tell the story of a tragic murder and the search for information that hopefully will lead to the author of the crime.

Richard Althorpe, the tale's narrator, resides in the home of his uncle's family in the sparsely populated countryside of Pennsylvania, and on one particular evening, two guests, a Mr. Davis and his daughter Constantia, are also present in the house. Just as the Davises are about to retire from the hearth and prepare for bed, a messenger arrives with an urgent missive for Mr. Davis, who decides to set out immediately in order to return to his own home as soon as possible. Althorpe — in love with Constantia in spite of her being engaged to another and desperate not to lose what he considers his one and only opportunity to win her for himself— protests their night journey along a road and through a countryside unfamiliar to them. But Mr. Davis and his daughter reject both Althorpe's admonitions and his offers to accompany them.

In his dreams that night, the ardent Althorpe resolves to follow Constantia and her father but catches up with them too late to prevent Constantia's being shot by an unknown assailant. His dream continues over the course of a long investigation, during which he discovers the identity of his beloved's assassin and, in turn, guns down this guilty man.

By noon the next day, another messenger arrives with news that Constantia has indeed been shot on the road during the night, and Althorpe hurries to the home of Dr. Inglefield, a physician who lives near the scene of the tragedy. There Althorpe, as he had in his dream of the previous night, begins to piece together the story of how this terrible event happened: how Mr. Davis and Constantia began to catch glimpses of a man shadowing them on their way, a man they thought looked much like Althorpe himself; how they learned from an old Yankee farmer that this dark figure was probably a trickster named Nick Handyside, a madman who haunts the area but, besides a penchant for frightening travelers out of their wits by his appearance and screams, is relatively harmless; how, after father and daughter alighted from their carriage in order to walk through a rough portion of the road, a nearby shriek in the darkness caused their horse to bolt, wrecking the carriage against the gnarled trunk of a giant oak that grows in the center of the road; and finally how, as Mr. Davis returned from an ill-advised, futile attempt to catch the horse, he heard a single pistol shot and hurried to the oak to find Constantia mortally wounded and her attacker fled. "Every measure that humanity and professional skill could suggest were employed on this occasion," Althorpe concludes. "The dying lady was removed to the house. The ball had lodged in her brain, and to extract it was impossible. Why should I dwell on the remaining incidents of this tale? She languished till the next morning, and then expired.———" (3: 347).

Between the elliptical dashes with which the story begins and ends, with which Brown indicates that more of the story exists beyond the confines of the printed text of the fragment, Althorpe never discovers—except vaguely in his prophetic dream — who murdered Constantia Davis. But the reader understands that Althorpe himself certainly murdered her. He is the story's sleepwalker.[15] Brown's editorial headnote to "Somnambulism"—largely an apparent extract from the 14 June 1784 issue of the *Vienna Gazette*—provides the key to understanding this aspect of the fragment. The clipping reports the arrest of a male somnambulist for the murder of a young woman who "'was the object of his affection'" and on a "'journey ... which ... had given him the utmost anxiety for her safety.'" The young man commits the murder "'while asleep, and ... entirely unknown to himself'" (3: 335).[16] Brown explores in fiction the situation presented in the report as fact, giving emotional and psychological drama to the story of a distraught lover and sleepwalker.

One of the few detailed readings of "Somnambulism" is William J. Scheick's essay, "Assassin in Artful Disguise: The De-Signed Designs of Charles Brockden Brown's 'Somnambulism,'"[17] in the course of which Scheick identifies in the fragment the "perfect miniature of ... Brown's enigmatic literary manner" and then analyzes the work in terms of plot, moral stability, structure, readership, authorship, and aesthetic design. He suggests that

> [d]esign (as both intention and scheme) is effectively de-signed as the narrative signs of "Somnambulism" lead to various culs de sac of self-referential configurations. Brown's chronicle, which adumbrates *fin de siècle* Aestheticism, intimates that the mind is evidently ontologically bereft and epistemologically lost. It is nonetheless capable of unwittingly

inventing, rather than of consciously discovering, philosophical, moral, political, and social signification — design as intention and pattern [27].

The general tendency, however, of the remaining few mentions of the story in Brown scholarship has been to focus on its obvious relationship to "Sky-Walk"— Brown's first novel, never published and now lost — and to *Edgar Huntly*. Still, Sydney Krause and Alfred Weber each laid a strong foundation on which interpretations of "Somnambulism" might be built. In discussing the relationship between Althorpe's conscious life and his sleepwalking, Krause says that Brown begins "to show the tortured ego (technically the 'id' in this case) attempting to compensate for its practical defeat"— that is, Althorpe's inability to convince Constantia of the dangers of the night journey or of the reality of his love for her. The unconscious somnambulistic event not only "release[s] the inner man" but also sets in motion an unknown entity who "*acts*, often dangerously." "Also implied is the response of the pleasure-principle denied," Krause continues, "the backlash of man's raw emotional nature. And these energies are not simply worked off passively in the wish-fulfillment of a dream" ("Historical" 335). Unfortunately these intriguing ideas are presented in the context of a discussion of *Edgar Huntly* and are not deeply explored in relation to "Somnambulism" as a separate work. Approaching the story from a different angle, analyzing how Brown and his short fiction participate in the development of the American short story, Weber rightly identifies the tale as a mixture of Gothic romance, psychological study, and crime fiction and ultimately claims that it is "the first American detective story, published thirty-five years before Poe's 'Murders in the Rue Morgue'" ("Beginnings" 18, 12).[18]

In "Somnambulism," Brown applies the "intellectual forcefulness" Berthoff identifies in his fiction to the exploration of ideas forming at the point of tension between a fading eighteenth-century rationalism and a nascent nineteenth-century non-rational individualism. Althorpe lives his waking life in a world governed by neoclassical decorum, by reason, restraint, and order, the civic virtues promoted by the Federalist agenda of his time. Within this social and political context he struggles— often unsuccessfully — to manage his romantic spirit: "My imagination was vivid. My passions, when I allowed them sway, were uncontroulable. My conduct, as my feelings, was characterised by precipitation and headlong energy" (3: 337).

Mr. Davis and Constantia see no logical reason that they should not make the night journey that the father's business seems to demand. They have with them a guide, and they feel the various dangers of the American road pose no threat to them as long as they remain alert and cautious. But Althorpe's fears push him "to enumerate and magnify the possibilities" of danger, and his "emotions arose to terror." "The strength of a belief, when it is destitute of any rational foundation," he says in a rational observation on such irrational trains of thought, "seems, of itself, to furnish a new ground for credulity. We first admit a powerful persuasion, and then, from reflecting on the insufficiency of the ground on which it is built, instead of being prompted to dismiss it, we become more forcibly attached to it." His sense of himself as a romantic hero—one who feels he knows the road almost as well as his own "chamber floor"—leads him into a social blunder in relation to Mr. Davis and Constantia: "I made bold enquiries into the importance of the motives that should induce them to expose themselves to the least hazard." Thus he crosses the line of "scrupulous decorum" and deference, and his uncle's guests become suspicious of his motives (3: 337). Althorpe can find no rational grounds for his heightened emotions. The others see his imagination as misleading him into envisioning dangers that exist only in his own irrationality, an irrationality which Miss Davis will privately attribute to the young man's believing that he is in love (3: 341).

But the tension between the romantic and the neoclassical arises not only between Althorpe and the Davises but also within Althorpe as an individual. Once the father and daughter are resolved to leave without any assistance other than that of their hired guide, the intense struggle between imagination and reason moves to the interior of Althorpe's mind. Faced with reasonable arguments against his fears and forebodings, conscious also of a duty to be obedient to his uncle (who believes with the Davises that there is no real danger in their journey), Althorpe finds himself left with no choice but to relent and attempts to restore to his character and actions some sense of self-restraint and rational order. But he exhibits these neoclassical, republican virtues only while the outside community exerts pressure on him to do so. "As long as their representations rung in my ears," he says, "I allowed myself to be ashamed of my weakness, and conjured up a temporary persuasion that my attendance was, indeed, superfluous, and that I should show most wisdom in suffering them to depart alone" (3: 338). As this largely self-aware young man recognizes, however, his dutiful restraint of individual desires and humble submission to the will of his superiors—virtuous actions in a republican citizen—are only a "temporary persuasion," a "conjured" illusion. As soon as the communal influences of reason and social order are removed by the departure of the Davises and his uncle's retiring for the night, Althorpe's internal struggle resumes, and he finds himself "breathless with fear of some unknown and terrible disaster that awaited" father and daughter on the dark road (3: 338–39).

At this point, the upcoming somnambulistic event begins to take form, and soon Althorpe himself—an individual released from the restraints of republican society, released in this case by sleep—will become that "unknown" which he fears. "A hundred times I resolved to disregard their remonstrances," he says, "and hover near them till the morning." And as many times, he decides against this idea. At last, however, still wrestling with these alternating resolutions, he closes the gate and haltingly returns to his uncle's house. There he spends "a drooping and melancholy evening" during which his "imagination," he says, "continually hovered over our departed guests." Memory and "fancy" blend as he remembers his brief time with Miss Davis, and in an excess of sentiment, his "eyes overflowed with tears"; "[t]here insensibly arose a sort of persuasion," he concludes, "that destiny had irreversably decreed that I should never see her more." Sleep finally overtakes him, however, and he "sinks into a profound slumber" (3: 339).

In the dream which naturally follows the ideas and desires that consume his conscious mind, the dream in which he is unable to save Constantia but then tracks down and kills her assassin, Althorpe finds his thoughts "full of confusion and inaccuracy" (3: 340). This confused state reflects early psychology's understanding of dreams. As Allan Gardner Smith has shown, Brown—in *Wieland* and *Edgar Huntly*—made use of contemporary scientific ideas about sleep and dreams, especially as these ideas appear in Erasmus Darwin's *Zoonomia*. That Althorpe's dream is as typically confusing and inaccurate as most dreams are results from what Smith terms the "lack of volition." "Normally," Smith writes in describing Darwin's theories,

> the mind follows trains of association which are quite well established and incorporate some acts of volition within them, as we compare our passing trains of thought with our acquired knowledge of nature. But in sleep the lack of volition causes these habitual connections to be dissevered, and to fall into new "catenations." Therefore dreams display the kind of inconsequence that Brown describes so frequently, often in the form of nightmare. "Incubus," as Darwin calls it, is accounted for by a combination of uneasy sensations and profound sleep [12–13].[19]

Althorpe certainly experiences this "combination," and even though in waking life he finally exhibits self-control and does not follow Constantia and her father, in his dreams—and in his somnambulism—he follows to disastrous effect. Not only does the young man find himself unable to save his love in the dream (while killing her in reality), but he also is unable to adhere to either civil law or to a code of honor when in his nightmare he discovers her assailant; instead of acting in accordance with the waking "train of thought" that should, in a man of honor, demand the criminal either be brought to justice or faced in a fair fight, he murders the murderer in a fit of passion. As Althorpe himself puts it, "I did not employ the usual preliminaries which honour prescribes, but, stimulated by rage, attacked him with a pistol, and terminated his career by a mortal wound" (3: 340).

Having experienced this cathartic dream, having committed as well the unconscious and perhaps in some way cathartic action of assuring that Constantia will never belong to another, Althorpe—"quietly reposing in the chair in which I had fallen asleep"—awakes the next morning "refreshed and invigorated" and with a lighter heart goes about his daily chores until news comes of the tragic attack on Constantia.

Upon his arrival at the home of Dr. Inglefield, as Weber says, Althorpe, "the former first-person narrator, steps into the background and gives an objective, detailed, and graphic account of the nocturnal events, in which the father and daughter become the protagonists" ("Beginnings" 14). The remainder of the story is theirs. Having no concrete reason to fear anything along their way, and being as well on an errand of apparently important business, they set out on the dark American road that passes Althorpe's uncle's gate. "After they had parted from us," Althorpe says, spinning a narrative from the later accounts of Mr. Davis and the guide,

> they proceeded on their way for some time without molestation. The clouds disappearing, the star-light enabled them with less difficulty to discern their path. They met not a human being till they came within less than three miles of the oak which I have before described. Here Miss Davis looked forward with some curiosity and said to her father, "Do you not see some one in the road before us? I saw him this moment move across from the fence on the right hand and stand still in the middle of the road."
> "I see nothing, I must confess," said the father....
> The carriage slowly advancing, and the form remaining in the same spot, Mr. Davis at length perceived it, but was not allowed a clearer examination, for the person, having, as it seemed, ascertained the nature

> of the cavalcade, shot across the road, and disappeared. The behaviour of this unknown person furnished the travellers with a topic of abundant speculation.
> ...At length Mr. Davis said, "A thought has just occurred to me. The person whom we just now saw is young Althorpe."
> Miss Davis was startled: "Why, my dear father, should you think so? It is too dark to judge, at this distance, by resemblance of figure..." [3: 340–41].

For the next while, father and daughter grow increasingly uneasy. The mysterious figure comes and goes. "'As I live,' exclaimed Mr. Davis, 'that thing, whatever it be, haunts us. I do not like it. This is strange conduct for young Althorpe to adopt.'" Like Hawthorne's Goodman Brown on the dusky forest path, the Davises are unable to see anything distinctly either in the road ahead of them or alongside it. But whereas the young Puritan's inability to see shakes his "faith" in his education and in the Christian leaders of Salem Village, the Davises' inability to see shakes their rational certainty of control, their reasonable expectation of safety, and the strength of purpose with which they had set out on their journey. As the pair and their guide approach the point where the road disappears into a stand of forest, Mr. Davis seems more fearful and uncertain than Constantia: "'I know not how it is,' said he, 'but I begin to be affected with the fears of young Althorpe. I am half resolved not to enter this wood'" (3: 342).

Just then the Davises hear "a noise, at a small distance behind them, as of shutting a gate" (3: 342). They call out, and a Yankee farmer "approached the chaise, and enquired who they were, whence they came, whither they were going, and, lastly, what they wanted" (3: 342–43).[20] From him they learn that the figure shadowing them is probably that of a local character named Nick Handyside — "'a fellow that went about the country a' nights. A shocking fool to be sure, that loved to plague and frighten people.'" "'Nick is an odd soul to be sure; but he don't do nobody no harm, as ever I heard, except by scaring them,'" the farmer assures the Davises. "'He is easily skeart though, for that matter, himself. He loves to frighten folks, but he's shocking apt to be frightened himself. I reckon you took Nick for a ghost. That's a shocking good story, I declare. Yet it's happened hundreds and hundreds of times, I guess, and more'" (3: 343).[21]

Furnished with this rational explanation of the mysterious figure in the night, Mr. Davis and Constantia resume their journey somewhat more at ease, even developing a lively curiosity — perhaps typical of "enlightened" individuals with an empirical mindset — to see this strange native of the frontier and hear his screams. They hear "rustling leaves or stumbling footsteps," but the ghostly human only "occasionally hovered in their sight" and never approaches to perform for them (3: 344).

Almost as soon as Althorpe's narrative provides an apparently reasonable solution to the mystery, it begins to question that solution. Brown's use of language supplies a first hint that the figure in the night is indeed Althorpe and not Handyside. That whoever haunts the Davises sometimes "hovered" where he might be seen echoes Althorpe's earlier internal struggles: "A hundred times I resolved to disregard their remonstrances, and hover near them till the morning"; "[m]y imagination continually hovered over our departed guests" (3: 339). Moreover, the man who haunts the road does not behave according to Handyside's reputation. The idiot trickster, Althorpe says, "took pleasure in the effects which the sight of his own deformity produced, and betokened his satisfaction by a laugh, which might have served as a model to the poet who has depicted the ghastly risibilities of Death." Apparently satisfied with the Yankee farmer's explanation of the mystery, however, Mr. Davis and Constantia, along with Althorpe in his role in this section as third-person narrator, give too little consideration to the fact that their shadow exhibits an ominously different behavior: "On this occasion ... the monster behaved with unusual moderation. He never came near enough for his peculiarities to be distinguished by star-light. There was nothing fantastic in his motions, nor any thing surprising, but the celerity of his transitions. They were unaccompanied by those howls, which reminded you at one time of a troop of hungry wolves, and had, at another, something in them inexpressibly wild and melancholy." When the carriage arrives at the edge of the wood and Mr. and Miss Davis alight to walk, "the spectre, which, till now, had been occasionally visible, entirely disappeared" in direct contradiction to the manner in which Handyside was supposed to behave (3: 344).

In the darkness beneath the trees of this frontier wilderness, where, metaphorically, reason and rational order are on tenuous ground, father and daughter talk about Handyside, who is "no longer an object of terror"; Constantia "declared she should be highly pleased by hearing his outcries, and consoled herself with the belief, that he would not allow them to pass the limits which he had prescribed to his wanderings, without greeting them with a strain or two." Althorpe the sleepwalker stands hidden nearby, "at less than twenty paces from them," and he utters a "scream, dismally loud, and piercingly shrill," startling both the Davises and their horse (3: 345).

Why does Althorpe scream? Perhaps, knowing the caprices of Nick Handyside, Althorpe simply reacts to Constantia's spoken desire to hear the harmless madman scream; her wish either suggests to Althorpe that he is Handyside or prompts the somnambulistic young man so hopelessly in love with her — so focused on her in the disconnected world of a dream — to attempt to grant her request. Perhaps only the mere suggestion of screaming reached him where he stood, and he responded, experiencing that "lack of volition," as Smith calls it, which would have restrained him while conscious. Perhaps, sleepwalking within the dream recounted earlier in the story, Althorpe screams in the moment of uncontrollable "rage" that leads him to murder Constantia's assassin. Whatever its cause, the effect of the scream is to separate father and daughter. Mr. Davis goes after the bolted horse, leaving Constantia — at the story's tragic climax — unprotected against the lovelorn, sleepwalking, and tragically armed Althorpe.

What cultural work might "Somnambulism" have performed for readers of the *Literary Magazine* in 1805? Discussing in *Sensational Designs* Brown's *Wieland*, a story similarly set on the American frontier and similarly peopled with supposedly rational characters, Jane Tompkins says that "*Wieland*'s rural decencies are the seedbed of a holocaust. Dramatizing the precariousness of Crèvecoeur's 'perfect' society, the novel's plot offers a direct refutation of the Republican faith in men's capacity to govern themselves without the supports and constraints of an established order" (49).[22] Similarly, Christopher Looby writes that Brown promotes in *Wieland* "a politics that recognizes the necessity of a respect for traditional authority as the only bulwark against the uncertainties and distortions that can afflict reasoned discourse" in a revolutionary society, that in the novel Brown's "persuasions, dramatized and allegorized, reveal him to be a complex counter-revolutionary writer" (202). While in part true, what these readings fail to recognize is that Brown's novel provides at the same time a "direct refutation" of traditional, Federalist assumptions that "an established social order" was indeed possible. Thus *Wieland*, this "American Tale" of "Transformation,"[23] shows that, in the new nation's increasingly liberal society, faith in either rational order or social balance was just as precarious as the rising liberal individualism Brown himself promoted to a large extent in the *Literary Magazine*. Brown was no "*party-man*," as I have shown. *Wieland* critiques the agendas of both the Federalists' classical republicanism and the French Revolution's radical democracy. The same exploration or testing of ideas, I argue, takes place in "Somnambulism."

Popular fiction in the late eighteenth and early nineteenth centuries supplied example after example of individuals who go against Federalism's rational, moral agenda and pay dearly for their transgressions. Given the popularity of Rowson's *Charlotte Temple* and Foster's *The Coquette*, given as well the proliferation of sentimental, moralistic fictions in magazines available in America, Brown's readers must have been at least subconsciously aware of Federalist assumptions that life should be organized and coherent and that, in order to achieve such organization and coherence, citizens should behave morally and virtuously, subordinating their private desires to the public good.

Brown's "Somnambulism" attacks these assumptions. All of settled America was, to some degree, a frontier, a space between the established civilization and order of the Old World and the young American nation's own primitive hinterland, the wilderness to the west. Understood in this context, life in the New World was as yet uncertain, unpredictable, even dangerous. Brown suggests that neither rationalism nor republican civic virtue serves to protect the individual from the threat of physical and psychological unknowns. Mr. Davis and Constantia assure themselves and young Althorpe that the night journey holds no dangers, but their assurances are based on the known — darkness itself cannot hurt them, sloughs can be avoided, other impediments such as rocks and trees in the roadway are to be watched for, and so on. Even when the figure in the night begins to seem threatening to Mr. Davis, Constantia calmly defers to logic: "'Nay, my father, ... be not disturbed. What danger can be dreaded by two persons from one?'" (3: 342). This makes rational sense, of course, but the unknowns—the abilities, character, and condition of this particular "spectre," the unfamiliar road, the dark woods—call her judgment into question.[24] Out in the world, Brown suggests, rationalists such as the Davises deceive themselves into believing that life is ordered according to reason and that aberrations such as the figure that haunts the road—be he Nick Handyside or another "thing"—can be dealt with on rational terms.[25] Like the Enlightenment itself, which Brown believed did not exist on as wide a scale as European and American intellectual and political leaders claimed, rational republican order and balance do not exist on the frontier of liberal America.

Brown's story, however, attacks not only the agenda of rational Federalism but also that of radical democracy, exemplified by the chaos of the French Revolution. In his somnambulistic state, Althorpe is disconnected from all restraints, excepting physical limitations. The sleepwalker, like the revolutionaries in France, acts unconsciously, without reference to the authority of the individual's natural aristocracy — the reason, moral values, character, education, manners, and so on that prohibit an individual's acting from pure selfishness and licentiousness. Nick Handyside is obviously irrational, a social outcast, and one of the unknowns Mr. Davis and Constantia potentially face on the frontier, but his freaks are easily detected and easily stopped; the Yankee farmer explains the madman's behavior and tells the Davises that a stern, authoritative voice will serve to frighten him away. On the other hand, Althorpe, when conscious, is a known quantity — if sometimes a contrary one — in society as it is represented by Mr. Davis, Constantia, and his uncle. When separated from the restraint that society places on him, however, especially when his id is separated by sleep from the control of his ego, he becomes a far more dangerous unknown than Handyside. Had the Davises been able to see Althorpe clearly as he shadowed them, outwardly he would have seemed a recognizable, knowable, and probably a welcome member of the community, but inwardly he is a nightmare, like France during the Terror, of licentious freedom and irrational, radical democracy.

Readers of Rowson and Foster, taking up "Somnambulism," faced a dilemma for which there was no rational solution. Constantia dies the same as Charlotte Temple and Eliza Wharton, albeit more violently. But the story does not fit the Federalist model. What moral code, Brown's readers must have asked, has Constantia broken? She has neither been seduced by novels nor been a coquette and become pregnant. What crime against convention has she committed? She naturally chooses to accompany her father on the journey that leads to her death, but she could not have known she was making so fatal a choice. What instruction does the reader receive from her tragic end?

Like Brown's essay "Is a Free or Despotic Government Most Friendly to Human Happiness?"— published in March 1805, only two months before the story of Althorpe and Constantia appeared — "Somnambulism" suggests that elements moving within a free society often collide, sometimes violently. The violence of the collisions in this state of liberal individualism depends on the degree of the various physical, psychological, or ideological difference between the colliding elements. Understood in this context, "Somnambulism" represents an exploration of extreme oppositions: the violent collision of a man in love with a woman who does not return his love, of the incautiously rational and the uncontrollably irrational, a staunch Federalism and a radical democracy, neoclassical reason and romantic imagination. Had Althorpe remained "conscious," the worst collision in the story would have been that moment of argument over the night journey, when the democratic Althorpe displayed his inability to be governed by decorum and a virtuous sense of deference. Both parties in the conflict are ruled by self-interest, but dangerous violence erupts only when Mr. Davis and Constantia naïvely assume the world to be rational and knowable, and Althorpe loses consciousness—and with it his conscience—and becomes the unknowable in their path. For Brown, this view of the world and of human relations, although extreme, seems to have been more realistic—and more useful—than that of the sentimental, moralistic fiction appearing in contemporary novels and magazines. His own moral in "Somnambulism" suggests that to be educated and wide awake—conscious—provides an individual with a safeguard against such tragic experiences as those of Constantia Davis and Richard Althorpe.

II. "Memoirs of Carwin the Biloquist"

In the final sentence of her epistolary narrative of the horrific destruction of her family in pastoral Mettingen, Pennsylvania, Clara Wieland refers to Frank Carwin as "the double-tongued deceiver" (244). Carwin's reputation has broadened since the publication of Brown's first novel, but he is consistently cast in a dark or enigmatic light; twentieth-century critics have called him, among other things, "the Richardsonian seducer" (Fiedler 149), "the quintessential child of revolution" (Tompkins 52), and "no one and everyone, himself and a kosmos, one and many," the voice of "radical democracy in the revolutionary period" (Ruttenburg 185). Yet these labels attempt to define him as he appears in *Wieland*. Frank Carwin has his own story, or at least part of one. In the novelistic fragment "Memoirs of Carwin the Biloquist," Brown traces the development of the young man who would eventually wreak such havoc on the peaceful banks of the Schuylkill and reveals some sympathy for the biloquist as Carwin struggles to find and maintain an individual identity in the face of forces he does not fully understand.

Like Arthur Mervyn and Edgar Huntly, Frank Carwin locates his background in rural Pennsylvania, identifying himself as "the second son of a farmer" and revealing from the beginning that an interest in literary pursuits makes him unfit for life in his father's footsteps.[26] The family patriarch is a stern, authoritative figure who sees to it that Frank's elder brother rises to what is deemed a necessary level of education—"signing his name, and spelling out a chapter in the bible"—and that young Frank does not exceed this level, as "all beyond the mere capacity to write and read was useless or pernicious." In Carwin's opinion, his brother more nearly represents the model farmer's son: he is barely literate, void of ideas beyond those related to his immediate duties, and able at his work as long as fear of his father motivates him.[27] Carwin himself, however, has a much different character: "My thirst for knowledge was augmented in proportion as it was supplied with gratification. The more I heard or read, the more restless and unconquerable my curiosity became. My senses were perpetually alive to novelty, my fancy teemed with visions of the future, and my attention fastened upon every thing mysterious or unknown" (1: 100). The unnamed father recognizes these tendencies in his youngest son and, in an effort to curb them, beats him, assigns him difficult work, subjects him to the surveillance of the eldest son, and seeks out and destroys his books.[28] Carwin suffers this treatment from the age of six until he reaches fourteen, when he makes a momentous discovery.[29]

Carwin's father dispatches him one evening to a distant pasture with orders to bring home the cows, giving the boy only a certain amount of time to accomplish this chore; "I was menaced with severe chastisement," Carwin says, "if, according to my custom, I should stay beyond the period assigned." Arrived at the pasture, he discovers that the cows have broken out at a certain part of the fence. Rather than return home quickly to alert his father, Carwin dawdles, investigating the breach in the fence and attempting to figure out how the cows made their escape. Suddenly realizing that he has waited too long to get home by the appointed time, that he will not only be late but will also return with no cows, he searches for an alternate, more expedient route and discovers "a narrow pass" in the ridge that he normally skirts in going back and forth between his house and the pasture. In he plunges, desperate to return home within the allotted time. Deep in the heart of this detour, young Carwin discovers the seed of the talent that, in this story at least, marks his independence, sharpens his sense of himself as an individual, and ultimately becomes such a formative part of his identity that he will risk his life in order to maintain it as his secret alone.

The potential new way home, this passage through an unknown landscape, is an experiment, and Carwin finds himself frightened by the uncertainty of his journey through the darkened gorge:

> The path was narrow, steep, and overshadowed by rocks. The sun was nearly set, and the shadow of the cliff above, obscured the passage almost

as much as midnight would have done: I was accustomed to despise danger when it presented itself in a sensible form, but by a defect common in every one's education, goblins and spectres were to me the objects of the most violent apprehensions. These were unavoidably connected with solitude and darkness, and were present to my fears when I entered this gloomy recess [1: 101].

In order to diminish the fears inspired by this ominous landscape and his own superstitions, Carwin attempts to divert his attention "by hallowing as loud as organs of unusual compass and vigour" allow.[30] The first sound that comes to his mind under the influence of his groundless fears is, significantly, "the shrill tones of a Mohock savage," and he shouts in imitation of the voice of the characterizing inhabitant of the American wilderness.

In the Preface to *Edgar Huntly*, Brown had suggested that such an untamed American landscape as Carwin here enters and the possible presence in it of Native Americans—especially the "incidents of Indian hostility" that take place there (3)—should inform any attempts to create an American Gothic. By extension, the landscape and its inhabitants, Native or European Americans, should serve to characterize and localize American literature in general. The scene of Carwin in his "narrow pass" shouting like "a Mohock savage" thus identifies "Memoirs of Carwin the Biloquist" as a distinctly American tale. His first outcry immediately reconfigures the rugged detour through the ridge as "Indian territory" and the boy himself—beyond both the known, civilized world and his father's law—as a "savage" (Downes, "Constitutional" 106). The wilderness, its wildness aurally reinforced by the boy's wild cries, briefly becomes identified in "Memoirs" as a non-rational, ungoverned place—here a more positive version of such a place than the dark woods and the mind of the sleepwalker represent in "Somnambulism"—where Carwin is free to develop an individual character different from, even foreign to, the characters of his father, brother, and neighbors.

In this lawless, politically neutral space, Carwin discovers his "voice": "After finishing the [Mohock] strain, I paused. In a few seconds a voice, as I then imagined, uttered the same cry from the point of a rock some hundred feet behind me; the same words, with equal distinctness and deliberation, and in the same tone, appeared to be spoken." Young Frank finds this a somewhat confusing, even frightening event at first: "I was startled by this incident," he says, "and cast a fearful glance behind, to discover by whom it was uttered.... The speaker, however, was concealed from my view" (1: 102). On the surface, Carwin is simply shocked to think that someone unknown — perhaps even one of the wild inhabitants of the American wilderness— is apparently nearby in this uncharted passage. On a deeper level, however, Carwin possibly finds it disturbing to think his voice — not only his protection against his fears but also a singular marker of his individuality — has been appropriated by another.

That Carwin is initially frightened by his own voice suggests that Brown understood the trepidation many Americans felt in the early republic regarding their Revolution and the slow but recognizable movement toward an apparent social, cultural, and political democracy that followed it. The people's voice that spoke from the Declaration of Independence and the Constitution signified the change —from an imperial, transatlantic British voice to a distinctively American "We the people"— by means of which life in the new United States, on both the collective and individual levels, was not to be the same again.[31] Similarly, democratic revolution and the rise of liberal individualism — both of which often found expression through one or another individual voice — signaled a new way of life in America, an independent life that was yet another unnerving unknown for the nation and its citizens. Discovering a voice, either in writing or speech, empowers a nation or an individual with a sense of autonomy, a sense not always the most comforting, especially when one is unaccustomed to it. In a colonial society on the brink of independence, such as that within which Carwin lives,[32] voice articulates a distinctive identity, a self-fashioning — on a national, regional, individual, or other level — that may be authentic or contrived, original or imitative. Carwin's voice is, in a sense, all of these.

Once fear of the voice heard in the "gloomy recess" subsides, the boy forgets that he is geographically and temporally outside the limits prescribed to him and begins to play. His toying with this extraordinary echo serves as his first step toward independence and an individual identity. After the first night in his "vocal glen" (1: 102), he returns at every opportunity, and soon the idea strikes him that he might learn to throw his voice without the aid of this echo: "To hear my own voice speak at a distance would have been formerly regarded as prodigious. To hear too, that voice, not uttered by another, by whom it might be mimicked, but by myself!" Such a talent would not only be entertaining — and, as he will later learn, an instrument of power — but, like an image of himself reflected in a mirror, the sound of his own voice returning to him from somewhere outside himself would reaffirm his individuality and sense of identity. Carwin soon masters the trick of "muscular motion" which allows him, he says, "to accommodate my voice to all the varieties of distance and direction," and after he has added his already developed imitative skills to his new abilities, the biloquist is born (1: 103).[33]

Like Brown, young Carwin has a "literary passion" (1: 182), and in order to indulge this passion he must escape his father's farm, where "every thing that denoted intellectual exertion was a crime" (1: 103). An opportunity for escape exists in Philadelphia in the form of an aunt, who "had often expressed her desire that her nephew Frank, whom she always considered as a sprightly and promising lad, should be put under her care"; towards this end, he says, "She offered to be at the expense of my education, and to bequeath to me at her death her slender patrimony" (1: 181). Carwin's father flatly refuses his sister's offer. But the boy recognizes that his vocal abilities—his newfound biloquism combined with his lifelong talent for imitation—promise to cast a new light on this situation, and he hatches a plan:

> A thousand superstitious tales were current in the family. Apparitions had been seen, and voices had been heard on a multitude of occasions. My father was a confident believer in supernatural tokens. The voice of his wife, who had been many years dead, had twice been heard at midnight whispering at his pillow. I frequently asked myself whether a scheme favourable to my views might not be built upon these foundations. Suppose (thought I) my mother should be made to enjoin upon him compliance with my wishes?

To imitate at midnight a trusted voice—"to counterfeit a commission from heaven"—certainly raises ethical questions, but the youth's often expressed claims to religious conviction are easily relaxed in the face of such strong motivations as independence and self-interest. "I endeavoured to persuade myself," Carwin says, "that the end proposed, was, in the highest degree praiseworthy, and that the excellence of my purpose would justify the means employed to attain it" (1: 182). The young man makes one attempt to put this plan into action, but he is foiled by a violent electrical storm which, before he can perform at this father's ear, sets the barn on fire and forces him to wake the household. Before a second attempt is made, the elder Carwin—also portrayed as one powerfully influenced by self-interest—consents to let the boy go to Philadelphia, thinking that in this way he will eventually get his hands on his sister's money.

Carwin lives with his aunt for three years, and during that time he exercises his vocal talents often but largely for amusement rather than gain. Once, for example, with a gathering of friends in a garden just outside Philadelphia, he listens to a young lady play her harp and sing the songs of Shakespeare's Ariel. Playfully the boy casts his voice into the arbor above the group and sings,

> In the Cowslip's bell I lie,
> On the Bat's back I do fly...
> After summer merrily, &c.[34]

The company is naturally mystified and thrilled, but Carwin has little time to enjoy his secret triumph as news arrives from the city that his aunt "was suddenly taken sick, and that her life was in imminent danger" (1: 257). He returns to find her already dead and her estate—from which he (and his father) had expected much—left to Dorothy, her maid.

Homeless and penniless, Carwin again plans another self-interested use of his biloquism. Feeling that the will making Dorothy heir to his aunt's estate was written prior to his coming to Philadelphia, that a subsequent will had either been destroyed or hidden away, Carwin schemes once more to imitate a voice from beyond the grave in order to force Dorothy to sign his late aunt's property over to him, an event that would reestablish in reality the independence promised by his vocal gifts. But this scheme is also never put into action because, as he says, "fate interposed, as in the former instance, to save me" (1: 259).

Salvation this time comes in the form of a man named Ludloe. "He was from Ireland," Carwin says, "was a man of some rank and apparently rich: I had met with him before, but in mixed companies, where little direct intercourse had taken place between us. Our last meeting was in the arbour where Ariel was so unexpectedly introduced" (1: 257). In a chance one-on-one encounter on the banks of the Schuylkill, Ludloe mentions the Ariel incident, at once causing Carwin to suspect that he might be discovered and reinforcing his belief that his vocal talents could be used for gain:

> I was somewhat startled when he expressed his belief that the performer of this mystic strain was one of the company then present, who exerted, for this end, a faculty not commonly possessed. Who this person was he did not venture to guess, and [I] could not discover, by the tokens which he suffered to appear, that his suspicions glanced at me. He expatiated with great profoundness and fertility of ideas, on the uses to which a faculty

like this might be employed. No more powerful engine, he said, could be conceived, by which the ignorant and credulous might be moulded to our purposes; managed by a man of ordinary talents, it would open for him the straightest and surest avenues to wealth and power.

His remarks excited in my mind a new strain of thoughts. I had not hitherto considered the subject in this light, though vague ideas of the importance of this art could not fail to be occasionally suggested: I ventured to inquire into his ideas of the mode, in which an art like this could be employed, so as to effect the purposes he mentioned [1: 258].[35]

Fascinated with Ludloe's conversation, young Carwin visits him often while, with new faith in the personal usefulness of his talents, laying plans to dupe Dorothy. But Ludloe, having grown interested in Carwin, interrupts the scheme by inviting the boy to accompany him on his return to Ireland.

In the second half of "Memoirs," Carwin learns that the Godwinian Ludloe — who takes the young man under his wing and supports him financially because it is "the scope of his exertions to be just" (1: 333) — is a member of a secret political society with plans to establish a utopian community that would eventually "overflow the habitable world" (1: 416). Ludloe's revelations regarding the existence of this society and its plans, although their exact nature is never revealed,[36] appear in guarded increments during conversations between the two, but he clearly intends that Carwin should be his protégé and ultimately his successor in the secret society.

At his home in Dublin, Ludloe provides Carwin with room, board, and library access, demanding nothing in return but that Carwin believe himself justly entitled to such treatment. From this base, Carwin roams where he will and studies what he will; Ludloe even sends him for a time to Spain for the useful purpose "of inspecting the habits and manners of a nation, and investigating, on the spot, the causes of their happiness and misery" (1: 413). These, Carwin explains, are practical studies to finish the knowledge drawn from reading. In Spain, Carwin involves himself in a few "bivocal projects" (1: 415), but upon his return to Dublin he refrains, studiously maintaining silence regarding his secret talents when in the company of Ludloe.[37]

This silence, however, becomes a threat to Carwin's life as his benefactor begins the incremental process of introducing the young man to the secret society and its plans: "A number of persons are leagued together for an end of some moment," Ludloe says by way of introduction. "To make yourself one of these is submitted to your choice. Among the conditions of their alliance are mutual fidelity and secrecy" (2: 5). This secrecy, Carwin discovers, is to be absolute. Any slight betrayal of the society, whether by word, action, or accident, results in immediate death. Ludloe warns Carwin "that compared with this task, the task of inviolable secrecy, all others are easy" (2: 6). But at this point in the biloquist's relationship with Ludloe and the unknown, amorphous society he represents, secrecy regarding the sect's beliefs and movements, indeed its very existence, is not Carwin's difficulty. In addition to the absolute secrecy to be maintained in regards to the world outside the society, Ludloe tells him, members are expected to make full disclosure of their entire histories and personal secrets. Any withholding later discovered will also result in immediate death. In order to fulfill this requirement, of course, Carwin must reveal his biloquism. "If secrecy were difficult to practice," he says, "sincerity, in that degree in which it was here demanded, was a task infinitely more arduous..." (2: 7).

Even under the threat of death, however, Carwin refuses to reveal his unique vocal talents in the various interviews with Ludloe preparatory to the young man's joining the secret society:

> Some fatal obstinacy ... got possession of me, and I persisted in the resolution of concealing *one thing*. We become fondly attached to objects and pursuits, frequently for no conceivable reason but the pain and trouble they cost us. In proportion to the danger in which they involve us do we cherish them. Our darling potion is the poison that scorches our vitals [3: 210].

But he has good reason for holding to this one secret, for being "guilty of a solemn and deliberate concealment" (3: 211): "My character," Carwin explains, "had been, in some degree, modelled by the faculty which I possessed" (2: 251). Inextricably interwoven with his identity as an individual, Carwin's biloquism defines him. Furthermore, it constitutes his independence. He discovered it in a moment of freedom found in a wild and lawless space, and, if his father's self-interest had not intervened, Carwin surely would have used his vocal talents to free himself from the farm on which he grew up and the stultifying life his father would have him live. Now in Dublin, his voice represents not only his independence but also his private self, and it remains all that prevents his complete absorption into Ludloe's sect.

With its protagonist embroiled in this conflict between secrecy and sincerity, concealment and disclosure, "Memoirs of Carwin the Biloquist" abruptly ends.[38] In the final pages of the text, Carwin seems resolved to proceed with the interviews leading to his membership in the secret society but determined — at the risk of his life — to remain silent about his defining biloquism.

Although "Memoirs" is set in the decade or so before the American Revolution, the ideas Brown attempts to portray and explore are certainly drawn from the social, cultural, and political situation that existed in the late eighteenth and early nineteenth centuries. In *The Republic Reborn*, Steven Watts says that "endorsements of the pursuit of self-interest were echoed in many early-nineteenth-century social tracts and gradually formed the conceptual centerpiece of an emerging liberal social ideology" (68). The notion of hard work and integrity as alone being the integral components of individual success began to give way to an understanding of the role played by self-interest. On the one hand, the influence of self-interest was seen as strengthening the commonweal; that is, as personal enterprise succeeded, the overall constitution of the community and the nation improved. On the other hand, self-interest had a dark side. It also encouraged a manipulation of social, economic, and political systems; those who best manipulated a particular system realized the greatest individual success. Concomitant with this underhanded aspect of self-interest was a weakening of the moral fiber of the individual: "Ultimately," Watts continues,

> the notion of 'moral free-agency' defined both the thrust and the difficulty in this maelstrom of culture and character in early–nineteenth-century America. In an atmosphere conducive to ambition and pursuit of the main chance, the individual was taking shape as the conceptual building-block of society. Older notions of an organic social order and traditional republican commitments to the commonweal were disappearing as restraints on individual action. The solitary citizen, many Americans became convinced, thus had to take responsibility for his own actions and destiny [113].

In this social context, individuals with a moral construction less than pure participated in the creation of "a shadowy social arena of calculating avarice, unscrupulous ambition, and deception" (Watts 111).

For readers of the *Literary Magazine* in the middle years of Jefferson's presidency, "Memoirs of Carwin the Biloquist" tests the ideas underlying the social situation Watts describes. Carwin's independence is rooted in the discovery of his particular voice. He understands the power of such a voice and, as narrator, refuses to describe the process by which he developed the physical talent from the mere suggestion of the extraordinary echo in his "vocal glen"; biloquism, he says by way of explanation, "is by far, too liable to perversion for a good man to desire to possess it, or to teach it to another" (1: 103). In this, he claims the appellation "a good man" for himself, but his own narrative calls his reliability into question. Although his moral conscience often whispers to him that his desires for escape, money, and distinction are wrong, usually only circumstance, "fate," or the self-interested intervention of another prevents his independent choices and actions from becoming successful — and unscrupulous — manipulation.

Brown portrays Carwin's increasing moral weakness as a counterbalance to his self-interested protection of his independence and identity. As a fourteen-year-old boy about to whisper his dead mother's voice in his father's ear, Carwin knows this is wicked work in a storm. In a romantic sense, the storm reflects his inner turmoil as he is about to perform his act: "I could not divest myself of secret dread. My heart faultered with a consciousness of wrong. Heaven seemed to be present and to disapprove my work; I listened to the thunder and the wind, as to the stern voice of this disapprobation. Big drops stood on my forehead, and my tremors almost incapacitated me from proceeding" (1: 182). But he proceeds in spite of his fear, being stopped only by the burning of the barn. The next time he intends to use ventriloquism for self-interested manipulation — the plan to "speak" to Dorothy about his aunt's estate — he evinces no similar scruples.

Except for his special vocal talents, Carwin is, I would argue, a representation of the typical individual caught up in the transformation of a liberalizing society, a representation somewhat anachronistic for the time period in which his story is set but not for Brown's readers. He tries to be a good person, but his attempts to be so are warped by ambition. Of the three years with his aunt, he says,

> My biloquial faculty was not neglected. I improved it by assiduous exercise; I deeply reflected on the use to which it might be applied. I was not destitute of pure intentions; I delighted not in evil; I was incapable of knowingly contributing to another's misery, but the sole or principal end of my endeavours was not the happiness of others.
>
> I was actuated by ambition. I was delighted to possess superior power; I was prone to manifest that superiority, and was satisfied if this were done, without much solicitude concerning consequences [1: 184].

In Carwin, Brown shows his readers a conflicted individual whose first intellectual and emotional impulse is to self-restraint but whose actions proceed solely from a second, overpowering impulse to self-interest.

Carwin ultimately becomes an allegorical figure of both the United States and the citizen at the beginning of the nineteenth century. In similar ways, the new nation and the independent individual looked forward with Carwin as he set sail for Ireland with Ludloe: "The world into which I was about to enter, was untried and unknown, and though I could consent to profit by the guidance, I was unwilling to rely on the support of others" (1: 334). Carwin's story allegorizes the early–nineteenth-century tension inherent in the nascent conflict between classical republicanism and liberal individualism, virtuous thought and self-interested action, a laudable drive for success and a dangerous desire for distinction. In Jeffersonian America, Carwin's individual impulse to independence, embodied in his refusal to lose his "voice" by revealing it to Ludloe, is set against the potential social and political disruption such a voice represents.

In a sense, "Memoirs of Carwin the Biloquist" allegorizes Brown and the *Literary Magazine* as well. Steven Watts has written that, for Brown, "speaking through other voices comprised the act of fiction writing" (*Romance* 185). While this is true, identifying the idea of authorial ventriloquism with fiction alone is too limiting in Brown's case. His ventriloquism speaks not only fiction but also subtle political instruction and nationalistic (as opposed to republican) sentiment, cultural analysis and liberal ideology. The lawless "narrow pass" in which Carwin discovers his voice — and, by extension, his independence and identity — can be understood as an allegorical representation of the miscellany itself. Here Brown's neutral editorial policy, governed by no overt ideology, creates a space that is to some degree as lawless as Carwin's gorge, a space which Brown is able to fill with whatever material and ideas he chooses. Unlike editors such as Joseph Dennie, whose Federalist ideology is openly promoted to his audience by Oliver Oldschool, Brown avoids face-to-face confrontations with — and overt influence of — his readers, preferring, like Carwin, to whisper from the republic of letters in many anonymous and pseudonymous but still authoritative voices.

Afterword

Without fanfare or farewell, Brown and his publishers ceased publication of the *Literary Magazine* with the December 1807 issue, making the miscellany itself something of a fragment.[1] At the conclusion of the seventh volume (January–June 1807), Brown appeared to be gathering new energy and resources to carry the magazine through its eighth volume and beyond;[2] his mind, however, was already turning towards his last major work as editor and man of letters, the *American Register, or General Repository of History, Politics, and Science*, an encyclopedic collection of public documents and documents of public interest — presidential messages, congressional actions, summary commercial reports, literary news, brief biographies, and Brown's own important "Annals of Europe and America."[3] The shape of Brown's literary career thus moves from the romantic musings of his Rhapsodist, whose participation in the eighteenth century's republic of letters is at best indirect, to the later work — in the *Literary Magazine* and in the *American Register*— of writing and compiling material that tends toward directness in its attempt to mold and inform America's citizen-reader.

Brown's notion of authorship was firmly rooted in eighteenth-century republican ideals of the relationship between publication and public life. Writing was to be done, as Brown similarly suggested regarding participation in party politics, in what time could be spared from private life and business by an author who sought, through publication, to be serviceable to the world of readers. In Brown's day, as he writes in "Authorship" (October 1803), only the long-established cultures of Europe provided examples of those who wrote by profession rather than inclination:

> IN Europe, Authorship is in some instances a *trade:* it is a calling by which those who pursue it, seek their daily bread as regularly as a carpenter or smith pursues the same end, by means of the adze or the anvil. But authorship, as a mere trade, seems to be held in very little estimation. There is no other *tradesman*, to whom the epithet *poor* is more usually applied. A *poor author* is a phrase so often employed, that the two words have almost coalesced into one. The latter, if used alone, signifies merely a man who writes and publishes; but if *poor* be prefixed, it clearly indicates a writer by trade.
>
> This trade is the refuge of idleness and poverty. Any thing that gives a permanent revenue, however scanty the sum, or laborious the service, is deemed preferable to authorship: but when a *poor* fellow has either too little steadiness, industry, or reputation, for the post of clerk in a banker's office, or usher in a school, or curacy in Wales, he betakes himself, as his last resource, to writing paragraphs for a newspaper, translating new novels or travels from the French or German, or spinning Romances from his own brain; and these enable him to live as well as habits of improvidence and heedlessness as to all economical matters, will allow him [1: 8–9].[4]

Brown had engaged in all of these activities identified as typical of the "*poor author*," but he seems to have understood his work as an editor of the *Literary Magazine*— perhaps grounded as it was by work with his brothers and a successful family life with his wife and children — as a more useful trade than that of author alone.

Authorship, Brown writes, if approached either as a performance of literary art or as a means of serving the public, is a worthy pursuit, and he continues with a description of the author he was desirous of being:

> While the *poor author*, that is to say, the author by trade, is regarded with indifference or contempt, the *author*, that is, the man who devotes to composition the leisure secured to him by hereditary affluence, or by a lucrative profession or office, obtains from mankind an higher, and more lasting, and more genuine reverence, than any other class of mortals. As there is nothing I should more fervently deprecate than to be enrolled in the former class, so there is nothing to which I more ardently aspire, than to be numbered among the latter. To write, because the employment is delightful, or because I have a passion for fame or for usefulness, is the summit of terrestrial joys, the pinnacle of human elevation [1: 9].

Seen in this light, Brown's aspirations as an author certainly reaffirm the understanding of the role of authorship in the public sphere of the early American republic. The writing he authored while under the influence of this ideology of letters, however, emerges not as a reaffirmation of eighteenth-century republican ideals and values but as an exploration of ideas inspired by the transformations taking place as the United States moved into the nineteenth century — the turn from the republican towards the democratic, from the neoclassical towards the romantic, from disinterested participation in the community towards self-interested action by the individual.

The *Literary Magazine* is a significant and accessible site in Brown's *oeuvre* for understanding why he wrote what he wrote. Having taken more years to produce than were devoted to the novels, having engaged the contemporary reality of the new nation and the transatlantic world during the first decade of the nineteenth century, the miscellany can neither be ignored as minor writing nor be dismissed as the work of a hack. I believe that to read Brown's essays regarding the French Revolution, for example, can shed new light on the characters and ideas explored in *Wieland* and *Ormond*. To develop an understanding of the many voices that speak from the magazine — even when the majority of them come from Brown himself — is to understand better the many voices woven together into the telling of *Arthur Mervyn*. To identify America as a frontier, as Brown often does, and to discover in the *Literary Magazine* the ways in which such a physical, geographical reality affects the character and culture of the American people provides insight for understanding the curious tale told in *Edgar Huntly*.

Brown continues in the miscellany to explore many of the same ideas that haunt his earlier fiction, but in his more mature thirties he wrote more clearly and addressed the issues more directly. His language and imagery are, on the whole, sharper in his essays, his subject matter more under his control. The essays, however, do not negate the novels and short stories; rather, they offer a ratiocinative foundation on which to build sound interpretations of the more intuitive fiction. Gaps certainly exist between the fiction and nonfiction, between the novelist and magazinist, but there seem to be more points at which a careful study of the two together would show their preconceptions and strategies to be similar, to overlap. Moreover, Brown's work as a writer of fiction had a demonstrable influence on his work as an editor and journalist. His allegorical turn of mind affects his approach to the essays, and there is a certain sense of novelistic indirectness in the way some topics — especially political ones — are treated for his readers. In addition to this, many pieces — "Pestilence and Bad Government Compared" and "Novel-Reading," for example — are a blend of fictional narrative and factual discussion. Thus the novels and the magazines compliment and enhance each other. For this reason there is no need to bemoan the fact, as many critics have done, that Brown did not continue writing in the same vein as his four major novels.

To speculate, seen in its entirety Charles Brockden Brown's literary career—from "The Rhapsodist" to the *American Register*—evolved naturally as he moved away from the youthful self-centeredness of his Rhapsodist to the more mature character of his "Editor," an evolution closely paralleling the stages identified with the human life cycle. Summarizing Erik Erikson's "formal program of life-cycle events," historian Peter Hoffer writes,

> A youth faces the challenge of finding an identity for himself, distinct from his role as a child and yet integrated with his past experience. The young adult must choose between intimacy and the sacrifice of self to others it entails, or isolation, with its potential for self-destruction. The mature individual can maintain his creativity, passing a lifetime of experience on to a new generation, or stagnate. The old man faces the task of achieving a sense of pride in self, an "ego integrity"—or falling into the snare of "feeling that this one chance has been wasted and has, in essence, been worthless" [2–3].[5]

When Brown began the *Literary Magazine* in 1803, he was thirty-two years old, an age early in the stage at which "[t]he mature individual can maintain his creativity, passing a lifetime of experience on to a new generation, or stagnate" (2). Rather than stagnate after the publication of his novels, Brown turned to the more "useful" vehicle of the miscellany. He sought in this middle magazine of his career to teach more than to entertain, to provide his audience with more instruction about how to read than information about what to read. "The compelling intellectual ambition of Brown," Warfel writes, "lay in the field of informational and didactic writing. To keep happy was to keep writing or at least disseminating useful information" (221). Given the relative longevity of the *Literary Magazine* and the arduous and thoughtful effort Brown invested to achieve it, this mature portion of his career was a "happy" success.

Brown was certainly disappointed that his writing between 1789 and 1809—as well as that of his American contemporaries—generally faltered because of the realities of the period's literary marketplace, but he was not necessarily disgruntled. "Brown did his best," Fred Lewis Pattee writes during his discussion of the role of the *Literary Magazine* in *The First Century of American Literature.* "With twice the energy of Dennie, with none of Dennie's procrastination and conviviality, he put his whole soul into his editing. Peculiarly was he fitted for such work. Like Poe in later years, he believed that the future of American literature was with the American magazines" (191). That around 1800 Brown changed his approach to his work as a man of letters is undeniable — although perhaps this change is not as drastic as critics have assumed. But the notion that he changed from a young radical to a middle-aged conservative is, I believe, certainly questionable. In the *Literary Magazine,* Brown promotes whatever is "just," be it considered radical or conservative, in relation to politics or culture. He appears strikingly Jeffersonian in the first decade of the nineteenth century; he promotes liberal individualism and recognizes the transformation of America from a community of republicans to a nation of individuals. It is thus that Charles Brockden Brown and his *Literary Magazine* truly "mark," as he put it in the miscellany's "Editors' Address," "the character of the age" (1: 5).

Notes

Introduction

1. The *Monthly Magazine, and American Review* (1799–1800) had been published in New York, where Brown carried on its editing and much of its writing while drafting and publishing *Edgar Huntly* (1799) and the second part of *Arthur Mervyn* (1800). Although the final issue of the *Monthly Magazine* appeared in December 1800, the review section, which had proven to be the magazine's most popular feature, continued; *The American Review, and Literary Journal* (1801–1802) began appearing quarterly in New York. Although Brown wrote the preface for the *American Review*, he was not its editor, at least not alone. Still, existing evidence suggests that he remained quite involved in its production. From New York, where he was most likely working on the magazine while visiting his future bride Elizabeth Linn, Brown wrote the following in an 8 July 1802 letter to Elizabeth's brother, Philadelphia minister John Blair Linn:

> The review is exceedingly behind hand, & my friends have imposed on me the task of reading & reviewing half a dozen books, which without their injunctions I should never have looked into. This has been an irksome undertaking & which nothing but a kind of necessity could reconcile me to. To criticise without reading would be absurd, & to read not for instruction or amusement would be galley slavery. The next number is very long in making its appearance & I suppose will scarcely issue from the press in less than a fortnight. When it reaches you, I am [afraid] you will be but little pleased with the alterations they have made in your pieces. I have prepared them to expect some displeasure from you, & they have earnestly besought me to apologize for them [qtd. in Clark 215].

The *American Review* closed its doors only a few months afterwards, near the end of 1802.

Some five years later, *The Literary Magazine, and American Register* gave way to Brown's final periodical: *The American Register, or General Repository of History, Politics, and Science*, a semiannual — also published by Conrad's company — five volumes of which Brown edited from 1806 until just before his death in February 1810.

2. While German Brown scholar Alfred Weber and his associates have recently been making available Brown's uncollected writing, only two books and one dissertation have studied Brown's later work in any depth: Wolfgang Schäfer's *Charles Brockden Brown als Literaturkritiker* (1991), Harald Mertz's *Charles Brockden Brown als Politischer Schriftsteller* (1994), and Mark Kamrath's "The 'Novel' Historicism of Charles Brockden Brown" (U of Nebraska, 1996). Neither Schäfer's nor Mertz's book is in print; Kamrath's dissertation, which focuses largely on Brown's historical writings in the *American Register*, is currently being revised and expanded for Kent State University Press publication.

3. Warfel's brief account of the *Literary Magazine* is too sketchy to provide clear insight into his understanding of the way the periodical fits into Brown's career. In general, he seems unaware of the amount of writing—

and the quality of writing — Brown did for the miscellany. Moreover, Warfel also includes some misinformation. He says, for example, that "Brown bowed to popular demand in his magazine. He refused to permit politics and theology to sully its pages with controversy" (223). In fact, Brown's seeming political neutrality put his magazine in the minority among productions of the American periodical press. According to Carol Sue Humphrey, "By the end of Jefferson's presidency, the number [of United States newspapers] had reached 329. Of those 329, all but 56 were identified, at least loosely, as supporters of one of the major political parties" (71). Likewise, of the three most important magazines in the first decade of the nineteenth century, only Brown's claimed to be politically neutral; Dennie's *Port Folio* and the *Monthly Anthology, and Boston Review* were staunchly Federalist.

4. LaCapra cites Heidegger's "The Origin of the Work in Art" as the source for the meaning of—as well as his use of—the term "worklike" (30n).

5. See Buell, "American Literary Emergence as a Postcolonial Phenomenon," *American Literary History* 4 (1992): 411–42.

Chapter One

1. As the title and text of the anonymous review imply, part of the credit for the success of the *Literary Magazine* is due to Philadelphia publisher John Conrad, whose association with Brown seems to have begun in 1801 when Conrad's company reprinted *Edgar Huntly* and published the first edition of *Jane Talbot*. "Conrad," Rosalind Remer writes, "headed a family of bookselling brothers in Philadelphia, Baltimore, Petersburg, Virginia, and Norfolk who published schoolbooks, literature, and a wide array of miscellaneous imprints" (71). The title page of the first volume of the *Literary Magazine* gives the detailed publisher's information: "Printed for John Conrad & Co. no. 30, Chestnut-Street, Philadelphia; M. & J. Conrad & Co. no. 138, Market-Street, Baltimore; Rapin, Conrad, & Co. Washington; Somervell & Conrad, Petersburg; and Bonsal, Conrad, & Co. Norfolk; at any of which places communications will be thankfully received." This network made his periodical venture with Brown the second most popular American magazine — after *The Port Folio*— during the first decade of the nineteenth century. Although no subscription list for the *Literary Magazine* is known to exist, Lewis Simpson writes in his introduction to a collection of essays drawn from the *Monthly Anthology, and Boston Review* that "the *Anthology* had only 440 subscribers, while Charles Brockden Brown's *Literary Messenger* [sic] had 600 and Joseph Dennie's *Port Folio* boasted 1,500" (20; Simpson's claims are based on a letter from Munroe and Francis, printers of the *Monthly Anthology*, to William Smith Shaw, a prominent member of the Anthology Society, an account of which appears in Joseph B. Felt's *Memorials of William Smith Shaw* [Boston, 1852]).

Conrad's publications included arithmetic, chemistry, grammar, and geography textbooks, government documents, almanacs, anti-slavery essays, sermons and religious tracts, conversion narratives, books of poetry, and British novels. In addition to Brown's magazine, political pamphlets, and translation of Volney's *A View of the Soil and Climate of the United States* (1804), the prolific Conrad and his publishing family are connected with more than sixty-five publications in the years between 1803 and 1807; a partial list includes Goldsmith's *The Vicar of Wakefield* (1803), editions of Johnson's *The Idler* and *The Rambler* (both in 1803), Isaac Watts's *Hymns and Spiritual Songs* (1803), an edition of Brackenridge's *Modern Chivalry* (1804), the second edition of Benjamin Rush's *Medical Inquiries and Observations* (1805), Zebulon Pike's *An Account of Expeditions to the Sources of the Mississippi* (1807), and Barlow's heroic attempt at an American national epic, *The Columbiad* (1807).

Conrad's imprint disappeared from the title page of the *Literary Magazine* with the January 1807 issue, the first of the seventh volume, and all issues thereafter were published by Thomas and George Palmer of 116 High Street in Philadelphia, a firm which had been the magazine's printers since the first issue dated October 1803. Conrad may have fallen on hard financial times for awhile. According to Remer, "The Conrads began having financial difficulties during Jefferson's Embargo of 1807-8, which prohibited exports" (119). Although the Embargo Act was not passed until December 1807, the end of Conrad's involvement with the miscellany almost a year earlier was still probably due to financial problems of some sort, because in 1813 he would file what Remer calls a "spectacular bankruptcy" (71). Conrad and Brown, however, were working together again by the end of 1807, as publisher and editor of Brown's final magazine.

2. By comparison, Boston's *Monthly Anthology*, begun in November 1803, provided its readers only forty-eight pages per issue. The weekly *Port Folio* was an "eight-page super-royal quarto" (Mott 223), which on a monthly basis provided only half the material Brown offered the public in each issue of the *Literary Magazine*.

3. In the *Literary Magazine* for November 1807 Brown's "Literary, Philosophical, Commercial, and Agricultural Intelligence" heralded the publication of Barlow's American epic:

> THERE will soon be published in Philadelphia a new and interesting work, entitled "the Columbiad, a poem, in ten books, by Joel Barlow." This work will be ornamented with twelve engravings, which have been done in England by the most eminent artists, and at great expence. They are in the first style of elegance. The typographical part, wholly American, is executed in a manner highly creditable to the several artists employed. The paper by Amies, the type by Binny and Ronaldson, and the printing, with consummate taste and care, by Fry and Kammerer; it will be published by C. and A. Conrad and Co., in one volume, quarto. A work like this, on a great national subject, must excite a high degree of interest. In the present instance, we are confident that the public expectation will not be disappointed; and while the Columbiad will be cited as a monument of American genius, the publishers are determined that this edition shall do equal honour to our arts [8: 204–05].

4. Although it seems to have been the first conceived, Franklin's was not the first magazine to be published in America. The inaugural issue of his *General Magazine* was dated January 1741 but did not actually appear until 16 February. In the meantime, a competing Philadelphia publisher, Andrew Bradford, preceded Franklin by three days. Here is the story as James Playsted Wood relates it:

> In the *Pennsylvania Gazette*, a weekly which Franklin had published since 1729, ... Franklin announced in November, 1740, his plans to publish *The General Magazine, and Historical Chronicle, for All the British Plantations in America*. Unfortunately Franklin offered the editorship of what was to be the pioneer American magazine to John Webbe, a Philadelphia lawyer, who quickly divulged his knowledge of the scheme to Andrew Bradford, son of Pennsylvania's first printer. Thereupon Bradford immediately announced a magazine of his own and, on February 13, 1741, with Webbe as editor, got out the first issue of his own *American Magazine, or a Monthly View of the Political State of the British Colonies*. Three days later, Franklin, acting now as his own editor, published the first issue of the *General Magazine* [10].

As was perhaps typical of him, Franklin had the last word: Bradford's magazine lasted for only three issues; Franklin's lasted for six.

5. In his *Specimens of Newspaper Literature* (1850), Joseph T. Buckingham remembers Dennie as he was during his days in Walpole, New Hampshire, where he was beginning his career as an author with the *Farmer's Museum*:

> He was particular attentive to his dress, which, when he appeared in the street on a pleasant day, approached the highest notch of fashion. I remember, one delightful morning in May, he came into the office dressed in a pea-green coat, white vest, nankin small-clothes, white silk stockings, and shoes, or *pumps*, fastened with silver buckles, which covered at least half the foot from the instep to the toe. His small-clothes were tied at the knees, with ribbons of the same color, in double bows, the ends reaching down to the ankles. He had just emerged from the barber's shop. His hair, *in front*, was well loaded with pomatum, frizzled, or *craped*, and powdered; the *ear-locks* had undergone the same process; *behind*, his natural hair was augmented by the addition of a large *queue* (called, vulgarly, the *false tail*), which, enrolled in some yards of black ribbon, reached half-way down his back [qtd. in Mott 224].

6. I borrow the idea of "redcoating" from Edward Watts, who offers it as a term describing how "republicanism attempted to recolonize the [American] reading public" (13). My usage is more restricted, however, and I employ the term in relation to the work of only those Anglophiles such as Dennie — and not early American republicans in general — who would have American writing and reading be merely imitations of British practices.

7. The work is definitely Brown's. According to Weber, Schäfer, and Holmes, "Although it is called 'The Editors' Address,' it is clear from the text that the editorial has only one

author. Since Brown was the sole editor of the magazine, he is definitely the author of the address" (*Literary* 240).

8. The four essays that make up "The Rhapsodist" originally appeared in Mathew Carey's *The Universal Asylum, and Columbian Magazine* 3 (1789): 464–67, 537–41, 587–601, 661–65.

It is from these publications that much of Brown's writing for periodicals has begun to be identified; these four personal essays were signed in succession B, R, O, and W. If a fifth entry had appeared in "The Rhapsodist" series, it would almost certainly have been signed N. The five letters of Brown's last name are used extensively among the items in both the *Monthly Magazine* and the *Literary Magazine*. Alfred Weber and his colleagues, who have collected many of Brown's short stories and periodical pieces, have discovered — or have confirmed the assumptions of various Brown scholars since the 1940s — that Brown also used the following letters from his first name: C, H, A, R (included in all three names), and E (see Weber's annotated bibliography in Brown's *Literary Essays and Reviews*). Of course, B, R, O, C, E, and N can be drawn from the letters of Brown's first and last names to form most of his middle name. No mention has been made, however, of the fact that most of the first and middle names are almost complete in the signature letters already identified. I would argue that internal evidence exists in Brown's magazines which suggests that he used all of the letters of his full name — including L, S, K, and D — in pseudonymously signing his articles. Wherever in this book I use articles signed with these letters, I will explain my reasons for assigning their authorship to Brown.

In addition to these letters, Brown often used X and sometimes Z. Weber identifies such combinations as A.Z. and C.E. as well. I have identified H.X. as another combination; "Remarks on the Russian Empire" appears with this signature in the *Monthly Magazine* (2: 99–102) and again in an only slightly revised form with the signature "R." in the *Literary Magazine* (6: 445–48). It is quite possible that Brown in other instances used various combinations of letters taken from his full name.

Although Brown far more often used letters for his signatures, he did from time to time use various more traditional eighteenth- and nineteenth-century periodical pseudonyms. Three of these have been identified by various Brown scholars: Alcander, Looker-On, and Philo. Evidence exists suggesting that Crito, Economus, and Alphonso are also among Brown's pseudonyms, and I will call attention to these as necessary.

9. Brown also made statements similar to those in the Advertisement that opened *Wieland* in his remarks prefatory to *Edgar Huntly*, but he gave the latter a more particularly American focus:

That new springs of action, and new motives to curiosity should operate; that the field of investigation, opened to us by our own country, should differ essentially from those which exist in Europe, may be readily conceived. The sources of amusement to the fancy and instruction to the heart, that are peculiar to ourselves, are equally numerous and inexhaustible.

He concludes his remarks by turning again to the American reader for approval: "The success of his efforts must be estimated by the liberal and candid reader" (3).

10. The metaphor of the mirror is taken from act 3, scene 2, of William Shakespeare's *Hamlet*:

Be not too tame neither, but let your own discretion be your tutor. Suit the action to the word, the word to the action, with this special observance, that you o'erstep not the modesty of nature. For anything so o'erdone is from the purpose of playing, whose end, both at the first and now, was and is to hold as 't were the mirror up to nature, to show virtue her feature, scorn her own image, and the very age and body of the time his form and pressure [1088–89].

11. The magazine's first issue contains a typical variety. The original communications include several essays: "Swift's Polite Conversation," "Fire," "Yellow Fever," "Authorship," "Pensions," "A Jaunt to Rockaway, in Long-Island," "Ascendancy of the French Language," "The Epithet Royal," "On the Eloquence of Pitt, Fox and Erskine," "Critical Notices," "Summary of Politics," and "Remarkable Occurrences." In addition to these there were "The Man with the Big Nose" (an imitation of Sterne), the first installment of a series called "The Traveller," and poems. There were also reviews of Drayton's *A View of South Carolina*, Abercrombie's *Two Compends for the Use of the Philadelphia Academy*, and D'Israeli's *Narrative Poems*. Among the selections included were "British Population," "Remarks on Female Dress," and "Miscellaneous Extracts."

12. Warner Berthoff, Steven Watts, and others have identified Brown as the writer of this preface, but his authorship in this case has been either assumed or rejected according to each particular scholar's understanding of Brown's relationship with the *American Review*. It is likely, however, that Brown is indeed the writer of this preface. As editor of *The Monthly Magazine, and American Review*, he was the driving force behind the popular review section which, when the *Monthly Magazine* closed its doors, continued for a time as the quarterly *American Review*. Furthermore, in Brown's 3 August 1807 broadside prospectus that introduced the eighth and final volume of the *Literary Magazine*, this same paragraph I have quoted appears — along with much of "The Editors' Address to the Public" — in an only slightly revised form:

In a new and commercial country like this, where so few can devote their sole attention to literature, *nothing, it is thought,* can be more useful *than those periodical publications which impart* a variety of *information in small portions; by which men, engaged in active occupations, may gradually acquire a degree of intellectual cultivation and improvement, without any infringement of the time allotted to their customary and necessary concerns* [qtd. in Kennedy 1760A; my emphasis of words and phrases that appear in both the 1802 preface to the *American Review* and Brown's 1807 prospectus].

The connection between these two pieces has gone unremarked until now, but it seems that, although Brown's editorship of the *American Review* is at best doubtful, his authorship of the magazine's preface is almost certain.

13. Although educational textbooks were in use in America before the Revolutionary War, few were compiled by Americans; as Michael Belok points out, "The colonists, for the most part, were content with their English heritage and saw no need to produce new books oriented to the American environment" (10–11). But this situation began to change after the Revolution. Noah Webster published part one of his *Grammatical Institutes, of the English Language* in Hartford in 1783, the very year independence was finally won. The second part appeared in 1784 and the third in 1785. These were, according to Belok, "unabashedly nationalistic," making use of "American pronunciations, an American orthography, and American names and places" (12). Around this same time, the *New England Primer* was revised to rid it of references to the new nation's former colonial situation. New manuals in arithmetic had to be written for the new national currency (11), and a handful of Americans began producing new spellers, geographies, readers, and other textbooks.

The readers were the most problematic of these. The third part of Federalist Webster's *Grammatical Institutes* was a reader, as well as "a manual of conduct, a text-book of moral philosophy, and a compendium of useful information" (Belok 12). But his was not the only one. In the second decade after independence, Caleb Bingham — "a Democratic Republican" (151) — published his *American Preceptor* (1794) and *Columbian Orator* (1797). Webster and Bingham's readers contained American materials: speeches by George Washington and patriotic addresses by other noted statesmen and orators; the Declaration of Independence; works by such poets as Barlow, Trumbull, and Freneau.

By the first decade of the nineteenth century, however, these readers had been replaced in popularity by those of Lindley Murray, who had been born in America but had emigrated to England where he compiled the *English Reader* (1795), *Sequel to the English Reader* (1800), and *Introduction to the English Reader* (1801), a reader for children. "Murray's books," Belok writes, "are free of any nationalism or glorification of Americans or any group. Instead, Murray's school-books stress the positive about all peoples and are heavily laden with selections aimed at promoting piety, virtue and stability of the state. Schoolboys nurtured on Murray's fare might be good, but whether they would be particularly patriotic is problematic" (22). Some pieces from the Bible and from classical writers such as Cicero appear in the pages of *The English Reader*, but whether understood as "free of any nationalism" or not, the fact remains that Murray's offerings were substantially British in origin: works from Dr. Hugh Blair, Dr. Johnson, Addison, Goldsmith, Hume, Cowper, Milton, Thomson, Pope, and Gray.

So it was while Americans were making regular use of Murray's readers that Brown began his *Literary Magazine*. He saw the need for reading material from the pens of Americans, and, at the same time, he recognized the need to explore and analyze the British writers Murray presented in order to understand them and their worth from an American point of view. Brown's miscellany tried to address both needs by offering itself as a substitute — or, perhaps more to the point, a supplemental — American reader.

14. Brown married Elizabeth Linn in November 1804 and on 20 February 1805 was dismissed from Philadelphia's Society of Friends. An item in the minutes of the Southern District Monthly Meeting regarding this matter reads as follows:

> Charles Brockden Brown of this city who had by birth a right of membership in our Religious Society having accomplished his marriage by the assistance of an hireling minister to a person not in profession with us, it became necessary tenderly to treat with him on that account. But not appearing sensible of the impropriety of his conduct, we testify that we cannot consider him a member among us, yet desire that through submission to the operation of Truth he may be qualified to condemn his transgression to the satisfaction of this meeting and become united in religious fellowship with us [qtd. in Moses 22].

The "hireling minister" was New York Presbyterian minister William Linn, Elizabeth's father.

15. See Warfel, *Charles Brockden Brown* 222; Ringe, *Charles Brockden Brown* 109; Ferguson, *Law* 133; and Steven Watts, *Romance* 144.

16. Although the title of "The Editors' Address to the Public" suggests that Brown could have hidden himself behind the insinuation that there was more than one editor of the magazine, the text of the essay never uses the plural first- or third-person voice.

17. This refusal to reveal his name follows a long passage in which Brown, Carwin-like, appropriates the voice of the public and questions himself as to his identity, background, and character:

> "This is somewhat more than a point of idle curiosity," my reader will say, "for, from my knowledge of the man must I infer how far he will be able or willing to fulfil his promises. Besides, it is [of] great importance to know, whether his sentiments on certain subjects, be agreeable or not to my own. In politics, for example, he may be a male-content: in religion an heretic. He may be an ardent advocate for all that I abhor, or he may be a celebrated champion of my favourite opinions. It is evident that these particulars must dictate the treatment you receive from me, and make me either your friend or enemy: your patron or your persecutor. Besides, I am anxious for some personal knowledge of you, that I may judge of your literary merits. You may, possibly, be one of these, who came hither from the old world to seek your fortune; who have handled the pen as others handle the awl or the needle: that is, for the sake of a livelihood: and who, therefore, are willing to work on any kind of cloth or leather, and to any model that may be in demand. You may, in the course of your trade, have accommodated yourself to twenty different fashions, and have served twenty classes of customers; have copied at one time a Parisian; and another, a London fashion: and have truckled to the humours, now of a precise enthusiast, and now of a smart freethinker.
>
> "'Tis of no manner of importance what creed you may publicly profess on this occasion, or on what side, religious or political, you may declare yourself enlisted. To judge of the value or sincerity of these professions: to form some notion how far you will faithfully or skilfully perform your part, I must know your character. By that knowledge, I shall regulate myself with more certainty than by any anonymous declaration you may think proper to make."

"I bow to the reasonableness of these observations," Brown writes in response to this fictional inquiry, "and shall therefore take no pains to conceal my name ... since an author or editor ... cannot fail of being known to as many as desire to know him" (1: 4). Still, the "Address" ends unsigned.

18. Elizabeth Drinker, a diarist and Brown's fellow Philadelphian, recorded her reading of at least four of the novels. Although she seems unsure of Brown's authorship in her first two entries, the final two entries identify Brown with certainty: "May 21st [1799]. Arthur Mervyn, or memoirs of the year 1793. said to be written by Charles Brown, son of Elijah Brown — It ends without finishing" (2: 1256); "July 1 [1802]. Edgar Huntly; or memoirs of a Sleep-Walker, To which is annexed The Death of Cicero, a Fragment. By the Author of Arthur Mervyn, wieland, ormond &c. supposed to be Charles Brown" (2: 1608); "30 [November 1803]. Jane Talbot, By Charles Brown" and "8 [December 1803]. Wieland or the Transformation — an American Tale. By Charles B. Brown" (3: 1722). If Drinker read *Ormond* and *Clara Howard*, she did not enter them in her diary.

19. "Our writings resemble our fashions,

various in their manner, but never simple," Brown wrote in 1805, "and our authors, like their fellow-citizens, are vying with each other in pomp and dignity. Hence the personal acquaintance of a modern author is always to his disadvantage; he has published himself a superior being; we approach and discover the imposture" (4: 165).

20. The first part of this declaration may have been true to the best of Brown's knowledge, but it was not true in fact. The *Medley; or, Monthly Miscellany* of Lexington, Kentucky, had begun publication in January 1803. Although it continued only until the following December, its demise did not leave Brown's magazine alone in the field of monthlies, for in November 1803 a group of intellectuals and clergy from the Boston area began publishing *The Monthly Anthology, and Boston Review.*

21. N. W.'s other suggestions include giving particular notice to contributors whose work was accepted for the *Literary Magazine* and ridiculing—for the purpose of entertaining his audience and "exalt[ing] the reputation of your critical sagacity in the general opinion"—those whose work was rejected. Of the latter purpose, N. W. writes, "Your stupidity or scrupulosity prevents you from reflecting that to *this* end an imaginary correspondent is just as useful as a real one" (3: 302).

22. On the one hand there exists external evidence that suggests Brown might be the author of "Duties of Editors." Almost a year earlier he had written and published under the pseudonym of "Alcander" an Addisonian personal essay "On Plagiarism." In this an author sits down at his desk "impelled, by some casual or extraneous motive, to write, without possessing either sentiments or subject" (2: 180–81). His wife enters the study and, after discovering his problem, suggests that he has "only to turn to any current book of essays, and marking with a pen in the margin what chanced to please me, varying perhaps the title and the signature, send it to the press as my own" (2: 281). There follows a discussion between author and wife as to what, on her side, would be the benefits of such plagiarism and what, on his, would be the drawbacks. Several of her suggestions correspond with those of N. W.: readers will be drawn to the piece because of its apparent originality; it is unlikely that anyone would recognize what they read as something they had read before; the piece could be presented anonymously without the originality claimed by any pseudonym or initial and without acknowledging the source. At the end of this clever essay, the discussion between the two people becomes the piece the author is trying to write: "Here then the debate ended, but my scruples being in no degree abated, and the muses continuing as deaf as ever to my supplication, I find I must, however reluctantly, relinquish my design, and lay down the pen without writing an essay" (2: 182).

On the other hand Brown's reply does not appear with N. W.'s letter but in the brief editor's column with which many issues concluded. That Brown is not N. W. is argued by the fact that Brown seems never to have responded to any of his own writing—those items identified by his commonly used signatures—in his editorial comments to correspondents. He definitely responds to N. W., which might suggest that he is not the author of "Duties of Editors."

23. Benjamin Franklin represents a striking precedent for Brown's seeing no conflict between a harmless dishonesty and sincerity. Honesty does not appear in the list of virtues Franklin presents in his *Autobiography*, but sincerity does. The precept Franklin uses to define sincerity is "Use no hurtful Deceit" (92). If Brown indeed wrote the N. W. essay, his presenting it as if he did not was ultimately an artful manipulation of his readers with no apparent intention to be insincere.

24. It was unusual for contributors to the *Literary Magazine* to sign names other than pseudonyms or initials to their original communications. Dr. Drake signed his few contributions, as did Bishop Horne. Some of the pieces Brown selected from other publications were signed by Mrs. Barbauld, Lady M. W. Montague, and Maria Edgeworth. Still, the great majority of items, especially the selected offerings, carry no attribution at all. A Boston weekly, *The Emerald*, took Brown to task for this. In its tenth number of 5 July 1806, there appeared the following paragraph under the heading "Literary Notices":

> The Literary Magazine and American Register, published by Conrad & Co. Philadelphia, is a periodical publication of merit. In typography it equals the best Monthly papers of England. Its original, prosaic communications are able. But the man, that can dress well himself, is under less temptations to wear as his own the adornments of others. We are therefore the more surprised, that noticing in this work, the frequent insertion of articles selected

without any other than internal evidence to distinguish them from original productions. We cannot believe these editors calculate that many are probably ignorant to whose credit this stock should be transferred, that few know its fair owners, that consequently gain will be greater than loss, and thus strike the balance in favor. Neither can they at this day doubt the right of literary property. The error probably arises from mere inattention and it is therefore we notice it [1: 117].

That Brown saw this review is unlikely, or if he did it made no great impact on his editorial practices. The most consistent recognition of authors or sources after this review appeared was in the *Literary Magazine*'s poetry department, where, among some few other items, "On the Discoveries of Captain Lewis" was recognized as "Written by Joel Barlow" and "Columbia's Eagle" as "From the Port Folio."

Chapter Two

1. Regarding the strength of hostile feelings between parties, Sharp suggests that a "dangerous crisis came in the winter of 1800–1801 with the deadlocked presidential election between Jefferson and Aaron Burr. As the Federalists sought to take advantage of the tie in order to retain power, the country skirted dangerously close to armed conflict" (13).

2. *The Monthly Anthology, and Boston Review*, conducted by members of the Boston Athenaeum, was also decidedly Federalist, but its anti-democratic and elitist language was softened by its neoclassicism and never matched Dennie's intensity, except, perhaps, on the rare occasion when the writer was Fisher Ames.

3. See Dowling's *Literary Federalism in the Age of Jefferson*, especially chapter 1.

4. Unfortunately for readers, there was no Joseph Dennie among the editors of the Republican magazines. The closest character the Republicans had to Dennie's "Oliver Oldschool" was perhaps "Toby Tickler, Esq.," whose biweekly *Corrector* appeared for only five weeks in spring 1804. To Tickler the Federalists were

> a set of villains as unprincipled as ever disgraced any nation on earth.—A mercenary, haughty, aristocratic faction, who under the garb of republicanism, seek to betray the people, and rob them of their most inestimable privileges; who, destitute of virtue, of patriotism, and of talents themselves, are endeavoring to destroy the reputation of every honest and upright man in the community.

The editor then points his finger at the "gentry who have for many months been so *tickled* with the slanders of a vagabond"—possibly a reference to Dennie, who on July 4 of the previous year had been brought before a grand jury and indicted on a charge of seditious libel (Mott 230–31). Tickler threatens the Federalist "gentry" with "an opportunity of examining their own caricatures" in the pages of his *Corrector* "unless they desist from the conduct they have hitherto pursued" (1).

5. The list also provides for Republicans who believed in "representative democracy" a defense against those Federalists who charged them with jacobinism:

> *Jacobins*— Dominican Friars, of the order of the dove, who had a hall in Paris, where before and after the commencement of the revolution, a political society met, and were from that denominated Jacobins.— This word not only became current in every country in Europe, but was introduced into America also, where it was liberally applied by every cunning knave and credulous fool to all who had the virtue and courage to raise their voices against aristocratical measures during the reign of terror [17].

6. Signed "X."

7. Intimately acquainted with the literature and language of the Greeks, Titus Pomponius left Rome in 88 BC and lived the next 23 years in Athens, for which reason he was given the additional name Atticus. He lived a peaceful life of study and business in Greece, far away for a time from the civil strife taking place at home. In 65 he returned to Rome, where the violent struggle that would transform the city from republican capital to imperial center was still raging.

The sketch is not Atticus's first appearance in Brown's work. To the second edition of *Edgar Huntly* (Philadelphia, 1800) Brown appended "The Death of Cicero, a Fragment," which was a work of historical short fiction in the form of a letter from Cicero's servant Tiro to Atticus.

8. By way of example Brown provides details of Atticus's dealings with the Roman factions:

> ...while he sent money to young Marius, whose father was declared an enemy of the

commonwealth, he was himself one of Sylla's chief favourites, and always near that general.

During the war between Caesar and Pompey, he still maintained the same conduct. After the death of Caesar, he sent money to Brutus in his troubles, and did a thousand good offices to Antony's wife and friends, when that party seemed ruined. Lastly, even in that bloody war between Antony and Augustus, Atticus still kept his place in both their friendships; insomuch that the first, ... whenever he was absent from Rome in any part of the empire, writ punctually to him what he was doing, what he read, and whither he intended to go; and the latter gave him constantly an exact account of all his affairs [5: 332].

9. Brown's was not the only magazine that refused to take part — at least overtly — in the political debates of the day. The prospectus opening the 15 December 1804 inaugural issue of Joseph Rakestraw's Philadelphia weekly *The Evening Fire-Side* claims that while "the political aspect of our country, and of the civilized world in general, is not to be altogether overlooked, ... it forms no part of the plan of this projected paper, to enter minutely into political, or personal controversies; nor does it aim to support any set of men or principles, independently of what decidedly appears to be the voice of truth" (1). He does not shun politics altogether. Later in the prospectus he says, "We should be pleased with a limited portion of *sterling* political information, but shall refrain from teizing our readers with the bickerings of the *pros* and *cons* and the squabbles of mere party men" (2).

John B. Colvin was even more restrictive on controversy in his *Baltimore Weekly Magazine*, first published on 26 April 1800. He declared his focus to be on "*Belle-Lettres* and their concomitants." The pages of his magazine, he promises, "shall ne'er be sullied by the rancorous spirit of party on the score of politics; *Modesty* will meet with nothing discordant to the ear; neither shall 'slander vile,' with all its train of character-blasting calumnies, find admittance here.— The dangerous, and too often malevolent, *theologist*, may keep aloof, for unless the disquisition is peculiarly and generally informing, it will not procure a place." Colvin follows with a definition of the belles lettres his magazine will include: "the Biographical Sketch, the Moral Essay, the Philosophical Enquiry, and Poetical Effusion," he writes, "I shall be happy to receive from the pens of the learned and sentimental" (1).

10. The essay is signed "S.," which until this writing has not been recognized as one of Brown's signatures. "Pestilence and Bad Government Compared" is—with only a few small changes—a reprint of section eleven of "The Man at Home," which originally appeared in Philadelphia's *Weekly Magazine* 1 (1798), 322–23, and then was reprinted in Warfel's edition of Brown's *The Rhapsodist and Other Uncollected Writings* (1977), 81–85.

11. In *Federalists in Dissent* Linda Kerber writes, "The Federalist anticipated violence ... because his countrymen had demonstrated their capacity for it during the Revolution, and because he saw developing a class of poor and unskilled laborers who might easily be encouraged to indulge what the Federalist knew to be a general human capacity for turmoil" (192). Because of this it was not unreasonable to fear that America's proven violent abilities might easily be roused against the government, just as had been the case in republican France.

12. The essay is unsigned, but it has been tentatively attributed to Brown by Steven Watts in *The Romance of Real Life* and by Alfred Weber and his editorial team currently editing an important work-in-progress called "The Uncollected Writings of Charles Brockden Brown." Both the content and the style of "Free or Despotic" lead me to concur with these attributions.

13. Despite his cover of anonymity, Brown removes himself yet one step further from the political ideas he is about to present by claiming that they are in the words of "a strenuous advocate" of such liberty, "with whose eloquence and ingenuity I was so much pleased, that I took the first opportunity of putting his declamation on paper" (3: 178).

14. Again, this essay is unsigned, but like "Free or Despotic" it has been identified as Brown's by Steven Watts and the editors of "The Uncollected Writings of Charles Brockden Brown." Ideas in "Merits"—that America's emotional reaction to the conflict overwhelmed the revolution's underlying good intentions, for example — bear a strong resemblance to those offered in the earlier essay. Furthermore, two other of Brown's essays—"French Legislation" (October 1806; signed "R.") and "The Spirit of Political Conversation" (December 1806; signed "L.")—reveal negative attitudes similar to those in "Merits" on the topics of French "republican" government

and the often destructive character of political debates between both political leaders and common citizens.

15. For a discussion of Brown's interests and abilities as a writer of history, see Mark Kamrath's excellent dissertation "The 'Novel' Historicism of Charles Brockden Brown."

16. Brown closes the section with the "memorable words of Hume, the most profound and philosophical of historians": "'By recent, as well as by ancient example, it was become evident, that illegal violence, with whatever pretences it may be covered, and whatever object it may pursue, must inevitably end at last in the arbitrary and despotic government of a single person'" (6: 354).

17. Brown questions whether or not a natural aristocracy actually existed in France. The French constituent assembly, he says, "which the enthusiasm of the public, and the misconduct of the privileged orders soon enabled to engross the whole power of the country, consisted almost entirely of persons without name or influence" (6: 357). Those who inhabited the usual spheres of influence available through "birth, fortune, or talents" (6: 355) existed within France's social structure in a way different from those in England and America. According to Brown, writing some years after the fact, "There was then in France no legitimate, wholesome, or real aristocracy. The noblesse, who were persecuted for bearing that name, were quite disconnected from the people. Their habits of perpetual residence in the capital, and their total independence of the good opinion of their vassals, had deprived them of any influence over the minds of the lower orders…" (6: 357). In England and America the elected representatives lived among the people they represented; the majority of their constituents naturally deferred to them in their home districts, making it easier for them to defer to the will of the Parliament or Congress of which that individual representative was a member. In France, Brown writes,

> the assembly possessed only the basis of talents or reputation; … it was by no means necessary that [a representative] should have previously possessed any influence or authority in the community; that he should be connected with powerful families, or supported by opulent and extensive associations[.] If he could dazzle and overawe in debate, if he could obtain the acclamations of the mob of Versailles, and make himself familiar to the eyes and ears of the assembly and its galleries, he was in a fair train for having a great share in the direction of an assembly, exercising absolute sovereignty over thirty millions of men [6: 357–58].

18. In "French Legislation" (signed "R.") Brown describes the character of France's representative government during the course of the Revolution. Disapproving of the radical democratic climate that characterized the legislature, he writes, "The tumultuous manner of proceeding, among the legislators of the French revolution, reminds us of nothing but a zealous mob or a factious town-meeting in old Rome" (6: 295). Where the Americans naturally, perhaps, resemble the British in the "dignity, solemnity, and good order" of their assemblies, the French "meetings appeared for ever verging to complete anarchy. It was extremely common for rival orators to enforce their rhetoric by grinning teeth, clenched fists, and brandished daggers; and a debate frequently ended in the president's abruptly putting on his hat, and the members rushing from the hall with one deafening roar of rage and phrenzy." After he particularly identifies this behavior with the "convention," making sure to distinguish it from the more dignified "constituent assembly" that existed before and in the early days of the French Revolution, Brown concludes: "We have reason to think highly of the wisdom of Bonaparte, in making his legislators dumb, in prohibiting them from saying any thing but yes and no. We cannot conceive of any other expedient for preventing riot and disorder" (6: 296), which in the American republic were the trademark characteristics of radical democracy.

19. In the tenth *Federalist*, James Madison is less specific in defining the qualifications of this group of leaders, saying only that they are individuals "who possess the most attractive merit and the most diffusive and established characters" (Hamilton, Madison, and Jay 83). Jefferson, in his well known 28 October 1813 letter to John Adams, identifies the "grounds" of the natural aristocracy as "virtue and talents." He also acknowledges the existence of an "artificial aristocracy," which is "founded on wealth and birth, without either virtue or talents; for with these it would belong to the first class" (534). Brown seems here to be assuming — perhaps rather dangerously — that "birth" and "fortune," even "talents," bring with them the necessary amount of virtue required for the prosperous management of the

nation, but he will later describe a balanced system between representatives and constituents by which beneficial legislative acts supposedly guaranteed by virtue in Jefferson's description are guaranteed either by the representative's loyalty or fear.

20. "Viator" has not been recognized as one of Brown's pseudonyms, but I consider it likely that Brown is the author of the "Holland" essay, at least, as well as another appearing with it in the same March 1805 issue, "On the American Constitution." Like "Thoughts on the Former and Present State of Holland," the essay "On the American Constitution" deals with the ideas of civil and political liberty. The style of their titles and content are similar and both typical of Brown. The essays appear back-to-back (188–92), and Brown sometimes tended to group his shorter essays together for those issues to which he contributed more than one. Furthermore, both essays make particular use of "the democratic cantons which once existed in Switzerland" as a point of comparison or contrast to their subjects—first to Holland's political liberty, then unfavorably comparing this "Helvetic league" to the United States under the Articles of Confederation. If this evidence suggests that the essays are by the same author, then that author is most likely Brown. The first essay on Holland is signed "Viator"; the second on the Constitution is unsigned. It does not seem typical editorial practice in the *Literary Magazine* to have one signed and one unsigned essay from the same correspondent; it was typical of Brown, however, regarding his own work, to keep shifting constantly between pseudonymous and anonymous contributions. It is at least possible, then, that Brown authored both essays.

21. Viewed in this light, the idea of government's being controlled by popular opinion anticipates Brown's own suggestion in "On the Merits of the Founders of the French Revolution" that if "[t]he whole weight and strength of the nation [is] bent on political improvement and reform," even the most despotic or tyrannical government must finally give way (6: 353).

22. The idea that a "*just* monarchy" provides liberty to a people that members of the free world would consider something akin to "slaves" echoes some of the sentiments of "Free or Despotic" and suggests that Brown may be the author of "National Liberty and Happiness." In "Free or Despotic" Brown puts forth the idea that "[t]he *fortunes* of men do not always decide their *feelings*" (3: 179). "We are, for the most part," he says, "little qualified to decide what is happy or miserable in the condition of other men at a distance. The inconveniences which we see, may be compensated in a way which we do not perceive.... Even those we call slaves ... are relieved of any anxiety for the future, and devolve every care on their master" (3: 180).

23. In the conclusion of "Force of Example," a three-part essay that appeared December 1804 through February 1805 (2: 652–53, 3: 10–12, 3: 118–19), one "Valverdi," a regular correspondent of the *Literary Magazine*, describes the influence of the natural aristocracy as a force that must be tempered with a sense of responsibility:

> SINCE example is so powerful an engine in the hands of the influential, how important a duty have they to fulfil, and how much vigilance and attention does not the exercise of it require! On them depends, in some measure, the formation of manners, and even the virtues and vices of mankind: mankind are placed in their hands, like clay in the hands of a potter, who moulds it into whatever form he pleases [3: 118].

In the 4 July 1804 letter to John Blair Linn, Brown claims that, except for one piece by Valverdi, he had written all the original prose for June 1804 issue. In addition to this he claims that he has written "the whole original department" for July, but, curiously, two pieces by Valverdi appear at the end of that section. Charles Bennett explains:

> It is possible, but not likely, that Brown shared the name with another author. The two essays signed Valverdi in the July issue are placed last in the department of original communications. That placement suggests that when Brown wrote Linn he had received no new contributions from Valverdi but sometime between 4 July and the time the issue was locked into the press Valverdi's essays were received and inserted, thus accounting for their position at the end of the department. In July Brown was no more Valverdi than he had been in June [106n].

I agree with Bennett that it is unlikely that Valverdi was always Brown, but I am not convinced that Brown did not share that name with another of his correspondents. Both of Valverdi's brief essays—"Political Instruction" and "Thoughts on Wealth"—are dated "*Philadelphia, July 7*" (the first in "*1803*," probably a misprint, the second in "*1804*"), the late date tending to support Bennett's suggestion that Valverdi's communications arrived after Brown wrote the letter to Linn. There is, however, one detail about the July 1804 issue that calls Bennett's full conclusion into question. Appended to the very end of the issue is a supplementary original communication called "Baron Humboldt," which sketches the South and North American travels of that Prussian-born adventurer. Does this indicate that Brown received the Humboldt piece even later than the Valverdi contributions and was thus unable to include it with the rest of the original department? Or might it suggest that Brown did in fact share the Valverdi pseudonym and the only late communication received for that July issue was the one on Baron Humboldt? Valverdi's contributions to the *Literary Magazine* are often strong pieces that add to the miscellany's American character, but unfortunately Valverdi has never been identified and no personal or publishing records seem to exist to settle this matter.

24. "Curioso" is not one of Brown's recognized signatures, but, as Bennett points out, the 4 July 1804 letter to John Blair Linn identifies Brown as the author of all original prose — with the possible exception of the two pieces by Valverdi and the piece on Baron Humboldt — in the July 1804 issue, of which "On the Life of Washington" is the opening piece. Characteristics of presentation and composition point to Brown as the author as well. As has been seen, the editor was not averse to writing letters to himself and presenting them as if they had come from some pen other than his own, thus removing himself one more step from possibly controversial opinions and allowing his magazine a broader range of voices. Given this, as well as the similarity in the language used and the literary concerns expressed in the essay, it is almost certain that Brown is Curioso.

25. Brown would later look somewhat more kindly on Marshall's work. In "A Sketch of American Literature for 1806-7," originally published in the *American Register* 1 (1806–1807), 173–86, Brown wrote,

[Washington's] life ... is the most magnificent theme, which the historian could select, and perhaps no historian possessed so fully as [Marshall] the materials of a copious and authentic narrative. We are not inclined to say that the execution of the present work is on a level with the exellence and greatness of the theme, but the most impartial reader must admit, considering merely the nature of the materials, that it is a most valuable accession to literature [*Literary Essays* 187].

See also Kamrath's dissertation, 53–54.

26. See Lowrance's "Biography and Autobiography," 71 and 81. Had Marshall used the Washington papers in the way Brown would have liked, the biography would have become a secular, nationalist version of the Puritan spiritual autobiography, which, like Franklin's, would "embrace, in a single life-chronicle, the values and attitudes of the people of these United States, embodying America in his own persona" (Lowrance 81).

27. This idea that personal writings—especially diaries and letters—are the most important source for discovering the character and beliefs of an individual is typical of Brown. In his September 1805 essay "On Self Biography" (signed "D."), he says that "diaries form that other self, which Shaftesbury has described every thinking being to possess; and which, to converse with, he justly accounts the highest wisdom. When Cato wishes that the breast of every man were a looking-glass, he only uses a metaphorical term for such a diary.... There are certain things which relate to ourselves, which no one else can know so well; a great genius obliges posterity when he records them" (4: 183). Moreover, it is through diaries and letters that the differences between individuals can become most apparent:

Every man, in whatever department he moves, has passions, which will vary even from those who are acting the same part as himself. Our souls, like our faces, bear the general resemblance of the species, but retain the form peculiar to the individual. He who studies his own mind, and has the industry to note down the fluctuations of his opinions, and the fallacies of his passions, will form a journal peculiarly interesting to himself, and, probably, not undeserving the meditations of others. Nothing which presents a faithful picture of humanity, is worthless to a human being [4: 182].

Brown's desire that individuals should record their own lives for the better understanding of the meanings of those lives is not only evident in his writing about Washington, but it also plays a significant role in the unsigned biographical sketches of Jefferson, Franklin, and Hamilton.

28. Again the connection between this "fervent wish" and Brown's "On Self Biography"

(4: 182–85) is clear, as is the connection between this essay's "animosities of the present age" and the "intemperance of party" in the *Literary Magazine*'s "Editors' Address."

29. In the selection "On Embracing a Party in Politics," which appeared in this "Jefferson" issue, the anonymous writer says, "Englishmen and Americans have been supposed peculiarly addicted to the contest and disputes which proceed from [party politics]; though I imagine this to be owing rather to the superior liberty they long enjoyed of following their inclinations in this respect, than to any peculiarity of temper" (2: 445).

30. Although Brown's political pamphlets are often harsh in their criticism of Jefferson's policies, Brown had shown some sense of admiration for the man himself. Near the end of the period during which Jefferson served as Adams's vice president, Brown, "a stranger to the person, though not to the character of Thomas Jefferson," sent to the Vice President a letter and a copy of one of his novels, probably *Wieland*. To "the most illustrious of his fellow citizens," Brown wrote, in part,

To request your perusal of a work, which at the same time, is confessed to be unworthy of perusal, would be an uncommon proof of absurdity. In this transmitting my book to you, I tacitly acknowledge my belief that it is capable of affording you pleasure &, of entitling the writer to some portion of your good opinion. If I had not this belief, I should be unavoidably silent [qtd. in Peden 66].

Despite suggestions by critics such as Charles C. Cole and Steven Watts that between the late 1790s and early 1800s Brown underwent a "conversion from radicalism to the anti–Jeffersonian camp" (Cole 254), the *Literary Magazine*, at least, carries no suggestion that Brown ever reversed the opinion of Jefferson as an individual suggested in this letter. Although the "Thomas Jefferson" sketch offers almost nothing that would indicate Brown's personal feelings, it contains a slight rhetorical hint as to what they were: of those Republicans and Federalists whose "hopes and fears" are inspired by Jefferson, the profile says, "A large number have laboured for his elevation, with all the zeal which *our* own interest is sure to inspire; while a number, scarcely less considerable, have laboured to degrade him, with all the perseverance and anxiety which men usually display to prevent *their* own fall" (2: 413; my emphasis). The switch from first to third person might be simply a rhetorical convention, but as the only such passage in the sketch, it provides the essay with two distinct yet subtle colorings: first, it reveals a possible democratic republican leaning, which to some degree dialogically undercuts the overall antiparty stance; second, "our interest" supports the rule of the majority, which, in light of the Constitution, would lend the piece a more nationalistic shading.

31. Two months earlier, in "Notices of American Writers and Publications" (August 1804), Brown writes,

The political and literary interests of this country have suffered a great loss in the death of general Alexander Hamilton. In every region of investigation, into which this man entered, he discovered a burning and intrepid genius. Our hearts bleed at the recollection of the manner in which he died; and most bitterly do we deplore that such a man has fallen in such a manner. The citizens of New York can never forget the rich displays of his capacious and overcoming eloquence, nor should America ever forget his services in the field and in the cabinet. Early in life, Hamilton discovered a brilliant fancy and correct taste. He wrote and delivered, at the request of his fellow students, an Essay on Duelling, which, even at that season of heated imagination, declared detestation of that savage practice. He pronounced, several years ago, an eulogium on the character of general Greene. We hope that both these productions may be discovered among his papers, and that these, in connection with his many political tracts, will be published in a uniform manner. During a year or more before his death, he meditated a work on government; but we are not informed that he had made any progress in such a great and desirable undertaking. In a future number of this Magazine, we propose to give a portrait, and a more particular account of this celebrated and extraordinary man [2: 345-46].

32. Brown biographer David Lee Clark identifies this essay as Brown's, saying, "The editor's gentle Quaker blood still boiled at the mere mention of dueling" (228), but Clark gives no other reason for assigning authorship to Brown.

33. The John Adams sketch naturally comes between Washington's and Jefferson's, while Franklin's follows Hamilton's and is in turn followed by Jay's.

The August 1804 issue's unsigned "Biographical Sketch of John Adams" briefly details the highlights of Adams's life, from his birth into an old and prominent Boston family to his retirement from the presidency. The writer notes that Adams was a lawyer by profession — a detail Brown would have taken particular notice of, having early on trained for the law himself — and acknowledges that his advocacy was for the "rights of his country, and of mankind at large" (2: 331). Identifying Adams's Federalism but not denominating it as such, the writer says the former president's "grand principle is, 'That the people's rights and liberties, and the democratical mixture in a constitution, can never be preserved without a strong executive; or, in other words, without separating the executive power from the legislative'" (2: 332). The essay concludes without going any further into Adams's political beliefs or career: "We purposely avoid entering into an exhibition of the public character of Mr. Adams, because political zeal has long since enlisted all men in the number of his friends or enemies, and we are desirous of avoiding, on this occasion, to offend any." Thus Brown maintains his magazine's political neutrality with only the slightest implication that Adams's Federalism — or the writer's portrayal of it — might be offensive to one portion or another of his readership.

The brief sketch of Franklin (November 1804) mentions the *Autobiography* and suggests that it would have been beneficial to his country if Franklin had finished his life through the Revolution and his world travels to his old age in Philadelphia.

John Jay's biographical notice (December 1804) makes note of his French ancestry and then focuses on his career as an American patriot. Like the Adams essay, this one mentions particularly the subject's legal career, especially his diplomacy work overseas. Jay's 1794 treaty with the British and its aftermath are briefly noticed, but the writer goes on to say that "most certain it is, that the true interests of his country constituted the only object of his labors." After seeing Jay into his "peaceful and modest retirement," the writer, probably Brown again, voices his request that a man such as Jay should write his own story in order "to throw the light of his own recorded experience on the momentous history of the revolution, in which he was so important and illustrious an actor" (2: 652).

34. Signed "A.B."

35. Brown argues against any distinction between private and public virtues, saying that while one set of philosophers are endeavouring to prove that man has not a soul, another set are taking equal pains to prove that he has *two souls*, one of which he employs at home, and the other abroad, in schemes which are diametrically opposite. Of what use this doctrine may be we cannot yet be certain, as it has not been pushed as far as it can go; but, in the mean time, it may not be amiss to consider, that the qualities of a highwayman are no great recommendation to public favour... [2: 95].

36. Signed "W."

37. See C. B. Macpherson's *The Political Theory of Possessive Individualism: Hobbes to Locke* (1962).

38. Signed "A." The essay continues the same line of thought as "On Habituating Ourselves to an Individual Pursuit" in that it again shows that particular "practice and experience" can improve almost any skill or ability. This time, however, the essay provides a broader picture of humankind in support of the idea that each member is a distinct individual.

39. Even though the nation was drawn together politically under a single government after the ratification of the Constitution, Brown and the *Literary Magazine* did not allow to go unnoticed the fact that the cultural character of the people — from region to region, state to state — varied widely (as it does now). See, for example, "The American Character," 2: 252–57, and "American Manners," 3: 291–92.

40. The library was that of Hoquet Caritat, the publisher of Brown's first two novels, *Wieland* and *Ormond*. The case appears to have been much the same with the American periodicals of the time. As Edward Chielens has pointed out, even patriotic publications printed at the height of the Revolutionary fervor, such as Isaiah Thomas's *The Royal American Magazine*, as well as those of the early national period that attempted to promote "American authors writing on American themes" (Chielens 95), reprinted substantial amounts of material from contemporary British periodicals.

41. This judgment concludes Brown's review of *Two Compends for the Use of the Philadelphia Academy* ... — the first dealing with elocution and the second with natural history — by James Abercrombie, who was, in addition to being an assistant minister at two of the city's churches, the director of the Philadelphia Academy (1: 38–39).

42. The article is called "List of New Publications in July," and of the seventeen published items mentioned, only three deal with American materials:

    A Map of Louisiana, compiled from a manuscript French map, Mr. Murray's map of the United States, and Hutchinson's map of the Mississippi, &c. and compared with the documents laid before Congress, 1803; drawn by Samuel Lewis; mounted on rollers. 1 doll. 25 cents...... Conrad & co.

    The Constitutions of the United States, according to the last amendments, to which are prefixed the Declaration of Independence and the Federal Constitution, the ordinance for the Government of the N.W. Territory, an act concerning the District of Columbia, an act to incorporate the City of Washington, the proposed Amendments to the Federal Constitution, and an act providing for the Government of Louisiana. 1 dollar.....Conrad & co.

    The American Distiller, or the theory and practice of distilling, according to the latest discoveries and improvements, including the most approved method of constructing Stills, and of rectification, by Michael Kraft of Bristol, Pennsylvania, Distiller, illustrated with copper-plates. 2 dollars.....Dobson [2: 319].

The first fourteen items include British travels, religious commentaries, and so on.

Chapter Three

1. That Brown wrote this piece under the guise of anonymity is not outside the realm of possibility. A year earlier, in the June 1804 number, an article readily identified as Brown's—according to his 4 July 1804 letter to John Blair Linn—expresses this same idea regarding the nightingale and American reading. In "The Spirit of Female Conversation," Brown writes about "a company of half a dozen ladies" and the subjects they touch on in talking together over the course of a few afternoon hours: flowers and shrubs, servants, birds, fruit and vegetables and their cost, housekeeping, and other such topics. During their conversation about singing birds, one particular young woman "threw in a hint, which was not attended to, about the nightingale, which European poets talk about so much, but which American readers know only by description." This idea is, of course, the same as that suggested by the anonymous writer of "The Nightingale and Mock-bird." Furthermore, another of the company mentions "a mocking-bird, who had by heart as many tunes as Haydn" (2: 188). The writer of "The Nightingale and Mock-bird" will make a similar claim about a mockingbird that he heard perform "a simple Scots air, in adagio time, of seventy-six notes" (3: 179). If Brown is indeed the author of this June 1805 essay comparing the two feathered singers, the allegorical reading I suggest in my discussion of "The Nightingale and Mock-bird" seems to me increasingly likely.

2. Shakespeare is quoted in support of this suggestion: "The nightingale, if she should sing by day, / When every goose is cackling, would be thought / No better a musician than the wren" (*Literary Magazine* 3: 418). The passage is from act 5, scene 1, of *The Merchant of Venice*.

3. In an essay on the "Voice of Birds" (signed "Q."), appearing earlier in the same June 1805 issue with "The Nightingale and Mock-bird," these "jerks" are described as "the short bursts of singing birds, contending with each other ... [and] distinguished from *song*" (3: 406). As Brown's anonymous foreign correspondent notices these sounds in the spring, the jerks are probably male nightingales competing for mates. The "Voice of Birds" makes no mention of the mockingbird.

4. These "*bars*" are the portions of the nightingale's music that have been identified by "a supposed affinity between the name and the thing signified. They are *sweet, sweet jug, jug sweet; water-bubble; pipe-rattle, bell-pipe, skroty; swat-swat-swatty; whitlow, whitlow, whitlow, &c.*" (3: 419).

5. In 1779, in the midst of the Revolution, David Ramsay wrote, "Ever since the flood, true religion, literature, arts, empire, and riches, have taken a slow and gradual course from east to west, and are now about fixing their long and favourite abode in this new western world" (qtd. in Free 12). The same was thought, at times, in England. Bishop Berkeley's eighteenth-century poem suggests that "Westward the course of empire takes its way" (qtd. in Matthews 48).

6. Although similar conflicts took place among the British, they seem not to have been as strident because they occurred in the context of a well established political and cultural order. Thus the nightingale metaphor continues to be appropriate as "the various *bars*" that

make up the nightingale's singular song reflect those voices contending within British society.

7. Benedict Anderson concurs with Watts to some extent, although he does not point a finger at republicanism. He says in *Imagined Communities* that often "successful revolutionaries ... inherit the wiring from the old state.... Like the complex electrical system in any large mansion when the owner has fled, the state awaits the new owner's hand at the switch to be very much its old brilliant self again." "One should therefore not be much surprised," Anderson concludes, "if revolutionary *leaderships*, consciously or unconsciously, come to play lord of the manor" (160). Far from linking republicanism with recolonization, however, Anderson seems to connect it to the revolution in culture that took place in the Americas in general once their individual countries were separated from the imperial centers in Europe (51).

8. On vocalism and the polyglot world of early America, see Christopher Looby's *Voicing America*, especially chapters four and five.

9. The headnote is identified as Brown's according to the 4 July 1804 letter to John Blair Linn, in which Brown claims, with a sense of regret, that he was forced to write all original material in the July 1804 issue. The headnote is, moreover, typical of Brown's editorial introductions to excerpted, reprinted, or pirated works, whether by native or foreign authors.

10. Martin Brückner has recently explored the ways in which American writers and public figures used the language of geography to construct the new American nation and promote the idea of unity within its borders. "Geographic characters, such as place names and the implied geographic image of the American continent," Brückner writes at one point, "provided post-revolutionary American orators and writers with more than a rhetorical device through which successfully to mesh personal authorship with authoritative cultural demands. Rather than actual 'nature' and its taxonomic accounts by natural histories, the map of the United States and the literary protocol of popular American geography books underpinned sermons arguing for the providential unity within the new American polity" (87–88). To this I would add the suggestion that, in essays like "The American Character," English and European writers sometimes reversed the American line of thinking and proposed that the United States was bound together by nothing more than its borders and a "congressional law" that "runs over all" (2: 254), that unity within those borders was an illusion created by maps and the Constitution.

11. Before the essay ends, the foreign author twice mentions the different effects of climate on the people of the United States. Brown later addressed this issue himself in "The Influence of Climate on the Mind" (signed "C."), an essay that opened the *Literary Magazine*'s May 1806 number: "Among the follies of the wise is a system which circumscribes the energies of the mind by the influence of climate. Though often confuted, it is still believed, for there are some whom no confutations can confute" (5: 323). He then discusses a list of Western philosophers and authors—from the ancient Aristotle to the modern Denina, Montesquieu, Baillet, Milton, Young, and Descartes—who tended to subscribe to the notion that climate, which for Brown includes both weather and soil, affects the character of a people. He answers that it is "the power which the *customs* and *government* of a people have over them" which leads to their character:

> Heroic and polished Greece and Rome are now barbarous and servile; and the gravity and superstition of the Spaniard, the politic and assassinating spirit of the Italian, the diligence and suppleness of the Scot, and the warmness and penetration of the Englishman, are derived from manners and government.... It is with nations as with individuals, and with individuals as with nations. The human mind is indeed influenced not by climate, but by government; not by soils, but by customs; not by heat and cold, but by servitude and freedom. A happy education, elegant leisure, and a passion for glory, must form a great man; as an excellent government, orderly liberty, and popular felicity, must form a great people.

Further removing the effects of climate and other factors in the formation of culture and nation, Brown suggests that "a great people" is always a new combination of influences and characteristics, as well as always somewhat surprising: "No system of education for the individual, or system of government for the people, has been discovered which can satisfy the rational mind; a great people, like a great man, must therefore be a sort of prodigy" (5: 326, 327).

12. Brown highlights only two perceived errors in the description of the New England

states: "*The Americans are all extremely inquisitive, owing, no doubt, to the practice of their earliest forefathers of inquiring news of their relations and friends in the mother country, from every new comer....*" and "*In their agricultural pursuits, they follow nearly the English system*" (2: 253).

13. The foreign essayist pays little attention to New Jersey and Delaware. New Jersey "is a great inland thoroughfare ... lying between the cities of New York and Philadelphia." Europe, it seems, knew little more of the state than what lay along this route. What Brown found to be a blunder in this brief description of New Jersey is that its "*inhabitants are principally of that sect denominated friends.... They are a very peaceable, quiet people, although numbers of them are of that class called fighting quakers, because they do not object to take up arms*" (2: 253). The state of Delaware "is scarcely, in any respect, distinguishable from Pennsylvania" (2: 254).

14. The writer eventually suggests that slavery may be the greatest force behind the obvious difference between North and South, saying, "There appears at present a decided superiority of the northern over the southern states, which, perhaps, the abolition of slavery in the latter may greatly diminish" (2: 254).

15. The writer provides the reader with this anecdote of a Virginia planter:
An Englishman calling upon a gentleman, whose house was situated a little distance from James river, was very hospitably received, although a stranger, and presently conducted to the stable to look at his racehorses, which were by no means remarkable. The Englishman, however, not to disappoint his entertainer, spoke more highly of them than he thought himself justified in doing. On their return to the house, the Englishman was struck with the beauty of the garden in front of the house, from whence it diverged to the river.... The Virginian informed him, it had been laid out by a Scots gentleman, to whom the house originally belonged. The Englishman, thinking to pay him a high compliment, told him he must bestow great pains to keep it in such fine order. "I, sir!" replied the Virginian, seemingly much nettled; "my Negroes do!!" [2: 254].
To make a broad, generalized interpretation of the anecdote is to see the British — the author of "The American Character" included — as praising Americans in order to avoid saying something disappointing. Moreover, it is important to note that the one aspect of the Virginian's life the Englishman enjoys was left the planter by a subject of Great Britain and maintained by the corrupt institution of slavery.

16. The writer defines the list of imported characteristics as "the frugality and plainness of the High and Low Dutch, the industry and parsimony of the Scots, the genius, conviviality, and want of economy of the English, the hardiness of the Irish, who are of the lower order, and the frivolity of the French" (2: 252–53). At this point, of course, the essay echoes Crèvecoeur and his ideas of America as a melting pot where "individuals of all nations are melted into a new race of men" (70).

17. Much of the remainder of the essay provides brief explanations of American legal practices, medical science, religious tolerance and variety, literature and art, music, architecture (both civil and naval), and education. American legal practices, the writer says, generally follow England in all but "those points where the fundamentals of a monarchial form of government are repugnant to those of a republican one." Religion is treated with a mixture of disdain and admiration: its "externals ... are exhibited in all its different sounds, aspects, and touches, of prayers, sighs, groans, kisses of love, of peace, of friendship, dancing, jumping, and tumbling"; "Deism is very prevalent, and in many places, as New York, &c. openly professed"; "[t]he spirit of fanaticism, so notorious, some time back, in the northern states, is totally obliterated, except some remains of outward show in Connecticut"; "yet it is but justice, however," the writer concludes, "to say, there are, in the clerical function, many pious, intelligent, liberal-minded men" (2: 255). All other elements mentioned — literature, art, music, architecture, and education — are judged inferior to the same in England, but they are considered to be improving.

18. The author's use of the plural when referring to the United States emphasizes the notion of the nation's being a collection of distinct peoples — and individuals — rather than a single entity. This practice, it appears, would remain in some usage for at least another fifty years. Walt Whitman, in his well known preface to the first edition of *Leaves of Grass* (1855), says, "The United States themselves are essentially the greatest poem." He unifies the image somewhat by closing it with a singular form, "poem," but in the following sentence he returns to the plural: "In the history of the

earth hitherto the largest and most stirring appear tame and orderly to *their* ampler largeness and stir" (711; my emphasis).

19. For a lucid overview of the problems of culture in early republican America, see Jean Matthews's *Toward a New Society*, especially chapter three.

20. This is from the important letter of 4 July 1804. Brown's request did not result in any sort of publication, probably due to the fact that Linn, whose health was failing, died only a few weeks later in August.

21. Here I am drawing on Dowling's "phenomenological reading" of Dennie's *Port Folio*. Dowling understands Dennie and his contributors as creating a separate world — Richard Poirier's "world elsewhere" — within the pages of the magazine, where "*The Port Folio* as a self-contained universe of discourse ... asks the reader to look outward from its own literary horizon upon the crowded scene of the early American republic" (x). But whereas Dennie — given his and the magazine's gradual withdrawal from the public sphere — expected the reader merely to mourn the increasing incongruities between idealized life in the republic of letters and actual life in the American republic, Brown seems to have hoped his readers would take what they read in his pages and work to mend the rift between the idealized and the actual.

22. Although not strictly a review, this essay addresses Richard Parkinson's *Experienced Farmer's Tour in America: A Tour in America in 1798, 1799, and 1800: Exhibiting Sketches of Society and Manners, and a Particular Account of the American System of Agriculture, with Its Recent Improvements*, 2 vols. (London, 1805). The *Literary Magazine*'s "Account" is unsigned, but it is probably by Brown, who, especially after the death of John Blair Linn in August 1804, wrote most items related to books.

23. Although a subtle addition, Brown's translation of shillings into dollars lends "An Account" an American point of view and helps localize the essay for his readers.

24. In a similar essay, "Cautions Respecting Emigration to America," selected for the February 1806 number, Brown likewise prefaces the warnings from another Old World emigrant with this headnote: "The following remarks are re-published from an English work for the *amusement* rather than the instruction of the American reader." Like Parkinson (and similarities suggest that the "English work" may in fact be Parkinson's), the author of "Cautions" sets out to disprove the "assertion ... that the new world holds out advantages not to be found in the old one." In this essay it is not — as it would be later in "An Emigrant in America" — largely the inexperience of the European in the New World that makes life difficult for those who would emigrate but the misconceptions of America as a place and the shortcomings of the land itself.

25. Given Brown's attitude in regards to Parkinson's work, it is difficult to know how far this condescension reaches in relation to the American farmer. The few purely agricultural items in the *Literary Magazine* carry no hint of cultural hostility towards those who worked the land in the United States. The same is not the case, however, in Brown's fiction. The fathers of Arthur Mervyn and Carwin are brutal and ignorant men. The same is true of Carwin's brother, and this description of him is typical:

> His wishes never led him astray from the hay-stack and the furrow. His ideas never ranged beyond the sphere of his vision, or suggested the possibility that to-morrow could differ from to-day. He could read and write, because he had no alternative between learning the lesson prescribed to him, and punishment. He was diligent, as long as fear urged him forward, but his exertions ceased with the cessation of this motive. The limits of his acquirements consisted in signing his name, and spelling out a chapter in the bible [1: 100].

It is likely that this poor usage of farmers in *Memoirs of Carwin the Biloquist* and *Arthur Mervyn* was more to serve the literary purpose of creating a foil for the protagonist than to condemn the intellectual abilities of farmers in general. Brown's animosity towards Parkinson and his narrative, therefore, seems rooted more in that writer's pretensions to portray America in a light to please the British court than in any negative opinion of farmers in general.

26. For example, the English feed their livestock hay; the Americans feed theirs "blades," which "proved to be the blades and tops of Indian corn." Brown allows Parkinson to tell the story of his search for hay when he arrived in America. The tale of his discovery of the general use of blades instead of hay includes accounts of American cows eating "'the dung of a horse, as naturally as an English cow does hay'"; of the streets of Norfolk being full of thieving local livestock, "'robbing every man's cart of the *blades* as they come to be sold, or

picking up any thing else they can find.'" Regarding this chaos, so different from the life of raising cattle in England, Parkinson writes, "'It appeared to me that a man's having land in or about that town was of no advantage to him in keeping cows, as it growed no grass; the street was the cheapest place to keep them in, and the best.'" Parkinson's voice drips with disgust at these practices, but Brown undercuts the story by closing the excerpt with an observation of his own: "It may be proper to add, however, that our author, in the sequel, found the trade of a cowfeeder a singularly profitable one; and that his horses approved exceedingly of those *blades*, 'which it was the practice to sell by the pound, in the same manner as tea in England'" (5: 221).

27. Brown summarizes Parkinson's beliefs, focusing particularly on the author's reasons for the harsh judgments of American land:

> Mr. Parkinson maintains that, after travelling repeatedly over the most favoured parts of the continent, and partly viewing, partly trying the soil, as an experienced farmer, he has been unable to find any which would be deemed worth the trouble of touching in England; that every appearance of poverty is to be met with in all parts of the country; that the labour required to preserve a wretched existence in America would procure the comforts of life any where else; that the nature of the climate and soil offers unsurmountable obstacles to the profitable employment of capital in agricultural speculations; and, in short, that Europeans have hitherto been more deceived in their ideas of America, than in the earliest descriptions of China [5: 219].

28. "'...[A]mong the white men in America,'" Parkinson writes, "'they are all *Mr.* and *sir*; so that, in conversation, you cannot discover which is the master, or which is the man. It is the same with the white women; they are all *madam* and *miss*. If you call at the door of any man, and ask the servant if his master is at home, he will say, 'Master! I have no master: do you want Mr. Such-a-one?' that is, the man he serves: and if you want a man that is a white servant, the master calls him in the same manner'" (5: 222).

29. At the same time that foreign travelers such as Parkinson were publishing their difficulties and disappointments in America, American travelers were out and about in their new nation as well. But Brown's choice of native travel narratives for *Literary Magazine* readers seems to have been rather limited. Little in the way of domestic travels through the South, New England, or the western states and territories appears in the miscellany; the focus remains largely concentrated on Pennsylvania, New Jersey, and New York, the locations—along with Connecticut—prominent in Brown's own travel experiences.

30. See also "Of the Mode of Education Proper in a Republic" in Benjamin Rush, *The Selected Writings of Benjamin Rush*, ed. Dagobert D. Runes (New York: Philosophical Library, 1947) 92.

31. Signed "B."

32. For a lucid discussion of educational reform in early republican America, see Linda Kerber's *Federalists in Dissent: Imagery and Ideology in Jeffersonian America*, especially chapter four, "Salvaging the Classical Tradition."

33. Here again the Federalist tendency toward an imitative rather than a creative culture should be kept in mind.

34. In an interesting turn on this idea, those who realized that Ovid wrote fiction sometimes wondered if the actual places the Roman writer used were real. Kerber presents this anecdote from Benjamin Rush's 24 February 1790 letter to John Adams: "One of Benjamin Rush's sons, studying Ovid, asked his father if there really was such a river as the Nile and if Egypt really existed: the question summed up, Rush thought, all that was wrong with 'that mode of education which makes the first knowledge of boys to consist in *fables*, and thereby leads them to reject truth, or to esteem it no more than gross errors and fictions of the ancient poets'" (qtd. in *Federalists* 112).

35. Signed "O."

36. Signed "W." Interestingly, this essay appears in the same issue as the second of the essays in the debate over education in the classics, "On the Anti-Christian Tendency of Classical Learning." In "On 'the Enlightened Public'" Brown refers to the heyday of Greece and Rome as having been one of those

> former periods [when] the human mind shot from a radical vigour, and flourished in the richest luxuriance. Among the ancients, the fine and mechanical arts have been considered to have exceeded our happiest efforts; and as for the intellectual powers and moral duties, though most of the compositions of these ancients have been lost, yet enough have remained to serve as models for our greatest poets; to

instruct our orators in the arts of eloquence; our historians in the composition of history, and to leave nothing for our moralists, but an amplification of the observations of Seneca and Epictetus [4: 112–13].

Yet Brown also understood — as he would reveal the following month in "Classical Learning No Anti-Christian Tendency"— that these "compositions" were by the period's most exceptional individuals and that the mass of the Greek and Roman people were, as he will say of moderns in the "enlightened" world, "vulgar and ignorant" (4: 191).

37. Although unsigned, David Lee Clark identifies this "plea" as Brown's but gives no explanation of his reason for doing so. This type of official item is typical of the "American Register" portion of the magazine, and Brown's interest in such government workings would eventually lead him to cease publication of the *Literary Magazine* and continue in this same vein with his *American Register*. Given Brown's interest in public documents and his position as editor, it is possible, even probable, that he wrote the introductory comments for this "Report."

38. A substantial population of German immigrants lived in Pennsylvania, and it is interesting to note that the children of this group were apparently to be taught in their own language. In those days before a commodified nationalism in the United States, there seems to have been little sense, at least in Pennsylvania, of English as the accepted national — and nationalizing — language. Brown makes no mention of the Germans' need to study English but only identifies the problem of teacher education by echoing the committee's report that "the great body of our schoolmasters [are] *deficient in the first principles of the language they attempt to teach*" (3: 386).

39. In "On 'the Enlightened Public'" Brown asks, "Is not opinion often local, and ever disguised by custom?" This is another example of why the Enlightenment was not in reality widespread. He seems to have believed that all locations — influenced by the character of the people, their past, their religions, and so on — maintained their own ideas of community. As a result, the Enlightenment could not exist on the basis of universally accepted truth so long as local custom dominated.

40. The italics here seem to identify phrases Brown drew from the original report of the committee. They are the important ends to which free education was the means, but the education — basic reading, writing, and arithmetic — set forth in the document was not sufficient, Brown seems to think, to achieve these ends.

41. Signed "D."

42. Again, here, Brown seems to anticipate Emerson and the opening lines of *Nature*.

43. Signed "N."

44. Brown reveals some practical secrets for improving reading skills. A reader can profit by any book, whether by positive or negative example, but individuals can profit most by keeping to the type of book that best suits her or his interest and temperament. Given the overwhelming proliferation of print in Brown's day, he suggests that it is not always necessary to read the whole of every book; a reader should understand the basic idea of a work and "examine some of the portions":

Of the little supplement at the close of a volume, few readers conceive the value; but some of the most eminent writers have been great adepts at the art of *index-reading*.... I, for my part, venerate the inventor of indices; and I know not to whom to yield the preference, either to Hippocrates, who was the first great anatomiser of the human body, or to that unknown labourer in literature, who first laid open the nerves and arteries of a book [5: 164].

In addition to keeping to one's interests and making good use of prefaces and indexes, Brown says that no one necessarily needs to read all the works written by a single author "but only those which have received the approbation of posterity." For example, Brown writes, "The best parts of Pope are his translations of Homer and Horace: these, with his moral essays, and his Art of Criticism, should be read, while his pastorals and his odes are forgotten, and his Wife of Bath, his Sappho, and his Eloisa should be reserved for the use of brothels." Similarly, readers should not be influenced by the reputation of an author, especially one who writes voluminously. Even "the best writers ... have a great deal of mediocrity; for whenever an author attains facility in composition, the success of his preceding labours ... stimulates him to new performances, ... and such being mostly writers by profession, most of their works are the products, not of inclination, but necessity" (5: 165).

In order to make reading most efficacious Brown makes further practical suggestions for the act of sitting down with a text. Recognizing that readers sometimes are, for whatever reason, unable "to settle on the subject" of the book, poem, or essay, he suggests that when they apply themselves, "with gentle violence, to the persual [sic] of an interesting work, the mind soon congenealizes with the subject; the disinclination is no more, and like Homer's chariot wheels, we kindle as we roll." Certain "mechanical aids" also make reading more profitable in the long run; while reading a work, readers will find it useful to "note in a blank leaf" the page numbers, "with a word of criticism," of the most interesting passages, thereby allowing those passages to be easily found should readers ever need to refer to them again (5: 166).

45. For a useful discussion of literacy, education, and reading, see Cathy N. Davidson's *Revolution and the Word* (1986), especially chapter four.

46. Signed "D."

47. Miscellaneous literature benefited writers as well as readers, according to Brown. Writing the short essays required by the genre
   is no task imposed on the mind of the writer for the mere ambition, but is generally a voluntary effusion, warm with all the sensations of a pathetic writer. In a word, they are the compositions of genius, on a subject in which it is most deeply interested, which it revolves on all its sides, which it paints in all its tints, and which it finishes with the same ardour it began [4: 166].

For the reader, Brown says, "A concise work preserves a common subject from insipidity, and an uncommon one from error. An essayist expresses himself with a more real enthusiasm, than the writer of a volume; for I have observed that the most fervid genius is apt to cool in a quarto" (4: 167). It is not difficult to see in these descriptions of the "miscellanist" at least a partial explanation of why Brown might have abandoned the novel for the magazine.

48. See for example such essays as "Fielding and Richardson" (2: 657–59), "Romances" (3: 6–7), "Novels" (3: 16–17), "Terrific Novels" (3: 288–89), "On Fleetwood, Godwin's Last Novel" (4: 60–66), and "Sketches of Some Recent Novels" (4: 207–08). Even more of Brown's literary essays regarding novels may be found in his first magazine, *The Monthly Magazine, and American Review* (1799–1800).

49. Although the essay is unsigned, several scholars such as David Lee Clark and Alfred Weber have attributed it to Brown. That "Popularity of Novels" strongly criticizes the sensational Gothic conventions of murder, ghosts, old castles, and such—clearly echoing feelings Brown put into words as early as the Preface to *Edgar Huntly* (1799) and later repeated in many other pieces easily identified as his—leads me to support this essay's attribution to him.

50. Brown describes such sentimental transformations from the common in life to the uncommon in fiction this way:
   Instead ... of a young couple walking regularly to church to be married, with their parents' consent, and their parents walking regularly with them (an incident so common as to occasion little or no notice), we have a pair of true lovers concealing from each other what they both are desirous to reveal, thwarted in their affection by cruel fathers and mothers, or guardians, beset with spies, their letters intercepted, rooms turned into prisons; and if an escape, usually called an elopement, be practicable, windows are turned into doors, and a ladder becomes a stair-case; post-horses are furnished with wings, and post-boys of the true Hounslow breed are converted into Cupids, while an old battered chaise is a hymeneal car [7: 411].

This sort of exaggeration seems not to disturb Brown. Individuals who read for ideas can apparently find value in spite of—or perhaps because of—the transfiguration of real life characteristic of these sentimental fictions. "By portraying dashing roués," Davidson writes, "sentimental novelists still allowed women to vicariously participate in a range of relationships with diverse suitors and to imagine what the aftermath of marriage to different men might be like" (113).

51. In the same year that saw the publication of *Wieland*, Brown attacked Britain's Gothic writers—writers who in some ways influenced his own *Wieland* and *Edgar Huntly*—for their use of such props or tricks in keeping readers buying, and reading, their fiction. In "A Receipt for a Modern Romance," originally published in Philadelphia's *Weekly Magazine* for 30 June 1798, writing under the pseudonym of "Anti-Ghost," Brown satirizes the traditional European Gothic romance by presenting the most common devices used by such authors as "Monk" Lewis. Brown's humorous criticism takes the form of a recipe: "Take an old castle; pull down a part of it, and allow the grass to grow on the battlements, and provide owls and bats with uninterrupted habitations among the ruins. Pour a sufficient

quantity of heavy rain upon the hinges and bolts of the gates, so that when they are attempted to be opened, they creak most fearfully." He goes on mixing all the customary ingredients of the Gothic novel until the beautiful young heroine, who is a staple of this recipe, after many strange experiences in the castle, "has been dissolved to a jelly with her fears," and is "delivered by the man of her heart, and married ..." (*Literary Essays* 8).

52. Although unsigned, the "Student's Diary" series has been identified as Brown's by Clark, Ernest Marchand, and Bennett, among others. Weber and Schäfer, editors of Brown's *Literary Essays and Reviews*, write that the series is "certainly by Brown: First, many of the articles reveal Brown's biographical background; they seem to be actually taken out of his diary. Second, there are so many references and relationships to other articles that have been identified as by Brown, that his authorship is certain" (241). Furthermore, as this was actually the sixth installment of the series to appear in the *Literary Magazine*, Weber and Schäfer suggest that the numbering is wrong (244).

53. According to the ideal connection Davidson makes between "literateness" and "autonomy" (69), Miss ***** seems to be literate; she seems at the same time, however, to be no reader.

54. See especially the first two essays — "Daughters of Columbia: Educating Women for the Republic, 1787–1805" and "The Republican Mother: Women and the Enlightenment — An American Perspective" — in Kerber's *Toward an Intellectual History of Women* (1997).

55. See Brown's "On Habituating Ourselves to an Individual Pursuit" (5: 176–78), already discussed in my chapter two.

56. The piece is unsigned, but both content and style suggest Brown's authorship. Daniel Edwards Kennedy says, "The literary subject *Madelina a portrait* has his style, is written as a letter in response to a request, has Brown's ideas of women and dodges the personal side as he did in his letters to Rebecca Linn. It recalls those letters but who Madelina is, is unknown" (1838).

57. The essay is the lead article for this June 1806 number, and although unsigned, its author is probably Brown, as he regularly supplied the pieces that occupied that position. Furthermore, content — the article's focus on feminine issues, reading, and history — and style both suggest that the piece is most likely Brown's.

58. "The literary character of women," Brown writes, "might *exceed* that of every man who does not make study his profession. Their employments are not unfriendly to *reading:* occupied at their delicate works, their avocations are ever more agreeably pursued while the circle listens to a reader; frequent readings of this nature would render their taste more lively, and their meditations less interrupted than among those persons whose studies are casual..." (5: 407).

59. The author does cite Benjamin West and John Singleton Copley as evidence that American could produce painters of genius, "but, it must be confessed," he says, "they have flourished as exotics, who would have perished in their indigenous soil" (3: 255). Both painters were, of course, born in America but achieved fame, and spent their careers, in the Old World.

60. Signed "R."

61. Here Brown is most likely referring to West and Copley.

62. Brown opened the May 1807 number of the *Literary Magazine* with the text of this speech. Kennedy suggests that Brown may have been the president of the American Literary Association: "We know that James West, Roberts Vaux, James Chambers and William M. Descharms were members.... Chambers was secretary at one time and Descharms was secretary in 1808. The president is unknown being designated mysteriously by ———, which does not correspond to any of the [known] members and is significant in that it may stand for Charles Brockden Brown" (1787). In September 1807 Brown published a brief note entitled "The American Literary Association" (signed "S."). As is typical of many of Brown's pseudonymous contributions, the note is addressed "To the Editor, &c." Posing as a correspondent who had "frequently heard of this association, and ... made some inquiry respecting it," he declares "the design of the institution laudable and praiseworthy" (8: 94):

> By a fund, which is annually created among themselves, they are enabled to subscribe for all the periodical publications of the United States which are valuable, and also some of those most celebrated in England, to procure which, they assemble every fortnight, and, in order to make the convention subservient to more than one useful purpose, at every meeting two of their members read each an essay on either a scientific, moral, or literary

subject. To such an institution the friends of learning must wish success. It does not appear to be built of those flimsy materials which will wear out in a day; but having for its object the promotion of knowledge among its members, as well as the extension of patronage toward American papers, it has a fair claim to long existence, creditable and honourable to its founders [8: 95].

63. The essay is unsigned, but it has been tentatively attributed to Brown by Alfred Weber and the scholars working on "The Uncollected Writings."

Chapter Four

1. Fred Lewis Pattee, writing in *The Development of the American Short Story* (originally published in 1923), all but ignores any examples of short fiction before Irving; "Brown," he writes, "...produced not short stories, but abortive romances, tales begun as novels and abandoned..." (1). A more thorough survey of the history of American short fiction is Eugene Current-Garcia's study entitled *The American Short Story Before 1850* (1985). Current-Garcia does not mention Brown in particular, but he apparently understands better than Pattee the role played by such early forms as fictional epistles and literary fragments—forms Brown made much use of in his magazine work—in the development of the short story in America.

2. For example, Brown included in the first issue of the *Literary Magazine* a piece entitled "The Man with the Huge Nose. *In Imitation of the Manner of Sterne*" (October 1803), from which the following is a brief excerpt:

> MY uncle Toby, one cold December evening, sat smoking his pipe by the fire, involved in deep reverie, when Corporal Trim entered. Please, your honour, said the Corpral [sic], slowly approaching. My uncle Toby made no reply. There is a biting air abroad, your honour. My uncle Toby spoke not. Shall I help your honour to a cup of sack, continued the Corporal, raising his voice. Still my uncle Toby was silent. I have seen the man with the huge nose, said Trim. My uncle Toby dropped his pipe... [1: 23].

3. Brown's fiction in the *Monthly Magazine* includes the following: "Thessalonica: A Roman Story" (May 1799, 1: 99–117); "Portrait of an Immigrant: Extracted from a Letter" (June 1799, 161–64); "Lesson on Concealment; or, Memoirs of Mary Selwyn" (March 1800, 2: 174–207); "The Trials of Arden" (July 1800, 3: 19–36); "Original Letters" (August 1800, 101–111).

4. "Distinction between Poetry and Prose" (November 1804) is unsigned, but the essay has been identified as Brown's by Clark, Weber, and others. Both form and method are typical of Brown and his ongoing attempt to define for his readers certain literary ideas that would be useful to them. In questioning the commonly held understanding of the difference between poetry and prose, Brown writes,

> If it belong to poetry to exhibit exact and lively pictures of men and things; if it be the province of the poet's office to observe the objects best adapted to excite emotions, and represent them with such distinctness and force as to make a vivid impression on the reader's fancy; why may not these effects be produced in prose? The same objects lie before the eye, or imagination of the writer; he has access to the same magazine of words; and he has equal scope for the exercise of judgment and taste in the arrangement of his materials....
>
> It then appears, that the terms *poetry* and *prose* are not adverse to each other. Verse is the contrary of *prose*; and because poetry speaks the language of fancy, passion, and sentiment, and philosophy speaks the language of reason, these two terms should be considered as contraries, and writing should be divided, not into poetry and prose, but into *poetry* and *philosophy* [2: 584–85, 586].

5. The essay is signed "O." This review, along with Brown's discussions of John Drayton's *A View of South Carolina* in October 1803 and Samuel Miller's *A Brief Retrospect of the Eighteenth Century, First Part* in May 1804, constitute the bulk of Brown's extended reviews of American work in the *Literary Magazine*.

6. "Somnambulism," "Memoirs of Carwin the Biloquist," "The Romance of Real Life," "A Miser," "New Year's Day," and "The Honest Man" are definitely Brown's. Other stories possibly from Brown's pen include "Story of Celia," "The Child of Simplicity," "Pressing," "The Value of General Rules," "The Old Man and His Dog," and "Omar and Fatima; or, the Apothecary of Ispahan." Apart from these, the miscellany presents few other samples of

fiction: "A Fragment" by "Sabina," "The Modern Griselda" by Maria Edgeworth, and "The Language of Birds," which, Brown says, "was published by Dr. Johnson in the course of his Idler" (7: 427).

7. In a response to Isani, Edward W. Pitcher clearly shows that many of the fragments published in the magazines and newspapers of the early United States were, like much of the material in American periodicals from that time in general, lifted from the British press. As Pitcher himself suggests, Isani's analysis of the genre's characteristics remains valuable, but its value lies in advancing our understanding of a particular literary form rather than in deepening our understanding of the writing of fiction in early America.

8. I am thinking here of Hawthorne's *oeuvre* in particular, especially his several tales and sketches which refer to some larger work which does not exist but of which they claim to be parts or fragments—the Custom-house sketch (with its references to the collection of stories that were never included with the publication of *The Scarlet Letter*), "Passages from a Relinquished Work," "Fragments from the Journal of a Solitary Man," "Ethan Brand," and so on.

9. Signed "X."

10. "*Jan*. 1, 1805" appears at the end of the essay, opposite the signature. Brown would turn thirty-four a few days later on 17 January.

11. Brown had married Elizabeth Linn two months before in November 1804.

12. Although unpublished until Brown included it in the *Literary Magazine* for May 1805, "Somnambulism" is generally believed to have been written several years earlier, between the time in 1798 when Brown wrote an unpublished novel "Sky-Walk" and 1799 when *Edgar Huntly* appeared. The story has been identified by various scholars either as originally part of the former novel or as a false start for the latter. See Bennett's dissertation, "The Charles Brockden Brown Canon" (208–10), Krause's "Historical Essay" (332–36) and "Introduction" (xxii–xxiii), and Weber's "Bibliographical and Critical Notes" for his edition of Brown's *Somnambulism and Other Stories* (249–50).

13. "Memoirs of Carwin" appeared in the *Literary Magazine* in ten installments between November 1803—the second number of the miscellany—and March 1805. *Wieland*, in relation to which the Carwin fragment stands as a sort of prequel or interpolation rather than a more preparatory form such as an introduction or prologue (Cowie 337), was first published on 14 September 1798, by which time Brown had apparently already written the majority of his abortive narrative of Frank Carwin's early life. Elihu Hubbard Smith reported reading some of Carwin's story as early as 8 August 1798, but Brown wrote in a 4 September 1798 letter to William Dunlap that he had "desisted for the present from the prosecution of [the Carwin] plan & betook myself to another which I mean to extend to the size of Wieland." The new project was "Memoirs of Stephen Calvert," which would appear in serialization in the *Monthly Magazine* but, like "Memoirs of Carwin," would never be completed. Brown did not use any of the tale of Frank Carwin's youth in his *Monthly Magazine*, but held it instead for the later periodical. The original 1798 manuscript seems to have made up the initial seven installments: November 1803, 1: 100–04; December 1803, 1: 181–84; January 1804, 1: 255–59; February 1804, 1: 332–35; March 1804, 1: 412–16; April 1804, 2: 3–7; and May 1804, 2: 89–93. In the 4 July 1804 letter to John Blair Linn, Brown says, "The manuscript of Carwin is exhausted, and it was impossible to piece the thread and continue in due season for [the June 1804] number. It goes on, however, in the present (for July)...." According to this information, it seems likely that Brown wrote new material for the final three installments of "Memoirs of Carwin," and thus the story was resumed for one more installment in the magazine's second volume (July 1804, 248–52). The final two installments did not appear until spring of the following year. Brown published the penultimate section in February 1805 (3: 110–14) and seems to have intended writing until the story was complete, for in "Notes from the Editor" at the end of that February 1805 number, he wrote,

> The writer of the Memoirs of Carwin was influenced to discontinue the publication of that work from a persuasion that the narrative was of too grave a cast to be generally amusing. He has, however, received so many and such urgent intreaties to resume the story that he should not be justified in suppressing it any longer. Hereafter it will be continued with regularity [3: 160].

But this was not to be the case. The final installment of the fragment appeared the next month in the number for March 1805 (3: 210–14). See Bennett's "The Charles Brockden Brown Canon" (198), as well as Cowie's "Historical

Essay" and Reid's "Textual Essay" in Kent State's Bicentennial Edition of *Wieland* and *Memoirs of Carwin*.

14. The narrator of "Somnambulism" identifies the setting as "Norwood" (3: 344), a place whose name and description sound much like Norwalk, the landscape through which somnambulists Clithero Edny and Edgar Huntly roam in Brown's fourth novel. While both Norwood and Norwalk appear to be similar frontier areas, the latter seems somewhat wilder and more rugged.

15. For a lucid examination of the subject of somnambulism as it was understood in Brown's day, see Krause's "Historical Essay," especially section V, 336–57. Krause's discussion relates directly to *Edgar Huntly*, but much of the factual information presented and some of the literary interpretation suggested can be applied to "Somnambulism" as well.

16. The entire headnote reads as follows:
The following fragment will require no other preface or commentary than an extract from the Vienna gazette of June 14, 1784. "At Great Glogau, in Silesia, the attention of physicians, and of the people, has been excited by the case of a young man, whose behaviour indicates perfect health in all respects but one. He has a habit of rising in his sleep, and performing a great many actions with as much order and exactness as when awake. This habit for a long time showed itself in freaks and achievements merely innocent, or, at least, only troublesome and inconvenient, till about six weeks ago. At that period a shocking event took place about three leagues from the town, and in the neighbourhood where the youth's family resides. A young lady, travelling with her father by night, was shot dead upon the road, by some person unknown. The officers of justice took a good deal of pains to trace the author of the crime, and at length, by carefully comparing circumstances, a suspicion was fixed upon this youth. After an accurate scrutiny, by the tribunal of the circle, he has been declared the author of the murder: but what renders the case truly extraordinary is, that there are good reasons for believing that the deed was perpetuated by the youth while asleep, and was entirely unknown to himself. The young woman was the object of his affection, and the journey in which she had engaged had given him the utmost anxiety for her safety" [3: 335].

That Brown himself created this "extract" is possible. Scholars have been unable to locate this story either in the *Vienna Gazette* or in any of the periodical literature from that time. No one has been able to produce a copy of the article, nor has anyone been able to find for certain that the *Gazette* was even published in 1784 (Krause, "Historical" 334–35, n38).

17. Also, an earlier version of my own reading of the story appears as "Sleepwalking into the Nineteenth Century: Charles Brockden Brown's 'Somnambulism'" in *Journal of the Short Story in English: Les Cahiers de la Nouvelle* 39 (2002), pages 41–55.

18. I am indebted to Professor Weber for sending me the typescript of his essay, "The Beginnings of the American Short Story and Charles Brockden Brown," for use in this book.

19. Brown had easy access to at least the first two volumes of *Zoonomia* at the time he was writing "Somnambulism." The first volume had been published in 1796 by New York printers T. & J. Swords, who also printed *Wieland* and worked with Brown on the *Monthly Magazine*. In 1797 the second volume issued from the press of Philadelphia's Thomas Dobson. If Brown revised "Somnambulism" before its appearance in the May 1805 number of the *Literary Magazine*, he might also have seen all three parts of Darwin's work as they were published by Boston's Thomas and Andrews in 1803. Brown was probably familiar as well with the writings about sleep by his fellow Philadelphian Benjamin Rush, who suggests that "there are cases in which the change that is produced in the state of the brain, by means of sleep, affects the moral faculty likewise: hence we sometimes dream of doing and saying things, when asleep, which we shudder at, as soon as we awake" (qtd. in Smith 12). Thus only in sleep can Althorpe escape his inhibitions and follow the Davises in the night; his affected "moral faculty" might also have made it possible for him to shoot Constantia at the foot of the giant oak.

20. Although in the July 1804 number of the *Literary Magazine* Brown had disagreed with a foreign writer's judgment that extreme inquisitiveness was a prominent feature of the American character (2: 253), here in this Yankee farmer he creates just such an "inquisitive person." The character also represents one of Brown's most direct — and successful — attempts to recreate a provincial American personality and a colloquial American language:

"As to what you seed in the road," continued [the farmer], "I reckon it was nothing but a sheep or a cow. I am not more scary than some folks, but I never goes out a' nights without I sees some *sich* thing as that, that I takes for a man or woman, and am scared a little oftentimes, but not much. I'm sure after to find that it's not nothing but a cow, or hog, or tree, or something. If it wasn't some sich thing you seed, I reckon it was *Nick Handyside*" [3: 343].

21. At this point Althorpe interrupts the narrative to wonder why he or his uncle had not thought to warn the Davises about Handyside, whose apparently harmless freaks were the only unpredictable events to be wary of on the night journey. According to Althorpe's description, Handyside "was an idiot. He also merited the name of monster, if a projecting breast, a mis-shapen head, features horrid and distorted, and a voice that resembled nothing that was ever before heard, could entitle him to that appellation" (3: 343). Thus Handyside serves the plot by suddenly becoming the prime suspect in Constantia's murder. Moreover, in this unfortunate individual, as Weber suggests, "The ghost motif of the 'Gothic romance' has been transmuted into a figure whose appearance and whose actions have the same horror effect, but who, in spite of his ghost-like character, is given human traits" ("Beginnings" 15).

22. In the context of Tompkins's argument, the use of "Republican" here specifically refers to Jeffersonian Republicanism.

23. The full title of *Wieland* as it appears in Kent State's Bicentennial Edition is *Wieland; or The Transformation. An American Tale.*

24. True, she is alone in the darkness when the sleepwalking Althorpe attacks, but I would suggest that this situation is itself the result of her father's and her separating, an irrational act which he too late attempts to correct by giving up the hopeless pursuit of the horse and returning to his daughter.

25. In discussing Romanticism in Brown's *Wieland* and *Edgar Huntly*, Robert Hemenway says, "I believe that Brown's novels are 'Romantic' because he creates dilemmas which are insoluble through Neo-classical principles of coherence and rationality. Brown's novels are Romantic because he implies that *irrationality* is the governing force in human affairs, and that man's efforts at ordering existence, his presumptions of an ability to reason, are self-delusive" (97). "Somnambulism," I argue, participates in this same type of Romanticism.

26. Ironically, the last mention of Frank Carwin in *Wieland* suggests that he has in some sense returned to this beginning and is probably living out his life as a farmer. Clara says that, when he left Mettingen, Carwin intended "to hide himself in a remote district of Pennsylvania.... He is now probably engaged in the harmless pursuits of agriculture..." (239).

27. Carwin apparently writes his memoirs at the home of this brother—"'whose farm is situated in the bosom of a fertile desert, near the sources of the Lehigh'" (*Wieland* 214)—between the time of performing his vocal tricks at Mettingen and learning of the murder of Wieland's wife and children.

28. A neighbor in western Pennsylvania secretly supplies the boy with books, "prompted partly," Carwin says, "by benevolence and partly by enmity to my father, whom he could not more egregiously offend than by gratifying my perverse and pernicious curiosity" (1: 102).

29. It must be noted here that, as an older individual narrating past events, Carwin sees his father's efforts in a different light than that in which they appeared to him as a boy:

> My father's opposition to my schemes was incited by a sincere though unenlightened desire for my happiness. That all his efforts were secretly eluded or obstinately repelled, was a source of the bitterest regret. He has often lamented, with tears, what he called my incorrigible depravity, and encouraged himself to perseverance by the notion of ruin that would inevitably overtake me if I were allowed to persist in my present career. Perhaps the sufferings which arose to him from the disappointment, were equal to those which he inflicted on me [1:100].

30. Paul Downes suggests that Carwin's "hallowing" is, in a sense, a mental detour, much like the physical one the boy is already taking. His cries are "a detour around his apprehension" ("Constitutional" 105).

31. To some, the official voice that speaks from these founding documents of the United States was also a false voice. Seen in this light, "We the people" represents a misappropriation by America's Federalist elite of the voices of the nation's individuals. Patrick Henry, for example, understood the Preamble to the Constitution as just such a misappropriation: "What right had they to say, *We, the people*?

My political curiosity, exclusive of my anxious solicitude for the public welfare, leads me to ask: Who authorized them to speak the language of *We, the people*?" (qtd. in Edward Watts 3).

32. The events in "Memoirs of Carwin" probably take place between 1763 and 1766. In the Advertisement at the beginning of *Wieland*, Brown says that the story Clara tells "took place between the conclusion of the French and the beginning of the revolutionary war" (3). The French and Indian War ended in 1763, and Brown claims in "Memoirs" that the events in the fragment "are supposed to have taken place before the voyages of Bougainville and Cook" (299n). Bougainville's voyage began in 1766 and Cook's in 1768.

33. Carwin's voice, in addition to being one "of unusual compass and vigour," also allows him to be a talented mimic: "From my childhood, I was remarkably skilful at imitation. There were few voices whether of men or birds or beasts which I could not imitate with success" (1: 103).

34. The song appears in act 5, scene 1 of *The Tempest*. Brown uses only three lines of the seven-line passage:
> Where the bee sucks, there suck I;
> In a cowslip's bell I lie;
> There I couch when owls do cry.
> On the bat's back I do fly
> After summer merrily.
> Merrily, merrily shall I live now
> Under the blossom that hangs
>   on the bough.

35. In response to Carwin's query about how biloquism might best be used to realize the biloquist's "purposes," Ludloe speaks of how humans believe
> in the existence and energy of invisible powers, and in the duty of discovering and conforming to their will.... A voice coming from a quarter where no attendant form could be seen would, in most cases, be ascribed to supernal agency, and a command imposed on them, in this manner, would be obeyed with religious scrupulousness. Thus men might be imperiously directed in the disposal of their industry, their property, and even their lives. Men, actuated by a mistaken sense of duty, might, under this influence, be led to the commission of the most flagitious, as well as the most heroic acts: If it were his desire to accumulate wealth, or institute a new sect, he should need no other instrument [1: 258].

These speculations, in part, suggest to what ends Ludloe might use Carwin's gifts if he discovers them. Likewise, Carwin's secrecy about his vocal abilities, in part, serves to protect him as an individual from such misuse by another. At any rate, Ludloe's ideas here seem to represent the seed from which grows the tragedy at the Wieland retreat by the Schuylkill.

36. As Paul Downes says of this society, "we are encouraged to hear echoes of Rousseau and particularly Godwin in Ludloe's pronunciations.... More importantly, perhaps, Ludloe's organization calls to mind the movements that attracted the period's most profound political anxieties (the Jacobins, Illuminati and freemasons)" ("Constitutional" 109).

37. Carwin reports using his biloquism only once in the vicinity of Dublin. On a stroll late one evening, he happens upon a small group of highwaymen holding up a lady's carriage on a deserted stretch of road. Throwing his voice so that the sound appears to be coming from around a near bend, he imitates several men's voices, frightening the highwaymen away (2: 89–90). Carwin later learns that the lady in the carriage, a rich young widow named Mrs. Bennington, is one whom Ludloe would have him marry so as to put himself out of the reach of poverty's vices and temptations.

38. *Wieland* provides few clues regarding what Brown may have planned for the remainder of Carwin's story. The biloquist confesses to Clara that he is being pursued, presumably by Ludloe:
> "I left America, which is my native soil, in my youth. I have been engaged in various scenes of life, in which my peculiar talent has been exercised with more or less success. I was finally betrayed by one who called himself my friend, into acts which cannot be justified, although they are susceptible of apology.
> "The perfidy of this man compelled me to withdraw from Europe. I returned to my native country, uncertain whether silence and obscurity would save me from his malice..."] [199].

He has also been in both the secret society's utopia and in prison:
> "With regard to myself, ... I had warred against my peace and my fame: I had banished myself from the fellowship of vigorous and pure minds: I was self-expelled from a scene which the munificence of nature had adorned with unrivalled beauties,

and from haunts in which all the muses and humanities had taken refuge.

"I was torn by conflicting fears and tumultuous regrets [regarding his deceptions in Mettingen]. The night passed away in this state of confusion; and next morning in the gazette left at my obscure lodging, I read a description and an offer of reward for the apprehension of my person. I was said to have escaped from an Irish prison, in which I was confined as an offender convicted of enormous and complicated crimes.

"This was the work of an enemy, who, by falsehood and stratagem, had procured my condemnation. I was, indeed, a prisoner, but escaped, by the exertion of my powers, the fate to which I was doomed, but which I did not deserve. I had hoped that the malice of my foe was exhausted; but I now perceived that my precautions had been wise, for that the intervention of an ocean was insufficient for my security["] [211].

In her final chapter, Clara says, "It was easy for Carwin to elude the persecutions of Ludloe. It was merely requisite to hide himself in a remote district of Pennsylvania. This, when he parted from us, he determined to do" (239).

Afterword

1. By this time the magazine was being published by Thomas and George Palmer, who had been its printers since the beginning in October 1803.

2. In the editor's notes at the end of the issue for June 1807, Brown provides a prospectus for the next volume:

THE Editor, on closing his seventh volume, begs leave to return his grateful thanks for the additional patronage he has lately been favoured with, and to assure his readers, that no expence nor trouble shall be spared to render his miscellany more worthy of their favour. For this purpose he is endeavouring to secure a more extensive correspondence, and he has been promised the assistance of a number of literary gentlemen.... He has likewise taken steps to ensure a more regular supply of the European periodical works; and as he has early access to all the new publications ... he will occasionally insert analyses of, and extracts from, such as shall appear to him most worthy of notice.

It shall be the study of the editor, as it always has been, on all occasions to avoid meddling with politics: convinced that the rancorous passions engendered by party rage tend more to obstruct than facilitate the progress of literature, it shall be his endeavour to allay and soothe them, by turning the attention of his readers to more pleasing objects... [7: 472].

3. See Mark Kamrath's dissertation for an insightful and thorough discussion and analysis of Brown's "Annals" and the *American Register*.

The last issue in the *Literary Magazine*'s eighth and final volume concludes with a separate "American Register," a section which—despite the miscellany's long-standing title, *The Literary Magazine, and American Register*—had not previously been so distinct a part of Brown's monthly plan. Extending beyond forty pages, the "Register" has separate pagination and a different format—undivided pages instead of the *Literary Magazine*'s typical two columns per page. It includes President Jefferson's 1805 messages to Congress, commercial statements regarding foreign imports of goods, and the like. The section might indeed be described as the first number of Brown's *American Register*, the first volume of which had already appeared in November 1807 and presented President Jefferson's 1806 messages and made public other material "useful" to the well informed democratic republican citizen in America during the nineteenth century's first decade.

4. The brief essay appears as the fourth item in the first installment of "Extracts from a Student's Diary" (1: 6–14), the whole of which is signed "C. E." and is identified as "*For the American Register.*" Other items included are "Swift's Polite Conversation," "Fire," "Yellow Fever," "Pensions," and "A Jaunt to Rockaway, in Long-Island."

5. Hoffer uses this program to study the development of the young United States and the changes in the thoughts and beliefs of the Revolutionary generation.

Bibliography

Adams, Henry. *The United States in 1800*. Ithaca: Cornell UP, 1979.
Allen, Paul. *The Late Charles Brockden Brown*. Ed. Robert Hemenway and Joseph Katz. Columbia: Faust, 1976.
American Literary Magazines: The Eighteenth and Nineteenth Centuries. Ed. Edward E. Chielens. New York: Greenwood P, 1986.
Ames, Fisher. *Works of Fisher Ames. With a Selection from His Speeches and Correspondence*. Ed. Seth Ames. 2 vols. Boston: Little, 1854.
Amory, Hugh. "Appendix One: A Note on Statistics." *The Colonial Book in the Atlantic World*. Ed. Hugh Amory and David D. Hall. New York: Cambridge UP, 2000. 504–18.
Amory, Hugh, and David D. Hall, eds. Afterword. *The Colonial Book in the Atlantic World*. New York: Cambridge UP, 2000. 504–18.
Anderson, Benedict R. O'G. *Imagined Communities: Reflections on the Origin and Spread of Nationalism*. Rev. and extended ed. London: Verso, 1991.
Appleby, Joyce. *Capitalism and a New Social Order: The Republican Vision of the 1790s*. New York: New York UP, 1984.
Ashcroft, Bill, Gareth Griffiths, and Helen Tiffin. *The Empire Writes Back: Theory and Practice in Post-Colonial Literatures*. London: Routledge, 1989.
Axelrod, Alan. *Charles Brockden Brown: An American Tale*. Austin: U of Texas P, 1983.
Belok, Michael V. *Forming the American Minds: Early School-books & Their Compilers (1783–1837)*. Moti Katra, Agra-U.P. (India): Satish Book Enterprise, 1973.
Bennett, Charles E. "The Charles Brockden Brown Canon." Diss. U of North Carolina at Chapel Hill, 1974.
———. "Charles Brockden Brown: Man of Letters." *Critical Essays on Charles Brockden Brown*. Ed. Bernard Rosenthal. Boston: Hall, 1981. 212–23.
Bennett, Maurice J. "A Portrait of the Artist in Eighteenth-Century America: Charles Brockden Brown's *Memoirs of Steven Calvert*." *William and Mary Quarterly* 39.3 (1982): 492–507.
Berthoff, W. B. "Adventures of the Young Man: An Approach to Charles Brockden Brown." *American Quarterly* 9.4 (1957): 421–34.
———. "Charles Brockden Brown's Historical 'Sketches': A Consideration." *American Literature* 28 (1956–1957): 147–54.

Berthoff, Warner. "Brockden Brown: The Politics of the Man of Letters." *The Serif* 3.4 (1966): 3–11.

Berthoff, Warner B. "'A Lesson in Concealment': Brockden Brown's Method in Fiction." *Philological Quarterly* 37 (1958): 45–57.

Berthoff, Warner Bement. "The Literary Career of Charles Brockden Brown." Diss. Harvard U, 1954.

Bhabha, Homi K. *The Location of Culture*. London: Routledge, 1994.

Brodhead, Richard H. *Cultures of Letters: Scenes of Reading and Writing in Nineteenth-Century America*. Chicago: U of Chicago P, 1993.

Brown, Charles Brockden. *Alcuin: A Dialogue* with *Memoirs of Stephen Calvert*. *The Novels and Related Works of Charles Brockden Brown*. Ed. Sydney J. Krause, S. W. Reid, and Robert D. Arner. Bicentennial Ed. Vol. 6. Kent: Kent State UP, 1987.

———. *Clara Howard in a Series of Letters* with *Jane Talbot, a Novel*. *The Novels and Related Works of Charles Brockden Brown*. Ed. Sydney J. Krause, S.W. Reid, and Donald A. Ringe. Bicentennial Ed. Vol. 5. Kent: Kent State UP, 1986.

———. *Edgar Huntly; or, Memoirs of a Sleep-Walker*. *The Novels and Related Works of Charles Brockden Brown*. Ed. Sydney J. Krause and S. W. Reid. Bicentennial Ed. Vol. 4. Kent: Kent State UP, 1984.

———. *The Literary Magazine, and American Register*. 8 vols. Philadelphia: John Conrad, 1803–1807.

———. *Ormond; or The Secret Witness*. *The Novels and Related Works of Charles Brockden Brown*. Ed. Sydney J. Krause, S. W. Reid, and Russel B Nye. Bicentennial Ed. Vol. 2. Kent: Kent State UP, 1982.

———. Preface. *The American Review, and Literary Journal* 1 (1801): iii–vi.

———. *The Rhapsodist and Other Uncollected Writings*. Ed. Harry R. Warfel. Delmar, NY: Scholars' Facsimiles, 1977.

———. *Wieland; or The Transformation. An American Tale* with *Memoirs of Carwin the Biloquist*. Ed. Sydney J. Krause and S. W. Reid. 1977. Introd. Sydney J. Krause and S. W. Reid. Kent, OH: Kent State UP, 1978.

Brown, Clarence. *The Achievement of American Criticism*. New York: Ronald P, 1954.

Brown, Richard D. *Knowledge Is Power: The Diffusion of Information in Early America, 1700–1865*. New York: Oxford UP, 1989.

———. *The Strength of a People: The Idea of an Informed Citizenry in America, 1650–1870*. Chapel Hill: U of North Carolina P, 1996.

Brückner, Martin. "Models of World-Making: The Language of Geography in American Literature, 1750–1825." Diss. Brandeis U, 1997.

Buel, Richard, Jr. *Securing the Revolution: Ideology in American Politics, 1789–1815*. Ithaca: Cornell UP, 1972.

Chambers, William N. "Parties and Nation-Building in America." *Political Parties in American History: Volume 1, 1789–1828*. Ed. Winfred E. A. Bernhard. New York: Putnam's, 1973. 6–33.

Charvat, William. *The Profession of Authorship in America 1800–1870*. Ed. Matthew J. Bruccoli. New York: Columbia UP, 1992.

Chase, Richard. *The American Novel and Its Tradition*. Garden City: Doubleday, 1957.

Chielens, Edward E. "Periodicals and the Development of an American Literature." *Making America/Making American Literature: Franklin to Cooper*. Ed A. Robert Lee and W. M. Verhoeven. Amsterdam: Rodopi, 1996. 93–103.

Christophersen, Bill. *The Apparition in the Glass: Charles Brockden Brown's American Gothic*. Athens: U of Georgia P, 1993.

Clark, David Lee. *Charles Brockden Brown: Pioneer Voice of America*. Durham: Duke UP, 1952.

Cody, Michael. "Sleepwalking into the Nineteenth Century: Charles Brockden Brown's 'Somnambulism'," *Journal of the Short Story in English: Les Cahiers de la Nouvelle* 39 (2002): 41–55.

Cohen, Daniel A. "Arthur Mervyn and His Elders: The Ambivalence of Youth in the Early Republic." *William and Mary Quarterly* 43.3 (1986): 362–80.

Cole, Charles C., Jr. "Brockden Brown and the Jefferson Administration." *Pennsylvania Magazine of History and Biography* 72 (1948): 253–63.

"Conrad's Magazine." *The Port Folio* 5 (1805): 125–6.

Cowie, Alexander. "Historical Essay." *Wieland; or The Transformation. An American Tale and Memoirs of Carwin the Biloquist. The Novels and Related Works of Charles Brockden Brown.* Ed. Sydney J. Krause, S. W. Reid, and Alexander Cowie. Bicentennial Ed. Vol. 1. Kent: Kent State UP, 1977. 311–48.

Crèvecoeur, J. Hector St. John de. *Letters from an American Farmer* and *Sketches of Eighteenth-Century America*. Ed. Albert E. Stone. New York: Penguin, 1986.

Current-Garcia, Eugene. *The American Short Story Before 1850: A Critical History.* Boston: Twayne, 1985.

Curti, Merle. *The Growth of American Thought.* New York: n.p., 1943.

Cyganowski, Carol Klimick. *Magazine Editors and Professional Authors in Nineteenth-Century America: The Genteel Tradition and the American Dream.* New York: Garland, 1988.

Dauber, Kenneth. *The Idea of Authorship in America: Democratic Poetics from Franklin to Melville.* Madison: U of Wisconsin P, 1990.

Davidson, Cathy N. *Revolution and the Word: The Rise of the Novel in America.* New York: Oxford UP, 1986.

Dennis, Ian. *Nationalism and Desire in Early Historical Fiction.* New York: St. Martin's P, 1997.

Dowling, William C. *Literary Federalism in the Age of Jefferson: Joseph Dennie and* The Port Folio, *1801–1812.* Columbia: U of South Carolina P, 1999.

Downes, Paul. "Constitutional Secrets: 'Memoirs of Carwin' and the Politics of Concealment." *Criticism* 39.1 (1997): 89–117.

_____. "Sleep-Walking Out of the Revolution: Brown's *Edgar Huntly.*" *Eighteenth-Century Studies* 29.4 (1996): 413–431.

_____, Paul Bernard. "The Spell of Democracy: Literature and Politics in the Post-Revolutionary United States." Diss. Cornell U, 1996.

Drinker, Elizabeth. *The Diary of Elizabeth Drinker.* Ed. Elaine Forman Crane. 3 vols. Boston: Northeastern UP, 1991.

Dunlap, William. *The Life of Charles Brockden Brown: Together with Selections from the Rarest of His Printed Works, from His Original Letters, and from His Manuscripts Before Unpublished.* 2 vols. Philadelphia: James P. Parke, 1815.

Elkins, Stanley M., and Eric McKitrick. *The Age of Federalism.* New York: Oxford UP, 1993.

Elliott, Emory. *Revolutionary Writers: Literature and Authority in the New Republic, 1725–1810.* New York: Oxford UP, 1986.

[Emerson, Ralph Waldo]. *Nature.* Boston: James Munroe and Co., 1836.

_____. *An Oration Delivered Before the Phi Beta Kappa Society, at Cambridge, August 31, 1837.* Boston: James Munroe and Co., 1837.

[Emerson, William]. Preface. *The Monthly Anthology, and Boston Review* 1 (1804): i–iii.

Ferguson, Robert A. *Law and Letters in American Culture.* Cambridge: Harvard UP, 1984.

_____. "Literature and Vocation in the Early Republic: The Example of Charles Brockden Brown." *Modern Philology* 78.2 (1980): 139–52.

Fiedler, Leslie A. *Love and Death in the American Novel*. Rev. ed. New York: Stein, 1966.
Fliegelman, Jay, ed. Introduction. *Wieland* and *Memoirs of Carwin the Biloquist*. New York: Penguin, 1991. vii–xlii.
———. *Prodigals and Pilgrims: The American Revolution Against Patriarchal Authority, 1750–1800*. Cambridge: Cambridge UP, 1982.
Franklin, Benjamin. "Advertisement." *General Magazine, and Historical Chronicle, for All the British Plantations in America* 1.1 (1741): n.p.
———. *Autobiography and Other Writings*. Ed. Kenneth Silverman. New York: Penguin, 1986.
Free, William J. *The* Columbian Magazine *and American Literary Nationalism*. The Hague: Mouton, 1968.
Gardner, Jared. "Alien Nation: Edgar Huntly's Savage Awakening." *American Literature* 66.3 (1994): 429–61.
Gilmore, William J. *Reading Becomes a Necessity of Life: Material and Cultural Life in Rural New England, 1780–1835*. Knoxville: U of Tennessee P, 1989.
Grabo, Norman S. *The Coincidental Art of Charles Brockden Brown*. Chapel Hill: U of North Carolina P, 1981.
———, ed. Introduction. *Edgar Huntly; or, Memoirs of a Sleep-Walker*. New York: Penguin, 1988. vii–xxiii.
Hagenbuechle, Roland. "American Literature and the Nineteenth-Century Crisis in Epistemology: The Example of Charles Brockden Brown." *Early American Literature* 23.2 (1988): 121–51.
Hamilton, Alexander, James Madison, and John Jay. *The Federalist Papers*. Ed. Clinton Rossiter. New York: New American Library, 1961.
Hedges, William L. "Toward a Theory of American Literature, 1765–1800." *Early American Literature* 4.1 (1969): 5–14.
Hemenway, Robert. "Fiction in the Age of Jefferson: The Early American Novel as Intellectual Document." *Midcontinent American Studies Journal* 9 (1968): 91–102.
Hinds, Elizabeth Jane Wall. *Private Property: Charles Brockden Brown's Gendered Economics of Virtue*. Newark, DE: U of Delaware P, 1997.
Hirsch, David H. "Charles Brockden Brown as a Novelist of Ideas." *Books at Brown* 20 (1965): 165–84.
Hoffer, Peter Charles. *Revolution and Regeneration: Life Cycle and the Historical Vision of the Generation of 1776*. Athens: U of Georgia P, 1983.
Howe, Daniel Walker. *Making the American Self: Jonathan Edwards to Abraham Lincoln*. Cambridge: Harvard UP, 1997.
Humphrey, Carol Sue. *The Press of the Young Republic, 1783–1833*. Westport: Greenwood P, 1996.
Irving, Washington. *The Sketch-Book of Geoffrey Crayon, Gent*. Ed. Susan Manning. New York: Oxford UP, 1996.
Isani, Mukhtar Ali. "The 'Fragment' as Genre in Early American Literature." *Studies in Short Fiction* 18.1 (1981): 17–26.
Jefferson, Thomas. *The Portable Thomas Jefferson*. Ed. Merrill D. Peterson. New York: Penguin, 1975.
Jehlen, Myra. *American Incarnation: The Individual, the Nation, and the Continent*. Cambridge: Harvard UP, 1986.
Jones, Howard Mumford. *O Strange New World*. New York: Viking P, 1964.
Kennedy, Daniel Edwards. *Charles Brockden Brown: His Life and Works*. Ts. Kent State Brown Collection. Kent State U.
Kerber, Linda K. *Federalists in Dissent: Imagery and Ideology in Jeffersonian America*. Ithaca: Cornell UP, 1980.

_____. *Toward an Intellectual History of Women: Essays.* Chapel Hill: U of North Carolina P, 1997.

Kohl, Lawrence Frederick. *The Politics of Individualism: Parties and the American Character in the Jacksonian Era.* New York: Oxford UP, 1989.

Krause, Sydney J. "Historical Essay." *Edgar Huntly; or, Memoirs of a Sleep-Walker. The Novels and Related Works of Charles Brockden Brown.* Ed. Sydney J. Krause and S. W. Reid. Bicentennial Ed. Vol. 4. Kent: Kent State UP, 1984. 295–400.

_____. "Historical Notes." *Ormond; or The Secret Witness. The Novels and Related Works of Charles Brockden Brown.* Ed. Sydney J. Krause, S. W. Reid, and Russel B. Nye. Bicentennial Ed. Vol. 2. Kent: Kent State UP, 1982. 389–478.

_____. Introduction. *Edgar Huntly; or, Memoirs of a Sleep-Walker.* 1984. Ed. Sydney J. Krause and S. W. Reid. Kent: Kent State UP, 1987. vii–li.

_____. "Penn's Elm and *Edgar Huntly*: Dark 'Instruction to the Heart.'" *American Literature* 66.3 (1994): 463–84.

Krause, Sydney J., and S. W. Reid, eds. Introduction. *Wieland; or The Transformation. An American Tale* with *Memoirs of Carwin the Biloquist.* 1977. Kent: Kent State UP, 1978. vii–xxv.

Kropf, Carl R. "The Nationalistic Criticism of Early American Literature." *Early American Literature* 18.1 (1983): 17–30.

LaCapra, Dominick. *Rethinking Intellectual History: Texts, Contexts, Language.* Ithaca: Cornell UP, 1983.

Ladd, Everett Carll, Jr. *American Political Parties: Social Change and Political Response.* New York: Norton, 1970.

Larkin, Edward. "Inventing an American Public: Thomas Paine, the *Pennsylvania Magazine*, and American Revolutionary Political Discourse." *Early American Literature* 33.3 (1998): 250–76.

Lewis, R. W. B. *The American Adam: Innocence, Tragedy, and Tradition in the Nineteenth Century.* Chicago: U of Chicago P, 1955.

"Literature and Criticism ... Chapter I." *The Monthly Review and Literary Miscellany of the United States* 1 (1806): 1–23.

Looby, Christopher. *Voicing America: Language, Literary Form, and the Origins of the United States.* Chicago: U of Chicago P, 1996.

Lowrance, Mason I., Jr. "Biography and Autobiography." *Columbia Literary History of the United States.* Ed. Emory Elliot et al. New York: Columbia UP, 1988. 67–82.

Macedo, Stephen. *Liberal Virtues: Citizenship, Virtue, and Community in Liberal Constitutionalism.* Oxford: Clarendon P, 1990.

Machor, James L. "Fiction and Informed Reading in Early Nineteenth-Century America." *Nineteenth-Century Literature* 47.3 (1992): 320–48.

Macpherson, C. B. *The Political Theory of Possessive Individualism: Hobbes to Locke.* Oxford: Oxford UP, 1962.

Matthews, Jean V. *Toward a New Society: American Thought and Culture, 1800–1830.* Boston: Twayne, 1991.

McCoy, Drew R. *The Elusive Republic: Political Economy in Jeffersonian America.* Chapel Hill: U of North Carolina P, 1980.

Mertz, Harald. *Charles Brockden Brown als Politischer Schrifter.* Frankfurt am Main: Peter Lang, 1994.

Micklus, Robert. "The Delightful Instruction of Dr. Alexander Hamilton's *Itinerarium*." *American Literature* 60.3 (1988): 359–84.

Miller, Richard G. *Philadelphia — The Federalist City: A Study of Urban Politics, 1789–1801.* Port Washington, NY: Kennikat P, 1976.

Milton, John. *Complete Poems and Major Prose*. Ed. Merritt Y. Hughes. New York: Macmillan, 1959.

Moses, Richard P. "The Quakerism of Charles Brockden Brown." *Quaker History* 75.1 (1986): 12–25.

Mott, Frank Luther. *A History of American Magazines 1741–1850*. Cambridge: Harvard UP, 1957.

Murray, Lindley. *The English Reader; Or, Pieces in Prose and Poetry, Selected from the Best Writers, Designed to Assist Young Persons to Read with Propriety and Effect; to Improve Their Language and Sentiments; and to Inculcate Some of the Most Important Principles of Piety and Virtue. With Preliminary Observations on the Principles of Good Reading*. 2nd Philadelphia Edition. Philadelphia: B. & J. Johnson, 1800.

Nord, David Paul. "A Republican Literature: Magazine Reading and Readers in Late-Eighteenth-Century New York." *Reading in America*. Ed. Cathy N. Davidson. Baltimore: Johns Hopkins UP, 1989. 114–39.

Nye, Russel Blaine. *The Cultural Life of the New Nation*. New York: n.p., 1960.

Oberholtzer, Ellis Paxson. *The Literary History of Philadelphia*. Philadelphia: George W. Jacobs, 1906.

Parrington, Vernon Louis. *The Romantic Revolution in America 1800–1860*. New York: Harcourt, 1927.

Pattee, Fred Lewis. *The Development of the American Short Story: An Historical Survey*. New York: Harper, 1923. New York: Biblo, 1970.

―――. *The First Century of American Literature 1770–1870*. New York: Cooper Square, 1966.

Peden, William. "Thomas Jefferson and Charles Brockden Brown." *Maryland Quarterly* 2 (1944): 65–68.

Pitcher, Edward W. "The 'Fragment' in Early American Literature: A Response." *Studies in Short Fiction* 19.2 (1982): 169–72.

Poe, Edgar Allan. *Essays and Reviews*. Ed. G. R. Thompson. New York: Library of America, 1984.

"Political Definitions, Occasionally Exemplified in the Conduct and Opinions of Public Characters." *Connecticut Republican Magazine* 1 (1802): 16–18.

Pratt, Luther, ed. "To the Public." *Connecticut Republican Magazine* 1 (1802): 1–2.

Pratt, Mary Louise. *Imperial Eyes: Travel Writing and Transculturation*. London: Routledge, 1992.

Prescott, William H. *Biographical and Critical Miscellanies*. Vol. 1. 1904. Introd. Wilfred Harold Munro. New York: AMS, 1968.

Reid, S. W. "Textual Essay." *Wieland; or The Transformation. An American Tale* and *Memoirs of Carwin the Biloquist. The Novels and Related Works of Charles Brockden Brown*. Ed. Sydney J. Krause, S. W. Reid, and Alexander Cowie. Bicentennial Ed. Vol. 1. Kent: Kent State UP, 1977. 349–67.

Remer, Rosalind. *Printers and Men of Capital: Philadelphia Book Publishers in the New Republic*. Philadelphia: U of Pennsylvania P, 1996.

Rice, Grantland S. *The Transformation of Authorship in America*. Chicago: U of Chicago P, 1997.

Richardson, Edgar P. "The Athens of America 1800–1825." *Philadelphia: A 300-Year History*. Ed. Russell F. Weigley. New York: Norton, 1982. 208–57.

Richardson, Lyon N. *A History of Early American Magazines 1741–1789*. New York: Thomas Nelson, 1931.

Ringe, Donald A. *American Gothic: Imagination and Reason in Nineteenth-Century Fiction*. Lexington: UP of Kentucky, 1982.

———. "Charles Brockden Brown." *Major Writers of Early American Literature*. Madison: U of Wisconsin P, 1972.
———. *Charles Brockden Brown*. Rev. ed. Boston: Twayne, 1991.
———. "Historical Essay." *Clara Howard; In a Series of Letters* with *Jane Talbot, A Novel. The Novels and Related Works of Charles Brockden Brown*. Ed. Sydney J. Krause, S. W. Reid, and Donald A. Ringe. Bicentennial Ed. Vol. 5. Kent: Kent State UP, 1986. 433–74.
Rombes, Nicholas. "'All Was Lonely, Darksome, and Waste': *Wieland* and the Construction of the New Republic." *Studies in American Fiction* 22.1 (1994): 37–46.
Rosenthal, Bernard, ed. Introduction. *Critical Essays on Charles Brockden Brown*. Boston: Hall, 1981.
Rush, Benjamin. *The Selected Writings of Benjamin Rush*. Ed. Dagobert D. Runes. New York: Philosophical Library, 1943.
Russo, James R. "'The Chimeras of the Brain': Clara's Narrative in *Wieland*." *Early American Literature* 16.1 (1981): 60–88.
Ruttenburg, Nancy. *Democratic Personality: Popular Voice and the Trail of American Authorship*. Stanford: Stanford UP, 1998.
Schäfer, Wolfgang. *Charles Brockden Brown als Literaturkritiker*. Frankfurt am Main: Peter Lang, 1991.
Scheick, William J. "Assassin in Artful Disguise: The De-Signed Designs of Charles Brockden Brown's 'Somnambulism.'" *Charles Brockden Brown*. Ed. Marc Amfreville and Françoise Charras. Profils Americains 11. Montpellier, Fr.: Presses de l'Imprimerie d l'Université Paul-Valéry — Montpellier III, 1999. 27–45.
Schulz, Constance B. "'Of Bigotry in Politics and Religion': Jefferson's Religion, the Federalist Press, and the Syllabus." *Virginia Magazine of History and Biography* 91.1 (1983): 73–91.
Shakespeare, William. *The Complete Works of Shakespeare*. Ed. David Bevington. 4th ed. New York: Harper, 1992.
Sharp, James Roger. *American Politics in the Early Republic: The New Nation in Crisis*. New Haven: Yale UP, 1993.
Simpson, Lewis P. Introduction. *The Federalist Literary Mind: Selections from the Monthly Anthology and Boston Review, 1803–1811, Including Documents Relating to the Boston Athenaeum*. N.p.: Louisiana UP, 1962. 1–41.
Smith, Allan Gardner. *The Analysis of Motives: Early American Psychology and Fiction*. Amsterdam: Rodopi, 1980.
Smith, Susan Belasco, and Kenneth M. Price. "Introduction: Periodical Literature in Social and Historical Context." *Periodical Literature in Nineteenth-Century America*. Ed. Kenneth M. Price and Susan Belasco Smith. Charlottesville: UP of Virginia, 1995. 3–16.
Smith-Rosenberg, Carroll. "Subject Female: Authorizing American Identity." *American Literary History* 5.3 (1993): 481–511.
Smyth, Albert H. *The Philadelphia Magazines and Their Contributors 1741–1850*. Philadelphia: R. M. Lindsay, 1892. Freeport: Books for Libraries P, 1970.
Spenser, Benjamin T. *The Quest for Nationality*. Syracuse: Syracuse UP, 1957.
Tassin, Algernon. *The Magazine in America*. New York: Dodd, 1916.
Tebbel, John. *The American Magazine: A Compact History*. New York: Hawthorn, 1969.
———, and Mary Ellen Zuckerman. *The Magazine in America 1741–1990*. New York: Oxford UP, 1991.
Thoreau, Henry David. *Thoreau: Walden and Other Writings*. Ed. Joseph Wood Krutch. New York: Bantam, 1962.

Tompkins, Jane. *Sensational Designs: The Cultural Work of American Fiction, 1790–1860*. New York: Oxford UP, 1985.
Voloshin, Beverly R. "*Edgar Huntly* and the Coherence of the Self." *Early American Literature* 23.3 (1988): 262–80.
Waldstreicher, David. *In the Midst of Perpetual Fetes: The Making of American Nationalism, 1776–1820*. Chapel Hill: U of North Carolina P, 1997.
Warfel, Harry R. *Charles Brockden Brown: American Gothic Novelist*. Gainesville: U of Florida P, 1949.
———, ed. Introduction. *The Rhapsodist and Other Uncollected Writings*. By Charles Brockden Brown. 1943. Delmar: Scholars' Facsimiles, 1977.
Warner, Michael. *The Letters of the Republic: Publication and the Public Sphere in Eighteenth-Century America*. Cambridge: Harvard UP, 1990.
Watts, Edward. *Writing and Postcolonialism in the Early Republic*. Charlottesville: UP of Virginia, 1998.
Watts, Steven. *The Republic Reborn: War and the Making of Liberal America, 1790–1820*. Baltimore: Johns Hopkins UP, 1987.
———. *The Romance of Real Life: Charles Brockden Brown and the Origins of American Culture*. Baltimore: Johns Hopkins UP, 1994.
Weber, Alfred. "The Beginnings of the American Short Story and Charles Brockden Brown." Ts. Unpublished essay, n.d.
———, ed. Introduction. *Somnambulism and Other Stories*. By Charles Brockden Brown. Frankfurt am Main: Peter Lang, 1987. ix–xxiii.
Weber, Alfred, Wolfgang Schäfer, and John R. Holmes, eds. Introduction. *Literary Essays and Reviews*. By Charles Brockden Brown. Frankfurt am Main: Peter Lang, 1992. xi–xix.
Whitman, Walt. *Leaves of Grass: Authoritative Texts, Prefaces, Whitman on His Art, Criticism*. Norton Critical ed. Ed. Sculley Bradley and Harold. W. Blodgett. New York: Norton, 1973.
Wilentz, Sean. *Chants Democratic: New York City and the Rise of the American Working Class, 1788–1850*. New York: Oxford UP, 1984.
Williams, David R. *Wilderness Lost: The Religious Origins of the American Mind*. Selinsgrove: Susquehanna UP, 1987.
Wolf, Edwin. *The Book Culture of a Colonial American City: Philadelphia Books, Bookmen, and Booksellers*. New York: Oxford UP, 1988.
Wood, Gordon S., ed. *The Rising Glory of America 1760–1820*. New York: George Braziller, 1971.
Wood, James Playsted. *Magazines in the United States*. 2nd ed. New York: Ronald Press, 1956.
Zboray, Ronald J. *A Fictive People: Antebellum Economic Development and the American Reading Public*. New York: Oxford UP, 1993.
Ziff, Larzer. *Writing in the New Nation: Prose, Print, and Politics in the Early United States*. New Haven: Yale UP, 1991.

Index

Abercrombie, James, *Two Compends for the Use of the Philadelphia Academy* 174n41
"Account of Parkinson's Tour in America" 98–103
An Account of the Expeditions to the Sources of the Mississippi 162n1
Account of the Voyages ... in the Southern Hemisphere 95
Adams, John 38, 58, 62, 64, 86, 170n19, 173–74n33, 179n34
Addison, Joseph 17–18, 78, 118, 120, 165n13
Alcuin 120
American Constitution 41, 54, 58–59, 61–63, 72, 75, 147, 174n39, 175n42, 176n10
American Incarnation 97–98
American Literary Association 124
"American Literary Association" 182–83n62
American Magazine, or a Monthly View of the Political State of the British Colonies 163n4
American Philosophical Society 14
American Preceptor, Columbian Orator 165n13
American Register, or General Repository of History, Politics, and Science (C.B. Brown) 20, 155, 161n1, 172n25, 180n37
American Review, and Literary Journal 23, 161n1; Brown's Preface to 86, 161n1
American Revolution 12–14, 18, 34, 39, 46, 49, 54, 62–64, 72, 76, 78, 84, 124, 147, 165n13, 175n5
Ames, Fisher 18–19, 37, 47, 84, 168n2; "American Literature" 19, 84
Amory, Hugh 77
Anderson, Benedict, *Imagined Communities* 92, 176n7
Andros, Edmund 54
Anthology Club (Boston) 42, 162n1
Appleby, Joyce 84
Aristotle, *Poetics* 128
Arthur Mervyn 1, 9, 46, 144, 157, 161n1, 166n18, 178n25
Articles of Confederation 54, 58, 75
Ashcroft, Bill (with Gareth Griffiths and Helen Tiffin), *Empire Writes Back* 7–8, 99
Athens 110, 123
Atticus, Titus Pomponius 43–44, 168n7, 168–69n8
Aurora 14
Austen, Jane 129
"Authorship" 155–57

Bacon, Francis 125
Baltimore Weekly Magazine 169n9
Barbauld, Anna Laetitia Aiken 167n24
Barlow, Joel 15, 162n1, 163n3, 165n13; *Columbiad* 15, 162n1, 163n3
Belknap, Jeremy 125
Belles Lettres Club (Philadelphia) 21
Belok, Michael 165n13
Bentley, William 39
Berkeley, George (Bishop) 175n5

Index

Berthoff, Warner 2–3, 9, 12, 15, 18, 25, 132, 135, 165n12
Bhabha, Homi K. 83, 86
Bingham, Caleb, *American Preceptor, Columbian Orator* 165n13
Blair, Hugh 165n13
Boston 14–16, 39, 62, 90, 92, 128
Boston Athenaeum 168n2
Brackenridge, Hugh Henry, *Modern Chivalry* 129, 162n1
Bradford, Andrew (publisher), *American Magazine, or a Monthly View of the Political State of the British Colonies* 163n4
Bradford, William 26, 96
Brodhead, Richard 126
Brooks, Cleanth 4
Brown, Armitt 11
Brown, Elijah 166n18
Brown, Elizabeth Linn 161n1, 166n14, 184n11
Brown, James (James Brown and Company) 11
Brown, Richard D. 17, 39; *Knowledge Is Power* 17, 39; *Strength of a People* 17
Brückner, Martin 176n10
Buckingham, Joseph T. 163n5
Buel, Richard, Jr. 47
Buell, Lawrence 8, 162n5
Burr, Aaron 168n1

Carey, Mathew 14, 16, 164n8; *Universal Asylum, and Columbian Magazine* 164n8
Caritat, Hoquet 174n40
Chambers, William 67
"Character of Atticus" 43–44
Charles Brockden Brown als Politischer Schrifsteller 161n2
Charleston (SC) 90
Charlotte Temple 116, 142–43
Charvat, William 2, 6
Chaucer, Geoffrey 82
Chielens, Edward 174n40
Christianity 26, 107–109
Cicero 165n13, 166n18
civic virtue 38, 135–36
Clara Howard 11, 25, 77, 166n18
Clark, David Lee 3, 13, 180n37, 181n49
classical learning 106–110
"Classical Learning No Anti-Christian Tendency" 108–10, 180n36

Coleridge, Samuel Taylor 4
Columbian Magazine 93–94
Columbus 94, 124
Colvin, John B. 169n9
Connecticut 37, 88
Connecticut Republican Magazine 40–42, 84
Conrad, John 6, 12, 15, 78, 129, 161n1, 162n1, 163n1, 163n3, 167n24
Cooper, James Fenimore 89, 129
Copley, John Singleton 182n59
Coquette 142–43
Corrector 168n4
Cowper, William 81–82, 129, 165n13
Crèvecoeur, J. Hector St. John de 24, 141, 177n16
crime fiction 135
Current-Garcia, Eugene 127, 130, 183n1; *American Short Story Before 1850* 130, 183n1
Cyganowski, Carol 6

Daggett, David 106, 118
Darwin, Erasmus, *Zoonomia* 137, 185n19
Daughters of Columbia 118, 120
Davidson, Cathy N. 77, 115, 182n53
"Death of Cicero, a Fragment" 166n18, 168n7
"Death of Hamilton" 68–69
Declaration of Independence 14, 54, 72, 105, 147, 165n13, 175n42
deism 14, 26, 83
democracy 8, 84–85, 147, 157; pure or radical 41, 141–143, 170n18
Dennie, Joseph 1, 9, 11–12, 15, 18–19, 21, 33–34, 39–41, 47, 84–86, 92, 154, 162n3, 163n5, 163n6, 168n2, 168n4, 178n21; as "Oliver Oldschool, Esq." 9, 19–21, 39, 154
"Distinction between Poetry and Prose" 183n4
Dobson, Thomas 14–15, 78; *Encyclopaedia* 15
"Domestic Politics" 71
Dowling, William, *Literary Federalism in the Age of Jefferson* 33, 40, 178n21
Downes, Paul 146, 187n36
Drinker, Elizabeth 166n18
Dryden, John 19
Dunlap, William 1–2, 22, 184n13; *Life of Charles Brockden Brown* 1–2

Dwight, Thomas 37
Dwight, Timothy 40, 125; *Greenfield Hill* 40

Edgar Huntly 1, 9, 22, 133, 135, 137, 144, 146, 157, 161n1, 162n1, 164n9, 166n18, 168n7, 181n49, 181n51, 184n12, 185n14, 185n15, 186n25
Edgeworth, Maria 167n24
"Editors' Address to the Public" 20, 22–24, 26, 42, 44, 57, 90, 159, 163n7, 165n12, 166n16, 173n28
education 47, 103–113, 131, 144; literary 5
"Education in Scotland" 105–106, 110
election of 1800 37, 105
Eliot, T.S. 4
Embargo Act of 1807 105, 162n1
Emerald 167n24
Emerson, Ralph Waldo 25, 75, 98, 110, 112–13, 180n42; "American Scholar" 113; *Nature* 98, 180n42; "Self-Reliance" 75
Empire Writes Back 7–8, 99
Enlightenment 26, 67, 110–12, 139, 142
Erikson, Erik 158
Evening Fire-Side 169n9
expansionism 89–90

Farmer's Museum 163n5
Federalism 8–9, 18, 27, 33–34, 37, 39–40, 42, 49, 57, 64–66, 83, 84, 104, 106, 109, 135, 141, 143, 154, 162n3, 168n1, 168n4, 168n5, 169n11, 186n31; literary tradition 19
Felt, Joseph B., *Memorials of William Smith Shaw* 162n1
"Female Learning" 120
Ferguson, Robert 28
Fiedler, Leslie 144
Fielding, Henry 95, 129; *Tom Jones* 95
Fliegelman, Jay 46, 48
Foster, Hannah Webster, *Coquette* 142–43
fragment (literary) 130–33
Franklin, Benjamin 14–17, 28, 62, 64–65, 110, 125, 163n4, 167n23, 172n26, 174n33; *Autobiography* 17; *General Magazine* 15–16, 163n4; *Pennsylvania Gazette* 163n4
Frederick the Great 60–61
Free, William J. 15, 93–94, 175n5

freemasons 187n36
"French Legislation" 169n14, 170n18
French Revolution 37, 40–41, 46–48, 50–51, 53, 57–58, 61, 74, 85, 141–43, 157, 169n14, 170n18
Freneau, Philip 14, 165n13
Fuller, Margaret 56, 75

Gardiner, John Sylvester John 106
Georgia 88–89
Gibbon, Edward 125
Goldsmith, Oliver 82, 129, 162n1, 165n13; *Vicar of Wakefield* 162n1
Gothic literature 116–17, 130, 135, 181n51, 186n21; American 133, 146
Gray, Thomas 165n13
Greece (ancient) 45–46, 48, 106, 109, 123, 179–80n36

Habermas, Jürgen, *Structural Transformation of the Public Sphere* 52
Hall, David D. 77
Hamilton, Alexander 47, 58, 62, 64, 68–69
Hawkesworth, John, *Account of the Voyages ... in the Southern Hemisphere* 95
Hawthorne, Nathaniel 74, 139, 184n8; "Young Goodman Brown" 139
Heidegger, Martin 162n4
Hemenway, Robert 186n25
Henry, Patrick 186–87n31
Hobbes, Thomas 73, 97
Hoffer, Peter 158, 188n5
Holmes, John 163n7
Homer 108, 110
Howe, Daniel Walker, *Making the American Self* 56–57, 70–72
Hume, David 125, 165n13, 170n16
Humphrey, Carol Sue 162n3
Humphreys, David 125
Hymns and Spiritual Songs 162n1

Illuminati 187n36
Imagined Communities 92, 176n7
individualism 40, 72–75, 79; liberal 40, 74, 79, 97, 109–10, 141, 147, 154, 159; non-rational 135; possessive 73
"Influence of Climate on the Mind" 176n11
Irving, Washington 76, 127, 129; "Rip Van Winkle" 75–76; *Sketch-Book* 127

"Is a Free or Despotic Government Most Friendly to Human Happiness?" 48–50, 63, 143, 169n12, 169n14, 171n22
Isani, Mukhtar Ali 130

Jacobinism 40, 48, 168n5, 187n36
Jamestown 62
Jane Talbot 11, 162n1, 166n18
Jay, John 62, 64, 174n33
Jefferson, Thomas 37, 40–42, 47, 58, 62, 64, 66–69, 85–86, 104–05, 111, 132, 162n3, 162n1, 168n1, 170n19, 173n30, 188n3
Jeffersonian/Republican ideology 8, 14, 27, 33, 37, 39–40, 42, 49, 64, 79, 83–84, 104, 107, 159, 168n5
Jehlen, Myra, *American Incarnation* 97–98
Johnson, Samuel 19, 78, 82, 165n13

Kamrath, Mark 65, 161n2, 170n15
Kennedy, Daniel Edwards 165n12, 182n56, 182n62
Kentucky 88–89
Kerber, Linda 120–21, 169n11; *Federalists in Dissent* 169n11
Kohl, Lawrence Frederick, *The Politics of Individualism* 72
Krause, Sydney 135

LaCapra, Dominick 5, 44, 162n4
Larkin, Edward 20
Lewis, Matthew G. "Monk" 181n51
Life of Washington 15, 64–66, 172n24, 172n25, 172n26
Linn, Elizabeth *see* Brown, Elizabeth Linn
Linn, John Blair 161n1, 171n23, 172n24, 175n1, 176n9, 178n20, 184n13
Linn, Rebecca 182n56
Linn, William 166n14
"List of New Publications in July" 175n42
Literary Federalism in the Age of Jefferson 33, 40, 178n21
Literary Magazine, and American Register (works): "American Character" (anon.) 87–94, 101, 103, 123, 176n10, 177n15; "American Manners" (anon.) 91, 94; "Baron Humboldt" (anon.) 172n23; "Cautions Respecting Emigration to America" 178n24; "Duties of Editors" (N.W.) 31–32, 167n22; "Duty of Periodical Essayists" (Dr. Drake) 34; "Emigrant in America" (anon.) 96–98, 178n24; "Force of Example" (Valverdi) 171n23; "Has Classical Learning an Anti-Christian Tendency?" (anon.) 107; "Man with the Huge Nose. *In Imitation of the Manner of Sterne*" 183n2; "National Liberty and Happiness" (anon.) 59, 85, 171n22; "Nightingale and Mock-Bird" 81–83, 86, 175n1; "On Embracing a Party in Politics" 69–72, 173n29; "On the Anti-Christian Tendency of Classical Learning" 107–108, 179n36; "Plan for the Improvement and Diffusion of the Arts to the United States" 124; "Political Instruction" (Valverdi) 171–72n23; "Thoughts on Wealth" (Valverdi) 171–72n23
literary marketplace 42, 127, 158
"Literary, Philosophical, Commercial, and Agricultural Intelligence" 163n3
Locke, John 73, 97
London 111
Looby, Christopher 54, 141
Louis XVI 46

"Madelina. *A Female Portrait*" 122, 182n56
Madison, James 58, 62, 64, 170n19; *Federalist* 170n19
Madrid 111
Making the American Self 56–57, 70–72
"Man at Home" (series) 169n10
"Many Men, Many Minds" 74–75, 91
Marshall, John, *Life of Washington* 15, 64–66, 172n24, 172n25, 172n26
Maryland 89
Massachusetts 37, 88
Matthews, Jean 27, 38, 105, 175n5
Maxwell, Hugh 78
Medley; or, Monthly Miscellany 167n20
"Memoirs of Carwin the Biloquist" 132, 144–54, 178n25, 184n13
Memoirs of Stephen Calvert 127, 184n13
Memorials of William Smith Shaw 162n1
Mertz, Harald, *Charles Brockden Brown als Politischer Schriftsteller* 161n2
Micklus, Robert 94–95
Milton, John 19, 82, 125, 129, 165n13

mimicry 83–86, 129
miscellaneous literature 15–21, 116, 158
Modern Chivalry 129, 162n1
Montagu, Lady Mary Wortley 167n24
Monthly Anthology, and Boston Review 42, 92, 162n1, 162n3, 163n2, 167n20, 168n2
Monthly Magazine, and American Review (C.B. Brown) 12, 31, 65, 127, 161n1, 164n8, 165n12, 183n2, 184n13
More, Hannah, *Strictures on the Modern System of Female Education* 108
Mott, Frank Luther 2, 15, 163n2, 163n5, 168n4
Munroe and Francis (printers) 162n1
Murray, Lindley 165n13

Napoléon Bonaparte 39–40, 50, 59, 60, 85
natural aristocracy 54–55, 58, 59, 62, 64, 70–71, 109, 170n17, 170n19, 171n23
neoclassicism 136, 157
New Hampshire 88
"New Year's Day. A Fragment" 130–32
New York 8, 11, 14–16, 88, 90
Newton, Isaac 125
Nord, David 38
Norfolk (VA) 99
North Carolina 89
"Notes from the Editor" 184n13
"Notices of American Writers and Publications" 128, 173n31
"Novel-Reading" 118–20, 157

"On Habituating Ourselves to an Individual Pursuit" 72–74, 91
"On Miscellanies" 32, 116
"On Plagiarism" 167n20
"On Self Biography" 172n27, 172–73n28
"On the American Constitution" 61–63, 75, 171n20
"On the Cause of the Popularity of Novels" 116–118, 181n49
"On the Difference Between Learning and Knowledge" 112–14
"On 'the Enlightened Public' and 'the Age of Reason'" 110, 179–80n36, 180n39
"On the Influence of Women" 122
"On the Life of Washington, Now Publishing" 64–66

"On the Merits of the Founders of the French Revolution" 50–59, 62, 169n14, 171n21
Ormond 1, 48, 157, 166n18, 174n40
Ovid 108, 110, 179n34

Paine, Thomas 20, 101, 125
Palmer, George and Thomas (printers/publishers) 162n1, 188n1
Paris 111
Parkinson, Richard 98–103, 178n22
Parrington, Vernon Louis 13
Pattee, Fred Lewis 158–59; *Development of the American Short Story* 183n1; *First Century of American Literature* 158–59
Peale, Charles Willson 14
Pennsylvania 88, 106, 111
Pennsylvania Academy of Fine Arts 14, 124–25
"Pennsylvania Academy of Fine Arts" 124
Pennsylvania Magazine 20
periodical press 39, 42, 92, 127, 162n3
"Pestilence and Bad Government Compared" 58, 157
Philadelphia 1, 2, 6, 8, 11, 13–15, 16, 21, 29, 45, 58, 90, 93, 111, 148–49, 161n1; Academy 174n41; host of Constitutional Convention 14; host of Continental Congress 13–14
Pike, Zebulon, *An Account of the Expeditions to the Sources of the Mississippi* 162n1
Plutarch 116
Plymouth 62
Pocahontas 96
Poe, Edgar Allan 3, 4, 74, 82, 127, 135, 159; "Murders in the Rue Morgue" 135
Poetics 128
The Politics of Individualism 72
Pope, Alexander 19, 82, 125, 129, 165n13, 180n44
Port Folio 1, 9, 11–12, 15, 19, 33–34, 39, 40, 42, 84, 92, 94, 162n3, 163n2, 178n21
Pratt, Luther 40–41, 84–85
Pratt, Mary Louise 95–96
Preface to the *American Review* 86, 165n12
Prescott, William H. 2, 6

Price, Kenneth 5, 9
Priestley, Joseph 101
Prussia 60–61
Puritans (American) 54, 83, 132, 172n26

Quakers 3, 13–14, 26, 31, 166n14

Radcliffe, Ann 117
Rakestraw, Joseph 169n9
Ramsey, David 125, 175n5
Raphael 125
rationalism 135
reading in the United States 5, 94, 110, 114, 117–18, 121–22, 180n44
"Receipt for a Modern Romance" 181n51
"Remarks on Reading" 113–116, 126, 180n44
"Remarks on the Russian Empire" 164n8
Remer, Rosalind 162n1
"Report of the Committee Relative to the Establishment of Schools Throughout the State of Pennsylvania, in Such a Manner That the Poor May Be Taught Gratis" 111
republic of letters 34, 51–52, 79, 93, 96, 110, 114–15, 117, 154, 178n21
Republican Mother 120, 121
republicanism 6, 8–9, 17, 38, 41, 53, 84–85, 104, 126, 136, 157; classical 9, 38, 74, 141, 154; democratic 40, 61, 78–79, 121, 188n3; liberal 38, 79
"Rhapsodist" (series) 22 164n8
Rhapsodist and Other Uncollected Writings 169n10
Rhode Island 88
Rice, Grantland 30
Richardson, Edgar P. 13–15
Richardson, Lyon 16
Richardson, Samuel 129
Ringe, Donald 4, 6, 28
Rittenhouse, David 125
Robespierre, François-Maximilien-Joseph de 46
romanticism 131, 136, 157
Rome (ancient) 43, 48, 106–07, 109, 179–80n36
Rousseau, Jean-Jacques 97
Rowson, Susanna, *Charlotte Temple* 116, 142–43

Royal Magazine 174n40
Rush, Benjamin 14, 105–07, 162n1, 179n34; *Medical Inquiries and Observations* 162n1, 185n19
Ruttenburg, Nancy 144

Schäfer, Wolfgang 161n2, 163n7, 182n52; *Charles Brockden Brown als Literaturkritiker* 161n2, 163n7
Scheick, William J. 134–35
Schuylkill River 144, 149, 187n35
Scott, Walter 129
Second Great Awakening 26
self-interest 132, 144, 148–49, 152–54, 157
Seneca 116
Sensational Designs 141, 144
sentimentalism 131–32
Sergeant, Winthrop, "Boston" 128–29
Shakespeare, William 82, 129, 149, 164n10, 175n2, 187n34; *Hamlet* 164n10; *Merchant of Venice* 175n2; *Tempest* 187n34
Sharp, James Roger 37–38, 168n1
Shaw, William Smith 162n1
Shays's Rebellion 18, 49
Simpson, Lewis 162n1
Sinclair, John 98
"Sketch of American Literature for 1806-7" 172n25
"Sky-Walk" 135, 184n12
slavery 89, 177n14
Smith, Allan Gardner 137, 141
Smith, Charlotte 82
Smith, Elihu Hubbard 131, 184n13
Smith, John 95–96
Smith, Susan Belasco 5, 9
"Somnambulism. A Fragment" 132–144, 184n12, 185n15, 185n16
South Carolina 89
Spectator 17
Spencer, Edmund 82
"Spirit of Female Conversation" 175n1
"Spirit of Political Conversation" 169n14
Squanto 96
Steele, Richard 17
Sterne, Laurence 129
Strictures on the Modern System of Female Education 108
Structural Transformation of the Public Sphere 52
"Students Diary" (series) 118 120

Taylor, John 37
Tennessee 88–89
Themistocles 123
Thomas, Isaiah, *Royal Magazine* 174n40
"Thomas Jefferson" 66–68, 173n30
Thomson, James 165n13
Thoreau, Henry David 75, 79; "Life Without Principle" 79
"Thoughts on the Former and Present State of Holland" 59–60, 171n20
"To the Editor, &c." 87
"Toby Tickler, Esq." 168n4
Tompkins, Jane, *Sensational Designs* 141, 144
Transcendentalism 56
Transformation of Authorship in America 30
travel literature 94–95
Trumbull, John 165n13
Two Compends for the Use of the Philadelphia Academy 174n41

United States Gazette 14

Vaux, Robert 124–25
Vermont 88–89
Vienna Gazette 134
View of the Soil and Climate of the United States 162n1
Virgil 19, 81
Virginia 89
"Voices of Birds" 175n3
Volney, Constantin François de Chassebouef, *View of the Soil and Climate of the United States* 162n1

Warfel, Harry 2–3, 9, 11, 23–24, 28, 158, 161–62n3
Warner, Michael 19, 29–30, 51–52, 101; *Letters of the Republic* 19, 52; "principle of negativity" 29–30, 85
Warren, Robert Penn 4
Washington, D.C. 13, 93
Washington, George 16, 62, 64–66, 68, 98–99, 165n13; Mount Vernon 99
Watts, Edward 8, 18, 84, 163n6
Watts, Isaac, *Hymns and Spiritual Songs* 162n1
Watts, Steven 4, 6, 28–29, 56–57, 154, 165n12, 169n12; *Romance of Real Life* 4, 56, 154, 169n12; *Republic Reborn* 152
Webbe, John 163n4
Weber, Alfred 135, 138, 161n2, 163n7, 164n8, 169n12, 181n49, 182n52, 185n18, 186n21
Webster, Noah 24, 106, 165n13; *Grammatical Institutes, of the English Language* 165n13
Weekly Magazine 169n10
West, Benjamin 125, 182n59
Whiskey Rebellion 18, 49
Whitman, Walt 177n18
"Why Are the Arts Discouraged in America?" 125–26
Wieland 1, 11, 22, 31, 48, 133, 137, 141, 144, 157, 164n9, 166n18, 173n30, 174n40, 181n51, 184n13, 186n25, 186n26, 187n32, 187–88n38
Winthrop, John 26, 96
Wisneski, Richard 96–97
Wood, Gordon 27, 84
Wood, James Playsted 16, 163n4
Writing in the New Nation 7

yellow fever 45–46, 58

Ziff, Larzer, *Writing in the New Nation* 7
Zoonomia 137, 185n19

www.ingramcontent.com/pod-product-compliance
Lightning Source LLC
Chambersburg PA
CBHW032057300426
44116CB00007B/788